Political Anthropology
Yearbook I

Political Anthropology Yearbook I

Ideology and Interest: The Dialectics of Politics

edited by
Myron J. Aronoff

LONDON AND NEW YORK

First published 1980 by Transaction, Inc

Published 2019 by Routledge
2 Park Square, Milton Park, Abingdon, Oxon OX14 4RN
52 Vanderbilt Avenue, New York, NY 10017

First issued in paperback 2019

Routledge is an imprint of the Taylor & Francis Group, an informa business

Copyright © 1980 by Taylor & Francis

All rights reserved. No part of this book may be reprinted or reproduced or utilised in any form or by any electronic, mechanical, or other means, now known or hereafter invented, including photocopying and recording, or in any information storage or retrieval system, without permission in writing from the publishers.

Notice:
Product or corporate names may be trademarks or registered trademarks, and are used only for identification and explanation without intent to infringe.

Library of Congress Catalog Number: 79-92197

Library of Congress Cataloging in Publication Data

Main entry under title:

Political anthropology yearbook.

   CONTENTS: v. 1. Ideology and interest.
   1. Political anthropology. 2. Political sociology. I. Aronoff, Myron Joel.
GN492.P65.   306'.2   79-92197
ISBN 0-87855-371-1

ISBN 13: 978-1-138-51077-7 (pbk)
ISBN 13: 978-0-87855-371-6 (hbk)

Contents

1. Ideology and Interest: The Dialectics of Politics
   Myron J. Aronoff   1

2. Go Down, Moses: Revivalist Politics in a Caribbean Mini-State
   Frank E. Manning   31

3. Two-Dimensional Politics: Political Action and Meaning in Rural West Bengal
   Marvin Davis   57

4. Models of Solidarity, Structures of Power: The Politics of Community in Rural Bangladesh
   Peter J. Bertocci   97

5. Caste, Ideology, and Power in North-Central Nepal
   Harvey S. Blustain   127

6. A Description of the Discrepancy Between Sikh Political Ideals and Sikh Political Practice
   Joyce Pettigrew   151

7. The Fabrication of a Social Past: The Kazakhs of Central Asia
   Martha B. Olcott   193

Index   215

Chapter 1

Ideology and Interest:
The Dialectics of Politics [1]

Myron J. Aronoff

Introduction

In this essay I set forth a preliminary formulation of a conceptual framework for the study of the relationship between culture and politics. Geertz (1973, p. 312) has pointed out the extreme difficulty in attempting to formulate the link between politics and culture given the present lack of theory. Given this state of relative theoretical underdevelopment, I suggest the relationship between a selected number of conceptual themes which might form the foundation for building the needed theory. I have deliberately chosen to limit my discussion to a limited number of ideas and issues, and fully realize that many other potentially relevant ones have been ignored. I shall deliberately give greater attention to the conceptualization of culture and its constituent components, forms and expressions—political culture, ideology, symbol, myth, and ritual—than to the elaboration of the components of politics. I do so not because I think the former more important than the latter, but because the cultural dimension has generally received less attention in the literature.[2]

In the process of simplifying complex reality through the construction of abstract conceptual paradigms, many social scientists have tended to concentrate on a unidimensional focus on either sociopolitical structure (or action) or cultural structure (or process). A number of scholars have called our attention to the need for a two-dimensional focus of analysis on the interrelationship between the two dimensions of conceptualized patterns of human behavior.[3] This essay attempts to make a contribution to the formulation of a conceptual framework which emphasizes the necessity of such a two-dimensional approach for an understanding of sociopolitical phenomena.

Both dimensions, culture and politics, are different conceptual abstractions of the same phenomena. "Culture is the fabric of meaning in terms of which human beings interpret their experiences and guide their action; social structure is the form that action takes, the actually existing network of social relations. Culture and social structure are then but different abstractions for the same phenomena" (Geertz 1967, pp. 233-34). Although I formulate this relationship as a dialectic one (cf. A. Cohen 1969 and 1974; and Habermas 1973), the main "problem" or focus of research is the explication of the nature of this relationship. In this sense, the term "dialectic" serves as a convenient intuitive label used to name that which is still unknown or not well understood. This essay aspires to clarify some of the problematics of the relationship, and to tentatively suggest steps which may usefully guide research in the investigation of the problem.

Different scholars have formulated variations of the same problem. As mentioned above, Geertz talks about the relationship between culture and social structure (and politics), and Cohen stresses the relationship between power and symbolic action. In this volume each contributor formulates the problem slightly differently. For example, Marvin Davis discusses political action and meaning, Harvey Blustain focuses on ideology and social structures, and Joyce Pettigrew deals with the discrepancy between ideals and political practice. Therefore, we have adopted the formulation "ideology and interest," which thematically unites all of the contributions. This essay serves as a common frame of reference for the other essays which I shall discuss as they relate to the approach I am proposing.[4]

I first propose and adapt a concept of culture as a socially constructed structure of meanings. I then propose a formulation of ideology as a focused dimension of political culture, and discuss the type of symbols most frequently found as the components of ideology. Finally, I suggest adapting the concepts of myth, the oldest narrative form of cultural expression, and ritual, the most ancient behavioral cultural form, to help us to understand political culture and ideology in contemporary societies. I conclude with a summary formulation of the proposed framework.

Culture as a Socially Constructed Structure of Meanings

Different scholars from diverse disciplines have contributed to our understanding of man as preminently a conceptualizing and symbolizing animal. A substantial literature in anthropology shows the evolutionary development of human sociability as a variation of primate sociability; and with the development of the neocortex, growing human capacity for, and dependence upon, symbolization in the creation of culture. Leslie White observed that man is the only creature capable of being killed by a symbol; but even more striking is the fact that he is capable of voluntarily sacrificing himself for a symbol. Many of our intellectual forefathers, e.g., Max Weber and Fustel de Coulanges, have taught us that human behavior is incomprehensible without understanding the shared meanings which inform political behavior. As Geertz expressed metaphorically, ". . . man is an animal suspended in webs of significance he himself has spun, I take culture to be those webs, and the analysis of it to be therefore not an experimental science in search of law but an interpretive one in search of meaning" (Geertz 1973, p. 5).

One approach from which we can borrow important insights is from the studies of scholars working within the phenomenological paradigm. Although an important underlying assumption on which this approach is based is human abhorrence of chaos which drives man to create meaningful social order, as I indicated above, one need not accept this Hobbesian view of human nature to arrive at the same or a similar focus for analysis.[5] The nature of the relationship between humanly constructed sociopolitical institutions and order (in the face of anarchy), and culture in the form of humanly constructed systems of meaning (in the face of indeterminacy), is the most important contribution of this approach which I incorporate in my own conceptual framework. I shall therefore outline in some detail the points which I utilize, and shall try to make clear the revisions and additions which are necessary to make the approach more complete and useful for political anthropology.

My formulation of the socially constructed nature of society is largely derived from the seminal work of Berger and Luckmann (1966) which was in turn strongly influenced by the pioneering work of Alfred Schutz (1962 and 1964). This approach views social order as an ongoing human production resulting from processes of habitualization. When patterns of habitualized behavior become reciprocally typified, they are subsumed under social control, i.e. they have become institutionalized. When the institutionalized pattern of behavior becomes objectively real to the participants, it is given a normative meaning, i.e., it is considered to be the "natural" or "right" way of behaving in such circumstances. For example, I have observed a case where the seating arrangement of city council members had become so informally institutionalized that even after dramatic realignments in political coalitions, characterized by bitter personal antagonisms had taken place, the council members continued to follow their old seating arrangements. Although it forced them to sit next to their new political "enemies" they apparently felt compelled to sit in their "proper" places (cf. Aronoff 1974).

This approach does not assume an a priori functional integration in society, but, rather, views social integration—to the extent that it occurs in any given situation—as deriving from the creation of socially shared universes of meaning or knowledge. Since I am presenting certain postulates abstracted from a systematic theoretical treatise on the sociology of knowledge, I stress their heuristic "ideal-type" nature, by occasionally inserting the qualifying *ideally* as an incantation against the "evil eye" of reification which tends to plague social scientists. I shall elaborate this point shortly.

> Individuals perform discreet institutionalized actions within the context of their biography. This biography is a reflected-upon whole in which discreet actions are thought of not as isolated events, but as related parts in a subjectively meaningful universe whose meanings are not specific to the individual, but socially articulated and shared. Only by way of this detour of socially shared universes of meaning do we arrive at the need for institutional integration . . . If the integration of an institutional order can be understood only in terms of the "knowledge" that its members have of it, it fol-

lows that the analysis of such "knowledge" will be essential for an analysis of the institutional order in question. (Berger and Luckmann 1966, p.61).

The systematic transmission of such knowledge (or institutional meanings) necessitates educational procedures and implies procedures of control and legitimation. Specific sectors of the common stock of knowledge are mediated through roles which link the general societal universes of meaning to individuals and thereby make them subjectively real and meaningful. As societies become increasingly institutionally differentiated, problems of the integration of meanings become more likely. Institutional segmentation creates the possibility of socially segregated subuniverses of meaning which leads to special problems of legitimation.

Legitimation is a form of meaning which, ideally, integrates disparate institutional processes, thereby making sense of the totality of the societal order. It also makes subjectively meaningful the totality of an individual's life as he passes through various stages, processes, and institutions (both in the more specialized sense in which Berger and Luckmann use the term and in its more conventional meaning). Legitimation has both a cognitive and normative dimension. As Berger and Luckmann (1967, p.93) explain, "legitimation 'explains' the institutional order by ascribing cognitive validity to its objectivated meanings. Legitimation justifies the institutional order by giving a normative dignity to its practical imperatives."

There are different levels of legitimation ranging from the most elementary agreement on common definitions in the formation of language, through the development of rudimentary propositions such as those contained in proverbs and folk legends, to the development of explicit theories which legitimate institutions through a differentiated body of knowledge. Berger and Luckmann call the highest level of legitimation, those bodies of theoretical tradition that integrate different provinces of meaning and which encompass the institutional order in a symbolic totality, symbolic universes. Their term, symbolic universe, is virtually synonymous with the more commonly used term, cosmology. The symbolic universe (or cosmology), ideally, integrates all sectors of the institutional order or society within an all-embracing universe of meaning. At the individual level, it provides a frame of reference in which, ideally all human experience is made meaningful. It integrates marginal realities, discrepant meanings, orders and legitimates everyday roles, and puts them in perspective of the general frame of reference. It makes possible the ordering of the different stages of life, such as through rites of passage, attests to the "correctness" of the individual's subjective identity, and the "normality" or "saneness" of his social identity.

The legitimation of the societal order is critically important because, "the institutional order, like the order of the individual biography, is continually threatened by the presence of realities that are meaningless in *its* terms. The legitimation of the institutional order is also faced with the ongoing necessity of keeping chaos at bay. *All* social reality is precarious. *All* societies are constructions in the face of chaos. The constant possibility of anomic terror is actualized whenever the legitimations that obscure the precariousness are threatened or collapse" (Berger and Luckmann 1967, p.103).

Using the logic of Berger and Luckmann's formulation, I derive the following hypothesis: the degree to which a symbolic universe is problematic varies in inverse relation to the degree to which it is taken for granted. It is at this point that the disparity between the idealized analytic construct and the range of socio-political reality becomes important. There is a wide range of possible patterns of integration or lack thereof between socio-political structures and cultural systems of meaning. As Geertz has argued, "In most societies, where change is a characteristic rather than an abnormal occurrence, we shall expect to find more or less radical discontinuities between the two" (Geertz 1967, p. 233). Even in the most stable and least dynamic of societies, we are unlikely to find anything approaching a perfect fit between the two.

Light (1969), for example, has criticized Berger and Luckmann's lopsided emphasis upon the production of social certainty to the neglect of processes which consistently create mass uncertainty, thereby making symbolic universes chronically subject to collapse. Berger and Luckmann tend to ignore the important fact that in reality symbolic universes contain ambiguities and contradictions, which allow for various interpretations which are frequently related to different socio-economic and political categories of actors, contexts, and interests. As various technological, social, economic, and political conditions change, past "certainties" become undermined, thereby creating new "uncertainties." In fact, all human experience can only be made meaningful in an ideal construct, and in reality disparate institutional processes never achieve anything approaching perfect integration. For Berger and Luckmann to argue that imperfect socialization can lead to the calling into question of the taken-for-grantedness of symbolic universe implies that some kind of Skinnerian or Orwellian perfectly socialized world can exist. Fortunately, this appears not to be the case in even the most totalitarian societies known to man. Therefore, individual differences as well as group differences almost inevitably will lead to individual and group differences in the definition of reality.

Ideology as a Focused Dimension of Political Culture

The development of deviant versions of the symbolic universe or the introduction of alternative definitions of reality call into question the taken-for-grantedness of socially shared cultural meanings. The "counterculture" of the 1960s and the anti-Vietnam War protest movement are examples of this in recent American history. Former Marine Lieutenant Robert Muller, Executive Director of the Council of Vietnam Veterans, expressed the traumatic effect this process can have on an individual in the following statement: "You know, I remember joining the Marines and standing in my dress whites and hearing 'The Star-Spangled Banner' and crying like a baby. I cried out of pride. We were so idealistic . . . My dream was a fraud. For a lot of guys, the foundation in our life was shaken. We were told we were fools" (*The New York Times Magazine*, May 27, 1979, p. 31).

The confrontation between alternative definitions of reality inevitably involves conflicts of power. As Geertz has argued, ideas must "be carried by powerful social groups to have powerful social effects; someone must revere them, defend them, impose them. They have to be institutionalized in order to find not just an intellectual existence in society, but, so to speak, a material one as well" (Geertz 1973, p. 314). Rival definitions of reality can inspire, guide, and give legitimacy to groups challenging dominant definitions of reality and the groups that defend them. Berger and Luckmann discuss the employment of "machineries of universe maintenance," e.g., mythology, theology, and science, to assert and support the existence of meaningful order. They give less emphasis to the forms of coercion and repression that may be used in conjunction with them.

Berger and Luckmann distinguish ideology from symbolic universes by identifying the former with the struggle for power within a commonly accepted symbolic universe. "When a particular definition of reality comes to be attached to a concrete power interest, it may be called an ideology.... The distinctiveness of ideology is ... that the *same* overall universe is interpreted in different ways, depending upon the concrete vested interests within the society in question" (Berger and Luckmann 1967, pp. 123-124).

This conceptual formulation of ideology requires clarification. For example, in certain circumstances symbolic universes can be interpreted as giving legitimacy to power interests in the social order; and they can therefore be understood in such contexts to have ideological dimensions. It is important to analytically distinguish between the contexts in which symbolic universes are so related to the political process, and when they are not. This is one of the distinctions which political scientists have attempted to make between political culture and culture in general (not always with conspicuous success).[6] On the other hand, it is important to determine whether groups with competing interpretations of reality share a common overall symbolic universe or political culture. Recent events in Lebanon and Northern Ireland (among others) tragically indicate that this is a point of more than theoretical import.

I view ideology as representing a more specifically focused form of general political culture as it is manifest in the meanings which political actors ascribe to explain and to justify their behavior. Power struggles in day-to-day activities frequently draw upon wider symbolic universes, not only in their formulation, but also ultimately for their inspiration. Therefore, the general symbolic universes of shared meanings which constitute the political culture guide and channel, prescribe and constrain political behavior. Yet, because these meanings are never completely systematic, coherent, and unambiguous, different individuals and groups, given the contingencies of diverse socioeconomic interests and contexts, differentially perceive and interpret them: they may act thusly in part because of these various interpretations, and use the different interpretations to justify their actions. Although ideology is influenced by these different material conditions, it is not *merely* a reflection of them. I shall discuss this point in more detail later.

To summarize the argument thus far: culture is a system of socially constructed and shared meanings; political culture is constituted from those shared meanings which are related to the political process and to relations of power in society; and ideology is the focused expression of different shared meanings and different interpretations of the same meanings as they are related to specific socioeconomic and political interests. I would like to emphasize an additional point. I do not accept the extreme subjectivist position which some critics ascribe to some phenomenological positions. In other words, I stress that it is important to distinguish between the nature of sociopolitical reality as observed and analyzed by the scholar and the reality as it is perceived by the group being investigated. Whereas it is important to understand the meanings ascribed to political behavior and events by the actors involved, I am by no means arguing that these accounts should be accepted as a complete or sufficient explanation of events. Pettigrew's analysis (in this volume) provides strong evidence for the importance of making this distinction.

It should be clear that this conceptualization of ideology is a much broader one than is normally found in the literature in political science and sociology. In his critical survey of this literature, Geertz (1964) found the traditional approaches to the study of ideology inadequate. One type of approach, which he called "interest theory," views ideas as weapons used to disguise and legitimate individual, group, or class interests in the struggle for power. Geertz (1964, p.53) summarized the narrowness of this approach as follows: "The battlefield image of society as a clash of interests thinly disguised as a clash of principles turns attention away from the role that ideologies play in defining (or obscuring) social categories, stabilizing (or upsetting) social expectations, maintaining (or undermining) social norms, strengthening (or weakening) social consensus, relieving (or exacerbating) social tensions."

The second type of approach called "strain theory" focuses on strain at both the personal and societal levels. The major assumption of this approach is that society is chronically malintegrated. Discontinuities between different norms in various sectors of society, discrepant goals, and contradictory role expectations create strains in the society which are subjectively experienced by individuals. Ideology is then viewed as a symbolic outlet for emotional disturbances generated by social disequilibrium. Geertz distinguishes between four main types of explanation employed by strain theorists to stress the main role or functions of ideology. These are: (1) The cathartic, safety-valve, or scapegoat explanations (which are self-explanatory); (2) The moral explanation which views ideology as bridging the gap between desired states and reality; (3) The solidarity explanation which stresses the power of ideologies to unite groups; and (4) The advocatory explanation which is the articulation of strains and demands, thereby raising them in the agenda of public issues.

Both approaches fail to treat ideology as an entity in itself as an ordered system of cultural symbols. They ignore the autonomous process of symbolic formulation and fail to show how "ideologies transform sentiment into significance and so make it socially available" (Geertz 1964, p.57). Geertz views ideologies as "schematic images of social order." He says, "They are extrinsic sources of information in terms of which human life can be patterned—extrapersonal mechanisms for the perception, understanding, judgment, and manipulation of the world. Culture patterns . . . are 'programs'; they provide a template or blueprint for the organization of social and psychological processes . . ." (Geertz 1964, p.62). Geertz claims that, "The function of ideology is to make an autonomous politics possible by providing authoritative concepts that render it meaningful, the suasive images by means of which it can be sensibly grasped" (Ibid., p.65). He concludes:

> It is a confluence of socio-psychological strain and an absence of cultural resources by which to make . . . sense of that strain, each exacerbating the other, that sets the stage for the rise of systematic . . . ideologies . . . Whatever else ideologies may be—projections of unacknowledged fears, disguises for ulterior motives, phatic expressions of group solidarity—they are, most distinctively, *maps of problematic social reality and matrices for the creation of collective conscience* (Geertz 1964, p.64, emphasis added).

In order to analyze the internal structure of ideology as an ordered system of cultural symbols, we must distinguish the major types of symbols, and identify the categories most likely to play a key role in the construction of ideology. The following brief discussion is merely suggestive of the applications of the work in semiotics which might be most useful. There is a general distinction between discursive or elaborating symbols on one hand, and presentational or summarizing symbols on the other. The former appear to play a more dominant role in ideology than do the latter.

Discursive symbolism is cognitive in that it conveys a concept of an object. Language, according to Langer (1942), is the prototypical system of discursive symbolism. Langer's category of presentational symbols is closely akin to Ortner's type of summarizing symbols. Summarizing symbols "are those symbols which are seen as summing up, expressing, representing for the participants in an emotionally powerful and relatively undifferentiated way, what the system means to them" (Ortner 1973, p.1339). They are sacred symbols in the broadest sense in that they are objects of reverence and/or catalysts of strong emotion. In many cultures the flag encourages this kind of all-or-nothing allegiance in certain contexts. The Western Wall in Jerusalem is a powerful summarizing symbol for most Israelis and for many Jews throughout the world.

Elaborating symbols, like discursive symbols, work in the opposite direction. They provide vehicles for sorting out complex and undifferentiated feelings and ideas, thereby making them comprehensible to oneself, communicable to others, and translatable to orderly action. Elaborating symbols are accorded central status in the culture on the basis of their capacity to order experience: they are essentially analytic. Rarely are these symbols sacred in the conventional sense of being objects of great respect or foci of strong emotion; their key status is indicated primarily by their recurrence in cultural behavior or cultural symbolic systems. Ortner distinguishes between two modes of elaborating. Root metaphors have conceptual elaborating power. They are valued as a source of categories for conceptualizing the order of the world. Examples of root metaphors in social scientific culture are the machine for systems theory, the living organism for functional theory, and the computer for cybernetics. Key scenarios have primarily power to elaborate actions as mechanisms offering blueprints for successful action. Ortner gives the example of the Horatio Alger myth in the United States.

As can be seen, the two modes or types of symbols reflect two basic and interrelated functions of culture and ideology discussed in the previous sections. They provide cognitive meaning, and act as maps of problematic reality which provide programs for social action in relation to culturally defined goals. Ortner provides us with a valuable scheme for determining the relative importance, or as she puts it "keyness," of these two basic types of symbols.

> A given summarizing symbol is "key" to the system insofar as the meanings which it formulates are logically or affectively prior to other meanings of the system . . . (i.e.) many other cultural ideas and attitudes presuppose, and make sense only in the context of, those meanings formulated by the symbol. The key role of an elaborating symbol . . . derives . . . from its

formal or organizational role in relation to the system; . . . we may say such a symbol is "key" to the system insofar as it extensively and systematically formulates relationships, parallels, isomorphisms, complementarities, etc., between a wide range of diverse cultural elements (Ortner 1973, p.1343).

Frank Manning's analysis of revivalist politics in Bermuda is a sensitive and sophisticated illustration of the analysis of the symbolic content of ideology in specific contexts which I have proposed. He shows how Bermuda's opposition Progressive Labour Party (PLP) deliberately appropriated rhetorical and ritual symbols of revivalist Protestantism, thereby portraying the campaign in religious terms and fostering racial cohesion and greater political support for itself. In his analysis of the meanings of revivalism to Bermudians, Manning shows how they resonated with the two poles of the dual Caribbean value system. He persuasively argues the need to examine the functional relations of tropes generated by revivalism as well as their logical properties.

Having failed in previous elections, the PLP replaced its former radical and secular vocabulary for one of religious revivalism. Likening the campaign in the 1976 election to a religious crusade, Manning analyzes the biblical imagery, hymns, preaching style with audience participation and response, utilization of clergyman, and other attributes of revivalistic political techniques of the PLP. He shows how the emphasis on family fused the religious and racial sensitivities evoked through the manipulation of the symbols of evangelical Protestantism. Manning discusses two cross-cutting classification schemes. The first axis is built on the polar opposition between religious salvation and secular worldliness. The second axis, a social hierarchy, runs between reputation and respectability. Manning links the different symbols to these axes and the different constituencies to whom they appeal, e.g., sex and class. This analysis is then linked to an explanation of the political gains of the PLP.

Manning draws some interesting general theoretical implications from his case study. He indicates that contrasting tropes, i.e. those representing religion and race, can be employed in the same communicative context; and he stresses the critical importance of the function as well as the form of these tropes. Manning concludes with an analysis of the different functions of metaphor and metonymy and how they can "resonate together in a communicative situation to convey different domains of meaning and to wield separate forms of influence on the social process." He postulates that metaphor promotes change by extending meaning while metonymy retards change by reducing thought to the familiar; and he suggests that "the functional and semantic variation of these tropes accounts for their interplay within the same communicative events."

Similarities and Differences of Approach in this Volume

One of the many issues of dispute among scholars who have studied ideology has been whether interests or ideas are the prime movers of history. The great debate between Idealists and Materialists, or Hegelians and Marxists, as to whether ideas are causes or effects has found expression in the work of anthropologists as well. Among the contributors to this volume, Harvey Blustain and Joyce Pettigrew come closest to the materialist approach, albeit in a modified form. The idealist position is exemplified in anthropology by the work of David Schneider (1968 and 1972) which maintains "that analysis of cultures as systems of symbols can profitably be carried out independently of the 'actual states of affairs' one can observe as events and behaviors" (Keesing 1974, pp. 80-81). Among the contributors to this volume, Peter Bertocci, Marvin Davis, Frank Manning, and I explicitly identify with a middle position, characterized (among others) by the work of Clifford Geertz, which does not posit *a priori* primacy to either interests or to ideas. As Marvin Davis puts it in his essay in this volume, this position "raises as problematic the fit between systems of action and meaning."

In his analysis of Nepalese village politics, Harvey Blustain argues that ideologies are to a great extent determined by the context of political and economic relationships. However, he views group interests as being dynamic and constantly shifting which necessitates the consideration of a multiplicity of social relations. Blustain's stress on the dynamism and complexity of the social system offers a more sophisticated "fine-tuning" (to use his own expression) of the materialist approach.

Whereas I agree with Blustain's conclusion that "ideologies are embedded within—not independent of—power relationships," I would insist that they are not simply reflections of power relations. I also stress that ideology, when it reflects such interests, frequently does so obliquely and indirectly. I also agree that *generally* "different power relationships will result in the invocation of different ideologies"; but I stress that knowledge of power relationships, although necessary, is not sufficient to explain ideological positions. As Geertz observes, discerning such relationships "is more like interpreting a constellation of symptoms than tracing a chain of causes" (Geertz 1973, p. 316).

Blustain effectively documents and explains the manipulation of the multiple forms of ideology by various groups of actors. He also points out the constraints ideology imposes on these actors. For example, his ethnographic material on the rules governing food exchanges indicates that, "For most members of most castes, these rules did, in fact, serve as guidelines for their behavior." Even in the case where high caste men violated dietary taboos, they did so secretly at night. This seems to indicate that even though they were not bound by belief to observe the taboos, they were constrained from violating them publicly by their fear that were they to do so they would lose status in the eyes of peers who evidently continued to adhere to such beliefs. In addition to Blustain's persuasive analysis of the dynamics of ideological manipulation, he indicates how ideology also guides and constrains behavior as well.

Joyce Pettigrew argues that in certain circumstances ideology does not, in fact, cannot guide or constrain actions. She maintains that the Sikh desire for communal autonomy was impossible given the wider socioeconomic and political realities of contemporary Indian society. Sikh political leaders in their dealings with non-Sikh national leaders were forced to ignore certain important codes of traditional culture and ideology. Pettigrew rejects the Sikh followers account of this behavior as personal corruption. Her explanation is based on an analysis of the structural position of the Punjabi Sikhs as a communal minority between two majorities, and their dilemma of remaining faithful to communal tradition while needing to accommodate themselves to political realities which extended beyond communal boundaries.

Although Sikh leaders were therefore forced to violate certain important Sikh traditional ideals, Pettigrew explains they did so in part out of a sincere dedication to Sikh communal interests. Pettigrew convincingly demonstrates that the perception of the Sikh followers that their leaders were personally corrupt was a woefully inadequate explanation of their behavior. Yet this "wrong" explanation is essential to understand the loss of authority of the Sikh leaders. Her richly detailed account shows the complex interplay between various levels of interests and ideas, and vividly illustrates circumstances in which communal ideals cannot operate as realistic guides to pragmatic political behavior in arenas which extend beyond the boundaries in which they were intended to operate.

Yet this is but a more extreme example of a more general phenomena. Universally, political action necessitates to some degree the compromise of principles under certain conditions. Politics is called "the art of compromise." Seliger (1976, p. 120) has shown that, "Compromises cause ideology to bifurcate into the purer, and hence more dogmatic, fundamental dimension of argumentation and the more diluted, and hence more pragmatic, operative dimension." He argues that, "The tension between the two dimensions gives rise to the question of the sincerity of the valuations which are advanced," as is vividly illustrated by Pettigrew. Seliger continues: "Whereas out of the interaction between the two dimensions, which normally signifies an increase of ideological pluralism, arises the challenge of ideological change" (Seliger 1976, p. 120).

Peter Bertocci also compares the cultural model of solidarity and the structure of power and actual political practice of a community in rural Bangladesh. He analyzes the dialectic interaction between normative models of social solidarity based on religious corporate groups as moral units, and the actual power domains of local elites. He demonstrates that the power domains are formed with reference to the cultural model which gives them legitimacy. Bertocci convincingly argues that these activities are not merely cynical manipulations of the normative code, since they derive from the political actors' self-images as proper Muslims, and thereby provide certain constraints to their actions. As he says, "Thus, the model of solidarity informs the concrete, specific expression of the structure of power, which in turn provides the conditions under which solidarity is possible." Unlike the Sikh leaders, the politicians of rural Bangladesh in Bertocci's case function primarily within boundaries where their norms are appropriate, although they are far from perfectly congruent with the political structure.

The general lack of a perfect "fit" between ideology and changing socioeconomic and political structures provides the basis for the dialectic interplay between ideology and interests which is the thematic focus of this volume. I postulate that ideological formulations become increasingly more important as the taken-for-granted nature of the traditional manner of doing things is called into question and is undermined. Ideological formulations either reinforce and reassert the meaningfulness of the old definition of reality, alter it, or replace it with a new one more in congruence with the changed conditions. Each contribution to this volume illustrates this point in a different way.

Marvin Davis shows that in the village he studied in rural West Bengal, villagers see traditional leaders as being in charge of "village politics," which is perceived as protecting village customs based on divinely sanctioned inequalities of rank; and they view the statutory village council as doing "government politics," i.e., promoting change and progress. These two different forms and types of politics are not viewed as being mutually exclusive. Davis analyzes the role of political themes as ideologies, i.e., schematic images of a certain reality which the villagers use to type their competitions, thereby making them intelligible as part of more general cultural patterns. He shows how these ideological themes serve to map reality and to direct and rationalize activity. For example, an analysis of the politics of caste-climbing and the sanctioning of backsliders are interpreted by Davis as processes of regularization, which allow for adjustments within, but ultimately strengthen, the socio-cultural system of ranked inequality.

An additional point raised by Davis which bears on my previous argument is that, "traditionalism requires that changes be accommodated in a way that they are regarded not simply as new, but paradoxically as old, as reviving or restoring an original and better state." He shows that innovative government policy is falsely characterized as restorationist to gain support and legitimacy. Modern village councils were related to significantly different institutions which existed in a mythic past, a reputed "Golden Age" of ancient India. Davis relates several examples of Indira Gandhi's attempts to use traditionalism and myth as instruments of political innovation.

Myth is probably the most ancient mode of cultural expression and is therefore very important for the study of ideology. In fact, myths contained the oldest types of root metaphors and key scenarios. Myths have traditionally used the past as paradigms for the interpretation of present states of affairs. In a more contemporary version, Sorel saw myth as providing a vision of the future which makes the present understandable. In both cases, the present is related to another time dimension in order to make it more comprehensible. Tudor (1972, p.35) argues that the characteristic perspective of the myth-maker is that, "He orders his experience on the assumption that the present is an episode in a story, an incident in a dramatic development; and it is this . . . that enables him to distinguish between what is significant and what is not.". He also stresses that the meaning and purpose of myths can only be understood in terms of the specific circumstances in which they are told and heard, and that they are altered to fit changing circumstances and contingencies. I stress that this is true for all expressions of culture and ideology, symbols and ritual as well as myth.

Myth is the articulation of the desire for moral coherence in the world. Tudor (1972, p.114) says, "The awareness of this incoherence or absurdity endemic in practical existence inspires the demand for a morally coherent world; and this demand is, I suggest, the stuff of which political myths are made." Tudor insists that the definitive characteristic of myth as a symbolic form is that it tells a story, that it is a narrative of events cast in dramatic form that is used in practical argument.

Sorel defined ideology as myth that had been rationalized and thus laid open for discussion. Although not all ideology is based on myth, most ideologies, even the most rational ones, contain within them mythical elements. For example, modern Zionist ideology, which is both a product and a rejection of the "Enlightenment," owes much of its legitimacy and appeal to its incorporation of the historic eschatological myth of the "Exile" and the "Redemption" of the Jews which was cultivated by successive generations in every country to which Jews wandered and which bound them in a self-conscious union of fate and destiny, and kept alive their tie to the ancestral homeland.

One of the reasons for the strength of the myth is because it presents a more lucid and compelling image than do abstract principles. In addition, an account of the past which justifies a present course of action is attractive to most people. A political myth generally tells the story of a particular group or society. Tudor (1972, p.139) says, "It has as its hero or protagonist, not an individual, but a tribe, a nation, a race, a class, or even a chance collection of exiles and immigrants." Cuthbertson (1975) distinguishes between three major mythic themes: (1) Order—the justification of political authority and societal stratification; (2) Obligation—individual domestic and social duties and leadership responsibilities; and (3) Freedom.

Political myths tend to play a particularly crucial role in times of crisis. At times of societal disorder, or of a threat to societal order, an important means of mobilizing collective action is through the use of myths to generate collective responses to collective commitments and responsibilities. The saliency and credibility of such myths to respective publics is therefore crucial in determining whether collective responses can be successfuly mobilized. Certainly ascertaining the credibility and effectiveness of myths is a difficult task under the best possible circumstances, and when such research is of a highly politically sensitive nature in a fairly "closed" society, the difficulties are formidable. Therefore, Martha Olcott's study of the attempt by the Soviet Union to create a Kazakh nationalist and socialist Soviet culture is a particularly bold endeavor. Olcott poses the question: To what extent can a political regime succeed in deliberately selecting and manipulating the symbols and myths of a traditional culture to recreate a new political identity which is both linked to the past and still compatible with the political goals of the regime?

Olcott's conclusion is that the Soviet cultural policy enjoyed a rather "mixed" success. The government was most successful in creating a Kazakh Soviet national political identity which was nationalist in form and socialist in content from a traditional nomadic society based on tribal confederations. Although they clearly had an impact on the developing Kazakh culture, Olcott argues that the Kazakh culture of today represents the continuation of cultural tradition; and it is not an entirely new Soviet-created artifact.

The incorporation of Kazakh territory into the Russian Empire, the abandonment of the seminomadic lifestyle, the emergence of new intelligentsia, the impact of Islam, Russian culture, Western ideals, nascent nationalism, the Russian Revolution, forced collectivization and political oppression resulting in the elimination of traditional leadership, the loss of nearly two million Kazakh lives and the near destruction of the entire Kazakh herd, are some of the main forces and variables which influenced the development of Kazakh political identity and culture over the course of several centuries. Dealing with such a complex set of forces over such a long period of time, it is extremely difficult to weigh and measure the interaction between socioeconomic, and political forces, and the variations in policies of ideological manipulation carried out by different Russian regimes during this period.

The Soviets attempted to strip the Kazakhs of many of their historic heroes and supply them with new ones. It is difficult to evaluate, for example, how effective the identification of Stalin as a metaphoric eagle, i.e., Kazakh hero, was to a people whom he had helped to partially decimate. We know that many wept throughout the U.S.S.R. at the news of Stalin's death, but we have no confirmation of how genuine or widespread this remorse was among the Kazakhs. The speech of Olzhas Sulumaniov at the Sixth Conference of the Writers' Union of Kazakhstan in 1971 indicates that even politically reliable (i.e., loyal to the regime) members of the Kazakh elite are not satisifed with officially sanctioned Soviet heroes, but demand the right to know and pay homage to their own tradition and mythic heroes.

According to the conceptual framework I am putting forth, since the cultural and the political dimensions of social dynamics are dialectically linked, it is impossible to achieve a change in one dimension without affecting the other dimension. Therefore, if the Soviets succeeded in gaining the political allegiance and ideological support of the Kazakhs, through a combination of political pressure and symbolic manipulation, this must have had an impact on other aspects of Kazakh culture. On the other hand, if the Kazakhs have retained some degree of cultural continuity, and are asserting their rights to greater cultural autonomy, this must reflect on the evaluation of the relative success of the Soviets in creating a new Kazakh Soviet national identity. I have argued that there is a wide variation in the extent to which cultural and socio-political structures "fit." This case seems to indicate that in a situation of political domination when deliberate directed culture change is attempted, the subordinate unit can maintain some degree of continuity of cultural identity by selectively adapting those aspects of the dominant culture which it is forced and/or induced to adopt; and by syncretizing them with the elements of tradition which are most sacred, valued, compatible with changing conditions, and most tenaciously held, some degree of integration of the new with the old can be achieved. This is characteristic of most political change which has taken place in the Third World.

In order to understand in greater depth how this process works, we must examine this process in specific contexts and more limited historical periods. For example, one of the most important ways in which myths are taught, reinforced, and reinterpreted is through ritual activity.

The study of ritual by anthropologists has until recently, generally been limited to traditional societies, and one of the requisite characteristics which defined ritual in such circumstances was the presence of mystical beliefs. When political scientists, e.g., Nieberg

(1973), and sociologists, e.g., Bocock (1974), have attempted to analyze ritual behavior in contemporary industrialized society (the U.S. and the United Kingdom respectively in the examples mentioned), they have tended to apply the term to such a wide range of phenomena that the concept becomes a metaphor and loses much of its analytic explanatory value (cf. Aronoff 1977, and Goody 1977 for elaborations of this point).

In their introduction to the edited volume *Secular Ritual,* Moore and Meyerhoff (1977, p.3) argue that since the essential quality of the sacred is its unquestionability, and since many secular political ideologies contain unquestionable tenets, "secular ceremonies can present unquestionable doctrines and can dramatize social/moral imperatives without invoking the spirits at all."[7] Although they may not invoke the spirits, they frequently invoke the "spirit" of past leaders, e.g., Marx and Lenin, Mao, De Gaulle, Churchill, Ben-Gurion, or Lincoln, etc.; or, they may invoke the "spirit" of the Constitution, or the "spirit" of a past heroic epoch of history, e.g., the Golden Age of India, as Davis illustrates in his essay. In certain cases a social past can be fabricated, as Olcott shows in her study of the attempt by the Soviet Union to create a Kazakh Soviet culture.

Ritual aims to structure behavior and to shape the socially perceived nature of reality. "Ritual and ceremony are employed to structure and present particular interpretations of social reality in a way that endows them with legitimacy. Ritual not only belongs to the more structured side of social behavior, it also can be constructed as an attempt to structure the way people *think* about social life" (Moore and Meyerhoff 1977, p.4). Social anthropologists have generally followed Durkheim's paradigm and have tended to interpret rituals as reflections of social relationships. They have examined how rituals state, reiterate, or reinforce social ties, or express social conflicts, or delineate social roles.

More recent emphasis on the social meanings of ritual by anthropologists reveals how rituals can also help shape the cultural ideas which they express. The participants in the symposium on secular ritual agreed that "a balance should be sought between these two ways of looking at the problem of meaning"; and they consequently focused on "the *creation,* the *performance,* and the *outcome* of secular ceremonies, and . . . their myriad meanings" (Moore and Meyerhoff 1977, p.5). I therefore characterize this anthropological approach as the concern with the social, cultural, and political roles, functions, forms and meanings of rituals, and the symbols, myths, and ideologies expressed in them. This anthropological approach is distinguished from other approaches by its focus on the interpretation of symbolic meanings of ritual proceedings located in specific social, cultural, and political contexts. I stress that it is only within these specific situational contexts that symbolic, mythical and ritual meanings can be understood.

Different scholars give divergent definitions of ritual and emphasize various characteristics of them. Whereas my own formulation (Aronoff 1976 and 1977) was strongly influenced by my participation in the symposium on secular ritual, it differs somewhat from that of the editors of the volume. I emphasized that the primary characteristic of rituals is that they take place in controlled and bracketed social settings. This social framing is similar to the focused interaction in encounters formulated by Goffman (1961), in which the participants agree to sustain for a time a single focus of cognitive and visual attention. Myerhoff also asserts, "the most salient characteristic of ritual is its function as a frame. It is a deliberate and artificial demarcation. In ritual, a bit of behavior or interaction, an aspect of social life, a moment in time is selected, stopped, remarked upon" (Moore and Myerhoff 1977, p.200).

Because of this controlled nature of the ritual performance, the actions of the actors are to a certain extent prescribed or constrained, but within these limits considerable freedom and innovation can take place. For example, in my analysis of ritual proceedings among the secondary echelon of leaders of the Israel Labor Party (Aronoff 1976 and 1977) the devisive debates were relatively free and open, but were constrained by the necessity of reaching final consensual agreement in conformity with the policies of the top leaders; and any formulations vetoed by the top leaders were removed from the agenda of the national party conference. I contend that this freedom within clearly bracketed constraints appears to be particularly characteristic of modern secular rituals. The actors are at some level conscious of performing ritual acts; and the ritual actions have serious implications for those who perform them. I define one characteristic which precludes many otherwise rituallike activities from being classified within the ritual end of the continuum. I argue that the outcomes of ritual are determined in advance. For example, many commentators have remarked about the rituallike nature of elections. This criteria would distinguish between the ceremonial aspects of genuinely competitive elections and the more characteristically ritual nature of conspicuously rigged elections such as those in which there is a single candidate.

The ritual performers converse in symbols which, although multivocal, are understood by, and have meaning for, the ritual performers. Ritual can be an important means for dealing with ambivalent social roles, conflicting interests, and ideological world views which threaten the unity of the social unit in which they take place. Rituals can also be an important means for dealing with cognitive dissonance between ideology and social reality, particularly when the latter has changed to the point where it is no longer meaningfully explained by the former. In such cases:

> the wider world must be introduced, but in a controlled and disguised manner . . . the rules seem to exist to let something difficult be quietly expressed as much as to exclude it entirely from the scene. Given the dangers of expression, a disguise may function not so much as a way of concealing something as a way of revealing as much of it as can be tolerated . . . We fence our encounters in with gates; the very means by which we hold off a part of reality can be the means by which we can bear introducing it, (Goffman, 1961, pp.77-8).

Because rituals present aspects of reality symbolically in selective and sometimes disguised manner, they allow discourse on it to take place which can produce either conciliation, affirmation, or transformation of ideologies.

The determination of which of these alternative outcomes will prevail largely depends upon the specific socio-cultural contexts, and particularly the power relations in which they take place. For example, I demonstrate that the affirmation or assertion of ideology in the ritual proceedings in the Labor Party was largely determined by the dependence of the secondary leaders on the top leaders, the internalization of party norms by the secondary leaders, and their perception that they could do nothing to change the order of things at that particular juncture in time. My prediction that when the socio-cultural conditions and the power relations would change, that this would affect the types of ritual behavior and their outcomes was confirmed (Aronoff 1978). I have suggested a relationship between specific types of rituals and specific types of political systems; and it is clear that these relationships must be investigated over a much wider range of conditions so that the typologies can be tested, corrected, expanded, and developed.

Because of these special characteristics which I attribute to ritual, I argued in the previously mentioned publications that they will not take place in modern society on a society-wide basis. I would now rephrase this statement to read "generally" not take place in modern society on a society-wide basis. Because of the necessary conditions of control and bracketing, they are certainly more likely to take place in subgroups within contemporary society where these conditions are more likely to be found. For example, they are conspicuous in many of the different cults found to be so prevalent in the U.S. which have recently gained public attention through the tragic circumstances of the mass ritual suicide in Guyana. However, since all of the previously listed conditions are matters of degree, an analytic continuum of these characteristics could be projected which would allow for such phenomena as obviously rigged national elections (mentioned previously), or aspects of the cultural revolution in China and racial riots in Bermuda (Manning 1978) to be classified within the ritual end of the continuum of ceremonial behavior.

Conclusion

I have proposed an interpretation of culture as a socially constructed and shared structure of meanings. Those shared cultural meanings which guide, inform, and constrain political activity constitute the political culture. Ideology is a more focused dimension of the political culture, which is identified with the specific socioeconomic and political positions of power and interests of groups. It performs in a more specifically focused way the same functions of the wider culture of which it is a part, i.e. it provides both cognitive meaning and normative guides for social action. It is specifically linked to the legitimation process in politics, but is not exclusively confined to this function. In this respect approaches which postulate an a priori primacy to either ideology as a cultural system or to material power interests are inadequate. My position is that the reciprocal or dialectical relations between these two spheres (ideology and interests) provide one of the most challenging and appropriate foci for analysis in political anthropology.

Symbols, myth, and ritual are basic components and forms of culture. Symbols are the primary building blocks out of which all cultural forms are constructed. There are two main generic types of symbols—presentational or summarizing symbols and discursive or elaborating symbols. The latter type tend to play a more predominant role in ideological expression. These elaborating symbols can be subdivided into root metaphors which have conceptual explanatory power and key scenarios which are blueprints for successful social action, thereby corresponding to two of the major functions of culture.

Myth, which can contain both root metaphors and key scenarios, is one of the oldest narrative forms of cultural expression. Some scholars have considered myth to be either a prerational or an irrational form of ideology, and therefore confined to ancient or traditional societies or "primitive" regressions in contemporary society. Ritual is one of the most ancient forms of behavioral cultural expression. Many anthropologists have considered ritual to be a form of nonrational or nonpurposive behavior which, because it is dependent upon mystical beliefs, they consider to be confined to certain types of traditional societies. I have proposed that by refining and adapting these concepts to contemporary complex societies, important insights into the relationship between political culture/ideology and political power/interests can be gained. The most valuable results will be gained when ideology, symbol, myth and ritual are studied in specific socioeconomic, political, and cultural contexts.

Finally, I have postulated that the lack of perfectly logical symmetry within ideologies, and the lack of perfect congruence between ideology on the one hand and socio-economic and political structures and the power interests of groups within them on the other, constitutes a framework within which a dialectical process occurs. The dual nature of ideology which divides it between a more fundamental dogmatic dimension and a more pragmatic operative dimension corresponds with the dual function of ideology to provide both cognitive meaning and practical guides to action. Yet, these dual dimensions frequently pull in opposite directions. The degree to which individual actors within groups or parties, and groups or parties within a system will tend to align with either the more fundamental or the more operative dimension of ideology is largely (although not exclusively) a function of the structural position within the unit or system. For example, a leader is more likely to be more ideologically pragmatic than his followers; and a leader of a party in power is more likely to be more ideologically pragmatic than is the leader of an opposition party, particularly one that is rarely in power.

Ideologies, as definitions of reality related to more specific power interests, and more comprehensive symbolic universes never achieve perfect symmetry, coherence, and clarity. Therefore, the ambiguities and contradictions within them are constantly subject to varying interpretations and reinterpretations by different individuals and groups to justify their actions. The bases for differing interpretations are frequently, but not always, different material interests or positions of power. Therefore, as material conditions change, different definitions of reality arise and challenge older ones. The challenge of alternative definitions of reality is more likely than not to involve conflicts of power as there is a strong tendency for groups to try to impose their particular definition of reality on others. The nature of such competition will be affected by whether such competing groups share an overall symbolic universe or political culture.

Although the framework I have put forth is obviously a very preliminary formulation, hopefully it offers a useful focus for research and a basis for further conceptual refinement. This framework calls for an approach which should attempt to identify the extent to which there is a developed symbolic universe, the degree to which there are competing ideologies sharing a common symbolic universe, or the possibility that one dominates its competitors or potential competitors which do not share a common general symbolic frame of reference. This requires the analysis of the reciprocal relations between symbolic universe and/or ideologies, institutional structures, and relations of power in the society.

We shall want to pay careful attention to the role of experts in the definition of reality, the myth-makers and ideologues, in those systems where they are accorded special power and authority. Of particular interest are their relationships with their respective constituencies and with various power interests in the society. It is important to make intensive analyses of ideologies as symbolic systems in order to determine how they transform sentiment into significance thereby making it socially available. We shall want to examine the constituent parts of these maps of problematic social reality, by distinguishing between the cognitive, discursive, elaborating symbols (root metaphors and key scenarios) on the one hand, and the expressive, summarizing, presentational symbols on the other. It will be important to analyze the role of myths and paradigmatic metaphors in ideology and how they form programs for orderly social action in relation to culturally defined goals.

One important means of accomplishing the former goals is to focus analysis on political rituals in contemporary society. Since the analysis of the symbolic meanings of myth and ideology are explicable only in relation to specific situational contexts in which they order behavior and shape the perceptions of social reality, ritual proceedings offer an ideal setting in which to make the observations for such an analysis. Certainly rituals are not the only forms in which one can observe the important interaction of the forementioned variables. But, because rituals frame or bracket social occasions for special symbolic commentary, they provide a kind of laboratory situation for investigating how actors perceive the meaning of their socio-political relations, how they view themselves, and their societies. These self-perceptions and definitions of reality are the very essence of ideology. They constitute the socially shared "knowledge" which is the basis of institutional integration and the legitimation of the social order. Therefore, one of the most important research questions to be asked is: how effectively ideologies do this job in any given context, and what are the sociopolitical consequences when they are ineffective?

Notes

1. I gratefully acknowledge a grant from the Rutgers University Research Council which helped in the preparation of this essay for publication. I sincerely thank Saliba Sarsar for his able research assistance, and Professors P. Bertocci, H. Blustain, E. Davis, M. Davis, R. Kaufman, B. Lewis, A. Lucas, J. Pettigrew, R. Sigel, H. Waterman, C. S. Whitaker, Jr., and R. Wilson for their helpful comments on various drafts of this essay.
2. This is particularly the case in political science. The literature in political anthropology tends to be somewhat more balanced, cf. Aronoff 1979, Balandier 1967, Claessen 1974, A. Cohen 1969 and 1974, R. Cohen 1965, 1967, 1969, and 1970, Colson 1968, Easton 1959, Kurtz 1979, Seaton and Claessen, eds. 1969, M. G. Smith 1968, Swartz, Turner and Tuden, eds. 1966, Swartz 1968, Tiffany 1979, Tuden 1969, and Winkler 1970.
3. For example, cf. Berger and Luckmann 1966, A. Cohen 1969 and 1974, and Geertz 1973.
4. Most of the essays in this volume were originally presented at the Xth International Congress of Anthropological and Ethnological Sciences in New Delhi, India in December, 1978 at a panel on "Boundaries and Units of Analysis in Political Anthropology," which I organized. Others were added at my invitation because they contributed to the theme of this volume.

5. For example, Berger (1969, p.66) claims that man's propensity for order is a fundamental human trait: "Any historical society is an order, a protective structure of meaning, erected in the face of chaos. Within this order the life of the group as well as the life of the individual makes sense. Deprived of such order, both group and individual are threatened with the most fundamental terror, the terror of chaos that Emile Durkheim called anomie (literally, a state of being 'orderless')." Susanne K. Langer (1942, p.287) argues: "Now he (man) can adapt himself somehow to anything his imagination can cope with; but he cannot deal with chaos."
6. Cf. Almond and Verba 1963, Banfield 1958, Bluhm 1974, Devine 1972, Pye 1968, Pye and Verba, eds. 1965, Rosenbaum 1975, and Verba 1965.
7. In the summer of 1974 a symposium on secular ritual was held at the Burg Wartenstein Castle of the Wenner-Gren Foundation for Anthropological Research. My thinking on the subject was profoundly influenced by my participation in this conference.

References

Almond, Gabriel A., and Verba, Sidney. 1963. *The civic culture: political attitudes and democracy in five nations.* Princeton: Princeton University Press.
Aronoff, Myron J. 1974. *Frontiertown: the politics of community building in Israel.* Manchester: Manchester University Press, and Jerusalem: Jerusalem Academic Press.
Aronoff, Myron J. 1977. *Power and ritual in the Israel Labor Party: a study in political anthropology.* Amsterdam/Assen: Van Gorcum.
Aronoff, Myron J. ed. 1976. *Freedom and constraint: a memorial tribute to Max Gluckman.* Amsterdam/Assen: Van Gorcum.
Aronoff, Myron J. 1978. The decline of the Israeli Labor Party: causes and significance. In *Israel at the polls: the Knesset elections of 1977,* ed. Howard R. Penniman, pp. 115-45. Washington, D.C.: American Enterprise Institute Studies in Political and Social Processes.
Aronoff, Myron J. 1979. Ritual in consensual power relations: the Israel Labor Party. In *Political anthropology: the state of the art,* eds. S. Lee Seaton and Henri J. M. Claessen pp. 275-310. The Hague: Mouton.
Balandier, Georges. 1967 (1972 edition). *Political anthropology.* Harmondsworth: Penguin.
Banfield, Edward C. 1958. *The moral basis of a backward society.* Glencoe: Free Press.
Berger, Peter L. 1969. *A rumor of angels.* Garden City: Doubleday.
Berger, Peter L. and Luckmann, Thomas. 1966 and 1967 (Anchor Books edition). *The social construction of reality.* London: George Allen and Unwin.
Bluhm, William T. 1974. *Ideologies and attitudes: modern political culture.* Englewood Cliffs: Prentice-Hall.
Bocock, Robert. 1974. *Ritual in industrial society.* London: George Allen and Unwin.
Claessen, H.J.M. 1974. *Politieke antropologie.* Assen: Van Gorcum.

Cohen, Abner, 1969. Political anthropology: the analysis of the symbolism of power relations. *Man* 4, pp. 215-35.
Cohen, Abner. 1974. *Two-dimensional man*. London: Routledge & Kegan Paul.
Cohen, Ronald. 1965. Political anthropology: the future of a pioneer. *Anthropological Quarterly* 38, pp. 117-31.
Cohen, Ronald. 1967. Anthropology and political science: courtship or marriage? *The American Behavioral Scientist*, Nov/Dec, pp. 1-7.
Cohen, Ronald. 1969. Research directives in political anthropology. *Canadian Journal of African Studies* 3, pp. 23-30.
Cohen, Ronald. 1970. The political system. *Handbook of method in cultural anthropology*, eds. R. Naroll and R. Cohen, pp. 861-81. Garden City: Natural History Press.
Colson, Elizabeth. 1968. Political anthropology: the field. *International Encyclopedia of the Social Sciences*, ed. David L. Sills, pp. 189-92. New York: Macmillan and the Free Press.
Cuthbertson, Gilbert Morris. 1975. *Political myth and epic*. Ann Arbor: Michigan State University Press.
Devine, Donald J. 1972. *The political culture of the United States*. Boston: Little Brown.
Easton, David, 1959. Political anthropology. *Biennial review of anthropology*, ed. B. Siegal, pp. 210-62. Stanford: Stanford University Press.
Geertz, Clifford. 1964. Ideology as a cultural system. *Ideology and discontent*, ed. David Apter, pp. 55-72. New York: Free Press.
Geertz, Clifford. 1967. Ritual and social change: a Javanese example. *American Anthropologist* 59, pp. 32-55; reprinted in eds. N.J. Demerath and Richard A. Peterson. 1967. *System, change, and conflict*. New York: The Free Press, pp. 231-49.
Geertz, Clifford. 1973. *The interpretation of cultures*. New York: Basic Books, Inc.
Goffman, Erving. 1961. *Encounters: two studies in sociology of interaction*. Indianapolis: Bobbs-Merrill.
Goody, Jack. 1977. Against ritual: loosely structured thoughts on a loosely defined topic. *Secular ritual*, eds. Sally Moore and Barbara Myerhoff. Amsterdam/Assen: Van Gorcum.
Habermas, Jurgen. 1973. *Theory and practice*. Translated by John Viertel. Boston: Beacon Press.
Keesing, R.M. 1974. Theories of culture. *Annual review of anthropology*. Palo Alto, California: Annual Reviews, Inc.
Kurtz, Donald V. 1979. Political anthropology: issues and trends on the frontier. *Political anthropology: the state of the art*, eds. S. Lee Seaton and Henri J.M. Claessen, pp. 31-62. The Hague: Mouton.
Light, Ivan H. 1969. The social construction of uncertainty. *Berkeley Journal of Sociology* 14, pp. 189-99.
Langer, Susanne K. 1942. *Philosophy in a new key*. Cambridge: Harvard University Press.
Manning, Frank. 1978. Riot and revivalism: cultural tradition and political modernization in Bermuda. A paper presented at the International Congress of Anthropological and Ethnological Sciences, New Delhi, India.

Moore, Sally F. and Myerhoff, Barbara eds. 1977. *Secular ritual*. Amsterdam/Assen: Van Gorcum.

Myerhoff, Barbara. 1977. We don't wrap herring in a printed page: fusion, fictions and continuity in secular ritual. *Secular ritual*, eds. Sally F. Moore and Barbara Myerhoff. Amsterdam/Assen: Van Gorcum.

New York Times Magazine, May 27, 1979, p. 31.

Nieburg, H. L. 1973. *Culture storm: politics and the ritual order*. New York: St. Martin's Press.

Ortner, Sherry B. 1973. On key symbols. *American Anthropologist* 75, pp. 1338-46.

Pye, Lucian W. and Verba, Sidney eds. 1965. *Political culture and political development*. Princeton, New Jersey: Princeton University Press.

Pye, Lucian W. 1968. Political culture. *International encyclopedia of the social sciences*, ed. D.L. Sills, pp. 218-225. New York: Macmillan and the Free Press.

Rosenbaum, W. 1975. *Political culture*. New York: Praeger.

Schneider, David. 1968. *American kinship: a cultural account*. Englewood Cliffs, New Jersey: Prentice-Hall.

Schneider, David. 1972. What is kinship all about. *Kinship studies in the Morgan memorial year*, ed. P. Reining. Washington, D.C.: Anthropol. Soc. Washington.

Schurmann, Franz. 1966. *Ideology and organization in communist China*. Berkeley: University of California Press.

Schutz, Alfred. 1962. *Collected papers, vol. 1*. The Hague: Nijhoff.

Schutz, Alfred. 1964. *Collected papers, vol. 2*. The Hague: Nijhoff.

Seaton, S.L., and Claessen, Henri J. M. eds. 1969. *Political anthropology: the state of the art*. The Hague: Mouton.

Seliger, M. 1976. *Ideology and politics*. New York: The Free Press.

Smith, M. G. 1968. Political anthropology: political organization. *International encyclopedia of the social sciences*, ed. D. L. Sills, pp. 193-201. New York: Macmillan and the Free Press.

Sorel, G. 1950. *Reflections on violence*. Glencoe: Free Press.

Swarz, Marc J. ed. 1968. *Local-level politics*. Chicago: Aldine; London: University of London Press.

Swarz, Marc J., Turner, Victor, and Tuden, Arthur eds. 1966. *Political anthropology*. Chicago: Aldine.

Tiffany, Walter W. 1979. New directions in political anthropology: the use of corporate models for the analysis of political organization. *Political Anthropology: The State of the Art*, eds. S. Lee Seaton and Henri J. M. Claessen, pp. 63-75. The Hague: Mouton.

Tuden, A. 1969. Trends in political anthropology. *Proceedings of the American Philosophical Society* 113, pp. 336-40.

Tudor, Henry. 1972. *Political myth*. London: Pall Mall Press.

Verba, Sidney. 1965. Conclusion: comparative political culture. In *Political culture and political development*, eds. Sidney Verba and Lucian Pye. Princeton, N.J.: Princeton University Press.

Winkler, Edwin. 1970. Political anthropology. *Biennial review of anthropology*, ed. B. Siegel, pp. 301-86. Stanford: Stanford University Press.

Chapter 2

Go Down, Moses: Revivalist Politics in a Caribbean Mini-State [1]

Frank E. Manning

How do politicians get elected? How do they reach and persuade an audience? How do they relate the values and concerns of the public to their own ideas, interests, and programs? The general answer to this familiar line of questioning is obvious: effective communication. It is equally apparent that a politician's communication to the public, especially in an election campaign, is primarily a discourse and display of symbols: rhetorical figures, performance idioms, styles, slogans, emblems, appearances, mannerisms, and all of the other condensed expressive devices that are said to constitute an "image." It is knowing what symbols are appropriate and how to use them—a skill urged by Machiavelli four centuries ago—that makes one a winning politician.

Cohen's notion of politics as a "two-dimensional" process yields a useful approach to the problem of political communication. "Political Man," he advises, "is also Symbolist Man" (1974, p.v.). The struggle to gain or hold power is interrelated with the usage of symbols that are both expressions of the struggle and instruments within it. Politicians manipulate these symbols, often adroitly and to obvious advantage. The symbols themselves, however, are characteristically apart and autonomous from the political situation, rooted in such intimate, emotional, and deeply significant areas of culture as religion, kinship, and ethnic custom.

Nations newly independent or in the terminal phases of colonialism are often good examples of the dynamic and vital role played by symbolism in the political process. Decolonization may be an unchallenged ideal in the United Nations, but popular support for it is not readily forthcoming in societies where both indigenous traditions and the colonial legacy have left a cultural residue that is either opposed to nationalism, or, more likely, simply unattuned to it. The task of political leaders is revolutionary, but in a semantic rather than military sense. The weapon is meaning, not force.

The political struggle of Bermuda's Progressive Labour Party (PLP) richly illustrates these general considerations. Formed as a vehicle for decolonization and democratic reform, the PLP has yet to attain parliamentary power, although its fortunes dramatically improved in the most recent election campaign, that of 1976. This paper examines that campaign as a forum in which the PLP appropriated rhetorical and ritual symbols of revivalist Protestantism both to portray the campaign in religious terms and to foster racial cohesion. Following an ethnographic account of the case, I will offer a hermeneutic analysis of what revivalism means to Bermudians, and attempt to show that its principal meanings resonate positively with both the indigenous and colonial poles of a dual value system that permeates Caribbean social life. In conclusion, I will review various models of the tropes generated by revivalism, and propose that the role of those tropes in political communication must be examined in terms of functional relations as well as logical properties.

The Challenge to Oligarchy

A circum-Caribbean tourist resort and tax haven, Bermuda proudly claims the oldest parliament in the British Commonwealth overseas, an assembly that has met since 1620. Yet until two decades ago the actual form of government was closer to oligarchy than democracy. Power, political and economic, was tightly controlled by an aristocracy of white families descended from the original seventeenth century English settlers and known colloquially for the past few generations as either "Front Street" (their commercial address) or the "Forty Thieves" (their acquisitive style). Seafarers until the 1870s, agricultural import-export agents from then until the 1920s, and now an interlocking establishment of merchants, bankers, commission agents, and corporate lawyers, the aristocracy have used the instruments of patronage—jobs, loans, credit, sponsorship, recallable mortgages, charitable donations—both to sustain their position and to symbolize themselves as a paternal, benevolent, almost feudal ruling class.

Bermuda's client population are primarily black, descendants of African slaves and West Indian immigrants who now constitute three-fifths of the island's 55,000 persons. Their first political challenge to white hegemony began in the late nineteenth century with the gradual coalescence of a black bourgeoisie of small shopkeepers, successful tradesmen, and struggling professionals. Their goals, attempted through intermittently active, loosely formed associations, were modest: generally, to win one of the four seats allotted to each parish in the House of Assembly and to gain minority representation on the parish vestries. By the 1940s these objectives had been met in heavily black parishes, in part through the selection of candidates who were moderate and docile enough to be acceptable to the aristocracy. There were no changes in the restricted franchise system, which prevented those without land from voting while allowing landholders to vote in as many parishes as they owned property. As recently as 1958, parliamentary elections were spread out over three days, enabling the landed gentry to travel between polling stations at a leisurely pace.

Aided by Bermuda's first labor union, the black movement accelerated on all fronts during World War II, but declined again with the crippling of the union in the following decade. Major changes were delayed until the early 1960s, when a popular campaign for voting reforms gained a temporary concession that extended the franchise to all adults but raised the minimum age from twenty-one to twenty-five and gave property owners an extra or "plus" vote as compensation for the loss of unlimited plural voting. The new political potential of blacks inspired the formation of the Progressive Labour Party (PLP) three months before the 1963 general election. The PLP's advantage over the independents, who included both white aristocrats and a few blacks who disdained party politics, was quickly made apparent. The party coordinated all campaign activity—meetings, fund raising, publicity, canvassing—and offered a single, detailed platform to the voters. The PLP ran only nine candidates for the thirty-six seats in the House of Assembly, but six of them won victories over both white and black independents.

With the plus vote scheduled to be phased out and the voting age returned to twenty-one in that session of parliament, the fall of the *ancien regime* seemed a foregone conclusion. Instead, the aristocracy regained the offensive a year later by forming a coalition party with the growing white middle class and an influential segment of conservative, upwardly mobile blacks. Named the United Bermuda Party (UBP), the coalition arose as an economic reflex. The rapid expansion of tourism since World War II and the phenomenal growth of the international finance sector after 1960 had produced an economy that the aristocracy continued to dominate but no longer monopolized. The UBP was a pragmatic alliance of Bermuda's old and new money interests, brought together by their common stake in a buoyant but extremely fragile economy and their perception of the threat posed to that economy by a party aligned with organized labor and susceptible to influences from both the black American movement, then in its most radical phase, and the West Indian drive for national independence. Terrified by the specter of economic catastrophe, the UBP subdued racial and class divisions in a way that appeared on the surface to transcend the structural compartmentalization of Bermudian society.

The UBP co-opted the PLP's drive for constitutional and social reform, supporting representative government, full and equal adult suffrage, free secondary education, and the desegregation [2] of both public and private facilities. On other issues, notably Bermudianization of the work force and the replacement of private charities with public social services, it modified PLP proposals but nonetheless became identified with a liberal position. The strategy was aimed both at winning the marginal black vote and at the more subtle but crucial objective of forcing the PLP into a leftist position that would dramatize their radicalism and thereby enhance the solidarity of the UBP. The strategy worked. A serious split emerged early in the PLP's history between professionals and labor union representatives, a rift in which labor gained the upper hand through its covert financial support of the party and commensurate influence. In the mid-1960s, five of the six members of the parliamentary caucus either left or were expelled from the party, three to form a short-lived splinter party and two to come back with scars that never really healed. Other professionals—physicians, dentists, lawyers, teachers—also bolted from the party, in some cases joining the UBP and in others simply abandoning politics.

A drift toward ideological radicalism developed later in the decade, primarily through the influence of an intellectual fringe who formulated a loose rhetorical synthesis of American black power and notions of revolutionary socialism imported from Africa and the Caribbean. Besides further alienating conservative professionals, this stance also disturbed the PLP's core of working-class supporters, whose political goals are immediate and mundane and whose dream of advancement centers more on capitalist competition than socialist equality (Manning 1973, pp. 87-147). The party's most enthusiastic constituency became the black street gangs and paramilitary youth groups whose brief florescence in the late 1960s and early 1970s contributed to two race riots and a spate of killings, included the assassinations of the governor and the police commissioner.

Investigating the 1968 riot—which occurred only three weeks before the parliamentary election—a commission summarized the partisan controversy by observing that the UBP was generally seen as wanting "fraternization for the colony's good," while the PLP, stridently urging black nationalism, was viewed as representing a "denunciation of the colony's status" (Wooding 1969, p. 69). The UBP's advantage resulted in part from the skillful exploitation of their chief symbol: the "partnership" of the races, portrayed graphically by a handshake in black and white and depicted rhetorically as the harbinger of a new social order replacing segregation with integration, bigotry with tolerance, animosity with respect and trust. Contrastingly, the PLP was not only radical and militant in ideology, but monoracial in composition—an image that made them the scapegoat for racial division.

In the 1968 election the PLP won only a third of the popular vote and a quarter of the seats in the House of Assembly, making Bermuda the only country in the Antilles with a black majority to return a predominately white government in its first election under full and equal adult suffrage (Allen 1973, p. 122). Four years later, in the election of 1972, that phenomenon was repeated with an identical distribution of parliamentary seats. Surveys indicate that UBP candidates, three fifths of them white,[3] gained unanimous white support and a fifth of the black vote (Manning 1978, p. 36). On a constituency basis, the UBP won districts with voting populations as high as three-quarters black.

Preempted and humiliated, the PLP retreated from combat after the 1972 election. A few party veterans quietly disengaged from politics to devote more attention to occupational careers. Others who remained involved changed their views, generally concluding that radicalism and racial militancy were, after all, unsuited to Bermuda. Concurrently, a group of culturally bourgeois professionals, mainly teachers, took enough interest in the party to seek seats on the policy-making central committee, while small businessmen became active on the parish level and groomed themselves as future candidates. Rapport was built with socially respectable black organizations, notably the churches and particularly the African-Methodist Episcopal (AME) Church, the largest and most influential black denomination. Public relations was taken over by media and advertising specialists who cultivated an image aimed at the black middle and upper classes.

The diminishment of a militant black threat undercut the brokerage value of UBP blacks to their white partners, especially in view of the party's gesture of knighting a black and making him premier a few months before the 1972 election. In 1974, UBP blacks formed the Black Caucus, an internal pressure group modelled after its American namesake and aimed at gaining more "meaningful participation" in the party and the national economy. In a report (Black Caucus n.d.) written as a private party document but leaked to the press, the Black Caucus warned the UBP that the PLP remained a radical threat and that Bermuda would face socialist upheaval unless the demands of the report were met. The Black Caucus also charged that the UBP's "partnership" was a sham, and that whites retained firm control of the party and the country. Accordingly, they as UBP blacks were stigmatized in the public eye for having "betrayed" their race and having "somehow lost their manhood" (Black Caucus n.d., p. 1)—an arresting metaphor in that three of the eight signers were women!

These circumstances gave the PLP an unprecedented opportunity in the 1976 election. But to exploit that opportunity, they needed a repertory of symbolism that would ridicule and rebuke the UBP's exposed racism, reduce their own vulnerability to charges of racism, project a morally credible but politically uncontroversial ideological stance, and function practically to coalesce a precarious constituency of working-class blacks, the traditional (but disenchanted) core of supporters, and the black bourgeoisie, who had withdrawn their support in the previous decade but were timidly beginning to return it. The PLP sought that repertory of symbolism in the performative genre of revivalism.

Performance, Preaching, Politics

The performative orientation of speech behavior in Afro-American and Afro-Caribbean societies has long impressed sensitive observers. Formal verbal presentations are clearly histrionic, and even ordinary conversations are easily and frequently raised to a high level of showmanship. Cultural heroism is attained by the ablest masters of the spoken word: evangelists, comedians, broadcasters, entertainers of every description, and the "good talkers" who hold sway in the male peer group. Kochman (1970, pp. 145-162) postulates that black speech is generally expressive or expressive-directive, not simply a means of reporting information. The content of speech is important, of course, but it is only one component of meaning. The form of speech is both meaningful in itself and influential on the interpretation of what is actually said. In the context of performance, form and content together establish a sense of dynamic rapport between speaker and audience, the foremost criterion on which speech events are evaluated within the culture.

PLP campaign rallies have always been popular speech events as well as the party's chief means of reaching the voters. In the three weeks of the 1976 parliamentary campaign, the PLP held nine rallies, as well as a "victory meeting" a few days after the election. Attendance averaged about 300 persons, the capacity of most public auditoriums. As at church services, there were usually another fifty persons outside the building, milling around in small groups, listening through doors and windows, and occasionally venturing inside. By contrast, the UBP communicates through advertisements in the media, particularly newspapers. During the 1976 campaign the UBP held only three rallies, two of which drew fewer than a hundred persons.

Like political and parapolitical movements throughout the Caribbean, the PLP has characteristically embellished rhetoric with millenarian imagery. In the 1968 and 1972 campaigns, revolutionary socialism and black power were envisioned as the basis of a new order that would overturn a capitalist, colonial, and racist system. The prevailing sentiment was not only secular, but rather explicitly antireligious. Religion was depicted in Marxist terms, as an opiate against oppression and therefore a deterrent to necessary militancy. The black churches were often attacked for failing to support the political struggle and for allowing themselves to become instruments of the patronage system. A few prominent party figures professed atheism, and in general party activists shunned involvement in church groups.

In 1976, however, the vocabulary of secular radicalism was replaced by one of religious revivalism. The PLP maintained their espousal of decolonization and democratic reform, but related the issues rhetorically to an apocalypse constructed from religious symbolism. The campaign was likened to a crusade against social immorality, waged by a people whom God had chosen to remake and inherit the land. Party leader Lois Browne, a veteran of the radical period and the only member of the PLP's parliamentary group who remained loyal throughout the dissension of the 1960s, struck the theme as follows:

> God doesn't mean for oppression to win. So ultimately we will win. We must rededicate ourselves to the task.
>
> We have faith, strength. Even if we don't win, we're going to go on. It's inevitable. We know we're going up and the others are coming down. We will claim the victory in 1980, or 1984, or whenever. It is God's work to so take us there. . . .
>
> The party wants to build idealism and restore it to our lives and politics. Our members are quality people. They are made in the image of God, and will represent you.

Biblical imagery, especially Old Testament, was extensively tapped. One candidate said that the campaign reminded him of "Climbing Jacob's Ladder," a familiar hymn about the mystic ladder linking heaven and earth and representing the promise of redemption. "Like the people in the song," he said, "we are going higher, higher, higher." Another candidate used the Biblical dream archetype, relating his "vision" of the marginal parishes falling successively to the PLP: "I see Sandys. I see Warwick. I see Hamilton. And I see St. George. And the ugly head of the UBP is put down forever." As he called the names of the parishes there was a gathering crescendo of excitement and interpolation in the crowd. When he reached St. George, the seat needed for a majority, one supporter yelled: "Go down, Moses. He's leading us to victory."

With the partisan opposition defined in moral terms, UBP blacks could be excoriated as sinners rather than as "Uncle Toms," their more traditional stereotype. "They (UBP blacks) are clasping the hand that gives them money," charged Browne at the opening campaign rally, "and I think God is going to strike them dead." At the postelection victory meeting she used a converse religious image to congratulate the PLP's committed followers: "You have to be really baptized to be in the PLP. We don't have any lollipops to give away."

The form and performance style of rallies were based on the revivalist prototype. Rallies were opened with prayers and closed with benedictions and the singing of religio-political hymns such as "We Shall Overcome." A well-known gospel singer was recruited as a candidate and called upon several times to render "Oh, Freedom," "Sometimes I Feel Like a Motherless Child," and other favorites. Her appearances usually came after the prayers and opening remarks but before the main speeches, the same place given to solo singing in Pentecostal services.

A new and successful candidate borrowed a hallmark of preaching by keynoting his speech with a Biblical text: "Unless the Lord build a house, they labor in vain who build it." His theme was that the PLP's political philosophy carried out God's plan. By contrast, the UBP's efforts reflected materialism and man-made objectives.

As in black revivalism (cf. Manning 1977), evangelism passed easily into entertainment, introducing an element of fun and consciously calling attention to the act of playing with performance styles. The obvious analogy between collections at rallies and offerings in church inspired Browne to develop the following pitch:

> It's part of our heritage, our culture, to pass the bucket. At the Church of God (Bermuda's largest Pentecostal assembly) they say that one-tenth of what you have belongs to God. So give it to us now. We are his agents (laughter).

Besides the regular collections there were calls for pledges at the first two meetings of the campaign, raising about $3000 on each occasion. Browne comically compared the pledging decision to the salvation experience:

> You know, you wriggle around in your seat and you hope that you have another hoot before you get saved. And you sit there and you don't go up for prayer. I have a feeling that there's someone out there tonight who's going through that feeling. You want to make that pledge. But you just can't get the courage. Yes now. The woman out there has finally got the courage. Stand up.

While the decision to pledge was likened to conversion, the form of pledging resembled "testimony," the recitation in church services of personal religious experience. The layman's opportunity to preach, testimony is often an entertaining and somewhat competitive exchange with the pastor. The political counterpart had similar characteristics:

> PLEDGE DONOR: (after making his own pledge and praising the PLP). I'm going to pledge ten dollars from my father. And if you don't get it from him, I'll get it from him (laughter).
>
> BROWNE: (speaking first to recording secretary). Ten dollars from _____, from his son. I'm going to leave it just like that, so I'll know what it is. And if I don't get it from him, I'm going to come looking for you (laughter).
>
> Anybody else want to pledge for their fathers? You can pledge for your mothers, too (laughter).

After several other pledges were made in the same manner, Browne noticed a young woman with a tape recorder:

> Oh, you're taping it all down. I'm going to have to do something on the Flip Wilson show.[4] I know I missed my calling. I should have been an entertainer.

Audiences participated more spontaneously by interpolating speeches with shouts of agreement and encouragement, the form of response typically evoked by stirring preaching in revival services. The pattern evolved into a highly stylized choral dialogue at an early meeting when the Deputy Leader, Frederick Wade, introduced the campaign slogan: "Time for a Change. Send Jack[5] a Message. Vote PLP." He urged the crowd to repeat the slogan, and soon had them chanting loudly and in unison. Continuing his speech, he used the slogan again after each major point:

> Under the Westminster Model, it's either all power or no power. And that's why it's time for a change, send Jack a Message, vote PLP.
>
> The UBP stay in power because of gerrymandered districts. There should be one member per district, and all districts should be equal in population. That's why it's time for a change, send Jack a Message, vote PLP.

As the speech unfolded, it exemplified the familiar form of black oral expression that Keil describes as "constant repetition coupled with small but striking deviations" (1966, p. 97). The speaker introduced a litany of grievances and proposals, each affirmed by the rhythmic refrain of the campaign slogan. At the end of the speech the slogan was again chanted in cadence by the audience, with pauses for individuals to insert their own petitions. One woman followed "Time for a Change" with the comment, " 'Cause I'm tired of working. I want a pension."

PLP candidates made a concerted effort to associate themselves with religion. As a group, they attended one or more churches every Sunday throughout the campaign—a rhetoric of action to support their verbal rhetoric. Speeches frequently employed the black trope that Abrahams (1970, p. 164) calls the "intrusive I"—the intrusion of first person pronouns into narrative in order to relate speaker to subject. Recalling her childhood exposure to religion, Browne commented at one rally:

> My dear grandmother brought me up in the Christian church. She sent me to two and sometimes three churches—St. Augustine's (Anglican), the Salvation Army, and the Holy Rollers (Pentecostal)—to make sure that I didn't become a heathen or an atheist.

The cultural as well as chronological climax of the campaign was the final rally on election eve, held outdoors in a racetrack before an estimated 2,000 people. The adult choirs of the largest African Methodist Episcopal (AME) and Pentecostal assemblies appeared in their robes and mortarboards, introducing the program with a medley of gospel music. The starring role, however, was given to three black pastors. The candidates (aside from Browne, who spoke very briefly) merely sat on the stage and acknowledged introductions, much like invited dignitaries at special church programs.

The first pastor to speak was known for his friendship with the UBP and aversion to the PLP. He explained his presence as the audience suppressed laughter:

> Mr. _____ (the rally organizer and a key party strategist) called me and said, "You know, sometimes we tend to forget there's a God. We'd like you to come and remind us, and lead us in prayer." As a minister of this parish and a member of the community, I could not say no.

He then opened the meeting with a short prayer, and went home on the grounds that he was coming down with the flu.

His two colleagues, both known as PLP sympathizers but previously inactive politically, offered no such apologies or explanations for their presence. They not only led prayer, but went on to attack the government with all the flamboyance and drama of hellfire preaching. One of them, a Pentecostal who had recently had the mortgage on his church revoked by a white bank, began by joking about the racetrack setting and then observing:

> Some horses are black, and some are white. It's the horses that endure to the end who will win.

He continued:

> I have been praying and fasting that God will have his way in this election, and not a certain group of people. It's time God ruled this island. We know God uses men to do his work. It seems God is unsatisfied with the job that some folk have been doing. Tomorrow he might be satisfied to have the results a little different.

Later he debunked the partnership symbol:

> We've been hearing a lot lately about some kind of partnership. For so many years we never had this partnership. It's true we can look at our TV screens and see blacks shaking hands with whites. I'm not against it. God knows I'm not against it. But I like the real thing.

The Family

The PLP's symbolic counterpart to the UBP's partnership was the family. In the platform the family was mentioned eight times, typically as a rationale for the party's solution to social and economic problems. The following planks, often quoted or paraphrased at rallies, are representative:

> We view the steady deterioriation of family life with alarm, and undertake to institute social and economic measures designed to strengthen the family unit, and particularly as it is affected by unemployment.
>
> Every form of encouragement and support will be given to

> persons engaged in various forms of agricultural production . . . Home gardening encourages the strengthening of family units.
>
> A reconstructed, comprehensive social insurance programme will be instituted. Additional resources will be directed towards the strengthening of family life.
>
> Regulations will be instituted to ensure that TV and other forms of mass media are used to build and strengthen rather than destroy family life.
>
> In order to cater to the full development of family life, there must be available a proper layout of roads and houses along with adequate provisions for cultural and recreational facilities to occupy leisure hours.

While the type of family prescribed by the churches—the nuclear, monogamous unit based on formal marriage—was idealized, the PLP also spoke to the victim and the sinner. The popularity at rallies of the hymn "Sometimes I Feel Like a Motherless Child," attests, as Frazier (1964, pp. 15-16) pointed out, to the chronic instability of the black family and the resulting sense of loneliness. In a speech entitled "Restoring Humanity That Has Been Robbed," a physician recruited as a new candidate addressed the subject of illegitimacy, the most stigmatized deviation from the ideal family and the status of about two-fifths of black births.

> I don't accept the designation that some children are illegitimate. All children are legitimate because they are conceived in love. They must be loved the way only a mother can.

He continued by relating the child's need for maternal care to the chief problem of single mothers—the necessity to work and therefore by away from their children:

> One-fifth of a child's education occurs between the ages of four and six. Parents should read and sing to their children, and play with them. Mothers should be with their children, instead of working outside. The PLP will make this possible, because it is dedicated to the restoration of the family unit.

Interestingly, the physician was billed as a "family doctor," emphasizing his differences from the incumbent, a white neurosurgeon. Although making his first bid for office, he topped the poll over both the neurosurgeon and another long-term UBP incumbent.

The family was variously symbolized by the PLP in both words and action. The party encouraged candidates to bring their spouses and children to meetings, and to seat them on stage. In turn, candidates made a determined effort to recognize husbands and wives together in the audience, and to comment on their political and matrimonial unity. A popular bumper sticker read, "Our whole family is voting PLP." Receiving a pledge from her cousin at a rally, Browne commented:

> Ten dollars from my cousin. You know, PLP support runs right through my family. I have only one cousin and one auntie in the UBP. I've got some swell cousins. She was on crutches the other day. She was the subject of a hit and run accident. She's still on crutches but she's here tonight and she's pledging. I wish I could reach out and touch you, and feel you.

Her brief remarks at the election eve rally were more serious as she summarized the campaign by expounding on the "vital issue" faced by the voters:

> It's the question of family life, the quality of life, and what's going to happen to Bermuda. We have taken on this issue as a means of saving Bermuda from degradation and corruption. We have tried to impart the true social meaning and truth of life.
>
> There are big gaps between the PLP and the UBP. It's not just money. It's a question of values, dignity, love, and brotherhood.

The PLP lost again the following day, but gained four seats in parliament and six percentage points in the popular vote—the major electoral shift in Bermuda's brief history of party politics. Survey research (Manning 1978) revealed that the electoral gains came almost entirely from blacks, notably those who previously supported the UBP or previously failed to vote. The survey data also indicated a substantial opinion swing to the PLP among black women, particularly in the middle and upper classes. To appreciate the role of revivalist symbolism in this political shift, we must probe its range of meanings and their relationship to the conceptual and social structure of Bermudian life.

Winning Niggers

Recalling the effort to win Hamilton Parish, a predominately black area where the UBP had taken all four seats in 1968 and 1972, a PLP insider confessed how a new symbolic strategy was plotted for the 1976 campaign:

> We asked ourselves, "Man, how we gonna win those niggers down in Hamilton Parish?" Then the idea came—put on a revival! And everyone agreed. "Yeah, that's what we need—a revival. We'll take them to church!" We knew the UBP could never follow that act.

Later he mused, "Revivalism, blackness, PLP—it's all together."

While perhaps gilded by the PLP's exuberance at winning three of the four seats in Hamilton Parish (as well as the other election gains), these candid remarks point to two cultural sensitivities that were evoked by revivalist symbolism. The most obvious and direct, of course, is evangelical religion. Like most of the Protestant Caribbean, Bermuda is aptly described as a "Bible Belt" or what Cross (1950) called a "burned over district"—an area scorched by the fire of revivalism. The PLP tapped religious sentiment through the correspondence of campaign rallies to church services, the likening of political combat to a moral crusade, and the emphasis on family well-being. Ironically but suitably, evangelism was used to counteract one of its own traditional influences: the notion that politics is "worldly" and therefore sinful. The PLP reversed that definition by associating immorality with the political status quo and identifying itself as the agent of spiritual reform and millenarian hope. The idealized evangelical concept of being "born again," dramatically and totally, could also account for the PLP's ideological transformation from atheism, black power, and revolutionary socialism to religion and conservative morality. As sinners saved by grace, the party had a credibility that would have been hard to project apart from the symbolic model of conversion.

The second cultural sensitivity stirred by the PLP's campaign was racial identity. Although revivalism denotes religion, it is also an idiom of expression that is distinctively black. The call and response exchange between speaker and spectators, a generally high level of oral, kinetic, and emotional audience participation, the exaggeration of histrionics as a means of emphasis and self-mockery, the interplay of entertainment and proselytization, a preference for dramatic hyperbole rather than factual precision—all are modes of performance that blacks recognize as symbols of their cultural style. Moreover, while this recognition was articulated both in the reflexive jokes that punctuated campaign speeches and in the comments on strategy given by party workers, it is largely a bond of solidarity based on moral and aesthetic traditions rather than ideological formulations. Unlike the symbols of racial militancy, the vocabulary and style of revivalism neither polarized blacks nor gave whites a ground for decrying racial chauvinism.

The family symbol fused the religious and racial sensitivities. As an explicit theme, the family summarized the moral purpose of the campaign. Implicitly, the family stood in opposition to the partnership of the races—the UBP's chief symbol and slogan. While the partnership had an idealistic dimension, its principal rationale, even in UBP rhetoric, is economic; harmonious integration is proclaimed essential for the stability needed to attract tourists and international companies. By contrast, the family represents a social unit that is "natural" rather than contrived, diffuse rather than specific, moral rather than expedient. Above all, the family is monoracial and therefore an analogue of the PLP.

Religion is, however, more than a fundamental value, just as race is more than a basic principle of social formation. The deeper cultural importance of religion and race derives from their significance as foci and organizing themes of the black Bermudian conceptual universe. Two cross-cutting classification schemes, each constructed from native categories of thought and behavior, can be viewed as the coordinates of this universe. The first axis, a metaphysical and moral continuum, is built on the polar opposition between religious salvation and secular worldliness. The poles are ideally envisioned as absolutes, but it is also recognized that there are gradations between them both in individual practice and in the standards imposed by different churches. With reference to adherents of the two major denominations (both active and visible in the PLP's campaign), the rigid asceticism generally observed by a Pentecostal is likely to be compromised by an African Methodist, who will drink wine with dinner, wear sedate items of jewelry, and attend sporting events occasionally, but nonetheless stay clear of nightclubs, bars, and similar milieu that are unambiguously worldly. Conversely, among persons who are not practicing Christians, there are recognizable degrees of indulgence in drinking, dancing, extramarital sexual involvement, and other pleasures and habits that are deemed sinful.

The second axis, a social hierarchy, runs between reputation and respectability, opposing value systems discerned by Wilson (1973) in his seminal model of the conceptual order of Caribbean and circum-Caribbean societies. Respectability is predicated partly on socioeconomic prestige symbols that designate social rank: standards of education, occupation, residence, material posession, and so on. Respectability also derives from moral conventions imposed by the mainstream Christian churches and exemplified chiefly by the middle and upper classes: legal, monogamous marriage, a stable nuclear family, restrained (or at least discreet) sexual conduct, and those Protestant ethic virtues of sobriety, thrift, responsibility, and self-improvement. Contrasting religious and secular symbols are the characteristics of reputation. Religiously, reputation is associated with fundamentalist sects and syncretic cults that emphasize the mystical, often millennial, accrual of power. On the secular side, reputation is embodied in a behavioral ethos highlighted by competitive and performance abilities, verbal fluency, sexual prowess and potency, swagger and "badness" (toughness, hedonism, ostentation).

Traditionally, the reputation-respectability axis corresponded to opposite racial identifications. The symbols of reputation, religious and secular, express the value orientations of creole (black, indigenous [6]) culture, just as the religious and secular symbols of respectability are products of colonial tutelage and therefore white in cultural origin. But with the growth among blacks of racial awareness and assertiveness, the socioeconomic status designations and sense of moral righteousness connoted by respectability have shifted on the conscious level from a white to a black identification. The process is seen throughout the Caribbean, and has been documented in Jamaica by longitudinal surveys which show how, during the period from 1962 to 1974, the elite switched from Euro-American to Afro-Caribbean tastes in a wide variety of symbolic items: food, music, entertainment, literature, and educational curriculum (Bell and Robinson 1977). In Bermuda this general process has been long encouraged by the AME Church, whose proclivity toward respectability is suggested by local epithets (Black

Anglicanism, African Money Eaters) and whose racial self-awareness is maintained by the ceaseless propagation of the church's history (in Bermuda as in the United States) as a protest against indignities suffered by blacks both in white religious assemblies and in the wider society. To simplify, the change undergone by the black bourgeoisie has been from deliberately projecting a posture of whiteness to pairing the symbols of respectability with smug, almost chauvinistic, color consciousness. The closest American counterpart might be the readership of *Ebony*.

As diagrams have become *de rigueur* in academic presentations of worldview, and its relation to social order, let me venture the following:

Diagram 2.1

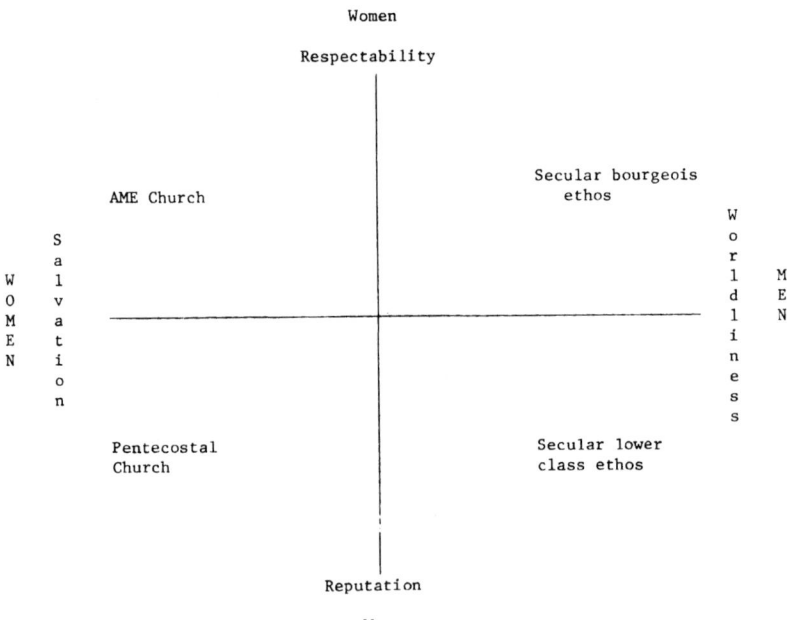

Importantly, the diagram relates the two axes of symbolic classification to the opposition between the sexes, one of the most striking sociocultural features of Afro-American and Afro-Caribbean social life (Keil 1966; Wilson 1973). The church constituency is made up preponderantly of women, while secular worldliness is closely associated with settings dominated by the male peer group: clubs, street corners, rum shops. Similarly, respectability is centered in the household and family, arenas controlled by women, while reputation is largely an expression of the stereotyped machismo complex. This should not imply, of course, that women are always "saved" and respectable, or that men are unable to achieve those statuses; rather, it is simply that female role models are generally predicated on religion and respectability, while the proclivity of male role models is toward the opposite values.

Relating the PLP's campaign symbolism to this conceptual schema, I would propose that the fundamentalist zeal, evangelistic imagery, and promise of millennial power stir the religious sensibilities of reputation, while the family theme and the general sense of moral righteousness signify the religious values of respectability. Alternately, the dramatic, flamboyant, and humorous orientation of rallies exemplifies implicitly the secular, worldly side of reputation, while the association with symbols of the black heritage, notably the church, conveys the type of racial-cultural identity that both the religious and secular faces of respectability consciously project. Moreover, the richness and diversity of the revivalist mode allows all of these meanings to be communicated in the same performance format. In the election eve rally, for instance, the preachers' hell-fire attack on a "wicked government" represented both sides of reputation, while the pose struck by the restrained, sedate candidates emitted a generalized respectability. Indeed, an informant recalled how the rally was orchestrated to convey such an image:

> If you can get a minister up before a few thousand people, he's got to preach. He can't resist. He's got a captive audience. So they (the preachers) came out swinging, and we (the candidates) stayed behind them like nice respectable niggers.

This line of interpretation is consistent with two striking patterns uncovered in survey research that I conducted in the weeks following the Bermuda election campaign. The first is that, while both sexes of blacks contributed equally to the PLP's popular vote gain, women alone, and particularly upper-class women, professed increased ideological agreement with the PLP; contrastingly, black men slightly diminished their agreement with the PLP (Manning 1978, pp. 80-83). The discussion here suggests that the emphasis on religion was a potent appeal to women, and that the appeal was intensified in the upper class by the emphasis on a "respectable" form of racial identification. At the same time, revivalism's resonance with the performance tropes of reputation gained increased voting support and prevented serious ideological erosion in the party's traditional base of strength, the (preponderantly male) black working class.

The second pattern pertained to issues that have been raised in public discussion and campaign platforms in recent years (Manning 1978, pp. 93-171). On economic and constitutional issues, there were significant opinion differences among blacks that correlated, as one would expect, with professed agreement for opposite parties. On religious and moral issues, such partisan differences disappeared almost entirely, but were replaced by outstanding differences correlating with sex and social class. These data suggest, first of all, that the meanings evoked by revivalism were likely influential in the voting and agreement shift to the PLP among blacks who had previously supported the UBP (Manning 1978, pp. 36-38). The data also suggest that the PLP's revivalist style played on black sociocultural variability without broaching the issues that divide blacks along partisan lines. Revivalism held different meanings for different segments of the black electorate, but all of them could see in it a basis of support for the PLP.

Political An-Trope-Ology: Forms and Functions

If nothing more, the Bermudian case should show that political communication is a highly symbolic enterprise, and that an understanding of it requires analysis of the conceptual universe in which communicative symbols operate. The politicians themselves—at least the ones I have encountered—realize that their craft is a traffic in symbols and that success depends on knowing and exploiting what is meaningful to the people. This awareness, to revert to Cohen's (1974) phrasing, is what makes politics a two-dimensional process, a dynamic interplay of semantic forms with circumstances and interests.

I have here examined a single phase of the process, an election campaign, and assessed the role of a symbolic theme both in imparting meaning and winning support. What implications—general, theoretical, or comparative—does the analysis have for political anthropology?

The thesis that symbols convey plural meanings has been widely advanced in recent years, notably in the voluminous and influential work of Turner.[7] He argues that dominant symbols are "multivocal" or "polysemous," and that they have opposite (sensory and social) poles of meaning. In the context of action (ritual, performance) the opposite poles are interrelated, integrating their meanings and communicating a holistic understanding. This "unification of disparate significata" is, for Turner, one of the fundamental attributes of symbolic action.

To an extent, this principle applies to the case before us. The two meanings of revivalism, religion and race, enhance each other and are mutually associated on a summary level. Recall my informant's observation: "Revivalism, blackness, PLP—it's all together." Yet it is also apparent that the two meanings wielded very different influences on sociopolitical thought, and that from the PLP's standpoint the separation of these influences was vitally important. The religious meaning fostered change. It gave PLP politics a new sense of purpose and value, encouraging broader participation and shifting political concern from issues on which blacks are divided along partisan lines to issues on which black differences are a matter of internal cultural variability, harmonized through revivalist symbolism. The racial meaning, on the other hand, implied a conservative response. Appealing to black awareness and solidarity, it maintained the traditional division of the races and rebuked the type of change proposed by the UBP—the move toward an integrated partnership.

The conceptual separation of religion and race was maintained through their representation in contrasting tropes of symbolic formulation, which are themselves predicated upon, and evocative of, contrasting modes of thought. As I will try to show briefly, classificatory models of these tropological contrasts tend to emphasize their relationship to radically different sociocultural formations, and to overlook functional differences. The Bermudian case, however, indicates that contrasting tropes can be employed in the same communicative context, and suggests further that the matter of function is of critical importance.

Rhetorically, the PLP's revivalist symbolism conveyed its religious meaning through metaphor and its racial meaning through metonymy. Metaphor is comparison, built on the symbolic construction of similarities. Metaphorically, the campaign took on significance as a moral and millennarian struggle, not merely a political contest or a drive for power. Metonymy, by contrast, derives from the perception of contiguity rather than similarity. In metonymy an entire phenomenon or field of meaning is represented through one of its parts—the principle of *pars pro toto*. Metonymically, the revivalist style—one aspect of black culture—evoked that culture in a general sense and identified the PLP as the party of the racial majority.

Recent anthropological discussions of the metaphor-metonymy contrast, an issue pondered by philosophers since the time of Plato and Aristotle, have proceeded from Levi-Strauss' (1966) contention that the tropes are logical opposites and transformations of each other. Fernandez (1974), in a comprehensive discussion of this approach, concludes that metaphor and metonymy share the same seven functions or "missions," all of them having to do with the conversion of pronouns from an inchoate and inappropriate condition. Throughout his discussion Fernandez presents metonymy as a parenthetical appendage of metaphor, a treatment suited to its imputed status as a logical transformation serving the same semantic role. Beck (1978) has criticized the Levi-Straussian position for pairing metaphor and metonymy as opposites that make sense only in relation to each other, but has taken a similar position in her own statement: "The metaphor and the metonym are two sides of a single device used to bridge the gap between rational and sensory thought processes" (1978, p. 87). None of these approaches really enlightens the problem of how metaphor and metonymy can resonate together in a communicative situation to convey different domains of meaning and to wield separate forms of influence on the social process.

The similarity-contiguity opposition, the cognitive basis of metaphor and metonymy, has recently been dismissed by Douglas (1978) as a distinction that is impossible to make. Nonetheless, her earlier (1970) typology of elaborated and restricted codes rests on that very distinction. Elaborated codes of symbolism, like metaphor, articulate meaning by expressing it in alternate contexts and semantic realms that are perceived as resembling the original. Restricted codes, like metonymy, articulate meaning by concentrating it on a limited number of its symbolic components. Douglas' central argument is that these opposite codes operate in radically different types of social formation. Elaborated codes are found in societies where the structures that control external boundaries ("group") and internal relationships ("grid") are weak, whereas restricted codes are found where group and grid are strong. She admits that in a modern pluralistic environment the two types of social formation may meet in the same arena, but depicts the result as division and miscommunication attributable to the incompatibility of symbolic codes.

Another pertinent classificatory model comes from Ortner (1973), who divides a culture's "key" symbols into two categories: summarizing and elaborating. Summarizing symbols are like metonymy and restricted codes: they subsume and unify a broad field of meaning under a single representation. Elaborating symbols are like metaphor and elaborated codes; they differentiate and expand meaning by relating it to alternate models and scenarios. Ortner also makes a point that is essentially precluded by Fernandez and Douglas: that her distinction pertains to symbolic function as well as symbolic type. "These (summarizing and elaborating) functions may be performed by any given symbol—at different times, or in different contexts, or even simultaneously by different levels of meaning" (1973, p. 1344).

But can a statement of greater heuristic value be made about function? I would submit that the symbolic pairs in all of these classificatory models—and the inventory of models could easily be expanded—have opposite general implications with respect to change. Metaphor promotes change by extending meaning, relating one form of comprehension to another, and urging the suitability of alternate interpretations and responses. Metonymy retards change by reducing thought to the familiar, containing it within images and experiences that are already known. Elaborated codes share the cognitive properties of metaphor, and flourish among those whose social ties are loose enough that they personalize moral and ideological mandates, relate traditional values to contemporary circumstances, and undertake the ventures that produce change. Restricted codes share the cognitive properties of metonymy, and flourish among those whose social structures closely encompass and regulate their lives, binding them to tradition. My contention is less easily related to Ortner's model, but it is notable that the characteristics of elaborating symbols—the differentiation and mobilization of meaning in an essentially profane context—are likely to be supportive of change, whereas summarizing symbols have a more conservative orientation based on their diacritical function of crystallizing commitment, catalyzing feeling, and conveying meaning "in an old fashioned way" (Ortner 1973, p. 1340).

I suggest, then, that the functional and semantic variation of these tropes accounts for their interplay within the same communicative events, and indeed (in the Bermuda case) within the same thematic field of symbolism. Popular political movements are likely not only to resonate with a diversity of sociocultural sentiments, but also to have a mixture of conservative and liberal objectives, an affinity with some kinds of change and a resistance to others. Political man is two-dimensional both in the sense of relating meaning to power, and in the further sense of trafficking with dualistic and contrastive tropes, concepts, and influences.

Notes

1. Part of the ethnographic data and a preliminary version of the analysis put forth in this paper were originally presented in a colloquium on political rhetoric at Memorial University of Newfoundland. The material was refined in guest lectures to anthropologists at the University of New Brunswick and to political scientists at St. John's University. I am grateful to participants in all three gatherings for their critical insights as well as their support and kindness.
2. Like the American South and the Bahamas, but unlike the British Commonwealth West Indies, Bermuda had a thoroughgoing system of racial segregation. The system was dismantled on a piecemeal basis in the 1960s, but *de facto* segregation maintains racial division. The awareness of racial separation remains Bermuda's most fundamental, ubiquitous, and intractable social reality (cf. Wooding 1969, pp. 86-7).
3. Of the UBP's successful candidates, however, 77 percent were white in 1968 and 70 percent in 1972. The discrepancy results from the UBP's policy of running heavily black slates in the PLP's safe constituencies.
4. The reference to black American comedian Flip Wilson is appropriate, in that he has developed a comedy routine around black revivalism.
5. In 1976, the UBP leader was "Jack" (now Sir John) Sharpe, who later stepped down as premier under the pressure of cabinet resignations. Sharpe's first name linked him with Sir Henry ("Jack") Tucker, the UBP's architect and chief personal symbol. The name Jack is also stereotypically white, in much the same humorous but deprecatory sense that Sambo is black.
6. Strictly speaking, there are no indigenous cultures in the Caribbean apart from those of the Amerindians, most of whom were decimated within the first century of European contact. But creole culture is regarded as indigenous in the sense that it is a synthesis of ground-level Caribbean experience with other influences, chiefly African retentions and derivations. As such, creole culture contrasts with cultural orientations that are recognizable colonial impositions.
7. A summary of Turner's major theoretical propositions and conceptual orientations is found in his recent book, coauthored with his wife (Turner and Turner 1978).

References

Abrahams, Roger, 1970. Patterns of performance in the British West Indies. In *Afro-American anthropology: contemporary perspectives*, ed.

Norman Whitten, Jr., and John Szwed, pp. 163-79. New York: The Free Press.
Allen, David, 1973. Bermuda: mid-Atlantic magnet, In *Guide to Caribbean, Bahamas and Bermuda,* ed. Eugene Fodor, pp. 119-64. London: Hodder and Stoughton.
Beck, Brenda, 1978. The metaphor as a mediator between semantic and analogic modes of thought. *Current Anthropology* 19, 1: 83-97.
Bell, Wendell, and Robinson, Robert V., 1977. European melody, African rhythm, or West Indian harmony? Paper read at annual meeting of International Studies Asociation, March 1977, St. Louis. Mimeographed.
Black Caucus, n.d. *Report to the Premier.* Hamilton, Bermuda. Mimeographed.
Cohen, Abner, 1974. *Two-dimensioned man.* Berkeley and Los Angeles: University of California Press.
Cross, Whitney, 1950. *The burned over district.* Ithaca: Cornell University Press.
Douglas, Mary, 1970. *Natural symbols.* Barrie and Rockliff: The Cresset Press.
Douglas, Mary, 1978. Comments. *Current Anthropology* 19, 1: 88.
Fernandez, James, 1974. The mission of metaphor in expressive culture. *Current Anthropology* 15, 2: 119-45.
Frazier, E. Franklin, 1964. *The Negro church in America.* New York: Schocken.
Keil, Charles, 1966. *Urban blues.* Chicago: University of Chicago Press.
Kochman, Thomas, 1970. Toward an ethnography of black American speech behavior. *Afro-American anthropology: contemporary perspectives,* ed. Norman Whitten, Jr. and John Szwed, pp. 145-62. New York: The Free Press.
Levi-Strauss, Claude, 1966. *The savage mind.* Chicago: University of Chicago Press.
Manning, Frank, 1973. *Black clubs in Bermuda.* Ithaca: Cornell University Press.
Manning, Frank, 1977. The salvation of a drunk. *American Ethnologist,* 4: 397-412.
Manning, Frank, 1978. *Bermudian politics in transition: race, voting, and public opinion.* Hamilton, Bermuda: Island Press.
Ortner, Sherry, 1973. On key symbols. *American Anthropologist* 75, 5: 1338-46.
Turner, Victor and Turner, Edith, 1978. *Image and pilgrimage in Christian culture.* New York: Columbia University Press.
Wilson, Peter, 1973. *Crab antics.* New Haven. Yale University Press.
Wooding, Hugh, et al., 1969. *Bermuda civil disorders 1968.* Hamilton, Bermuda. Government publication.

Chapter 3

Two-Dimensional Politics: Political Action and Meaning in Rural West Bengal *

Marvin Davis

This paper provides an account of how distinctions of rank in a West Bengal village are variously maintained or altered, supported or challenged through political competitions. It aims partly to add to the general fund of ethnography about politics in rural India, and partly to advance the kind of analysis being undertaken. With regard to this latter and more polemical aim, it is argued that our understanding of politics will be enhanced by complementing the usual concerns with political structure and process with an attention to political culture, and doing so in a manner that examines social structural and cultural material without treating either as in some sense secondary, derived, or epiphenomenal.

Two developments in anthropology are pertinent here. One is an increased interest in Marxist and other materialist approaches to the study of social structure and culture, which are seen as rooted in the material conditions of life. Ideas, concepts and the subjective meanings which inform behavior are seen by Marxists as dependent variables shaped in support of social structure, which itself emerges from subsistence activities and arrangements.[1] Materialists of another bent collapse the distinction between social structure and culture, and view culture as an adaptive system of socially transmitted behavior by which human populations adjust to changing physical and demographic environs. Explanations of this adaptive process separate the cultural materialism of Harris from the cultural evolutionism of Service, and distinguish cultural ecologists like Steward from human ecologists like Vayda, but all are alike in viewing ideational systems as derivative from economies and their social correlates of technology, labor organization, etc.

A second intellectual thrust reverses the explanatory emphasis of materialists, giving primacy to cognition, symbols and human intersubjectivity in the ongoing construction and explanation of reality. Here subsistence and other materially adaptive activities are seen as dependent for their form on systems of meaning, to be understood like social structure as an epiphenomenon of culture. The ethno-scientists Frake (1964), Metzger and Williams (1963), and Spradley (1970), among others, for example, share Ward Goodenough's (1957) view of culture as a cognitive or ideational system that does not consist of things, people, behavior or emotions, but of the organized knowledge required to act appropriately in a given society. Such knowledge is deemed prior to social structure much as grammar is deemed prior to speech; one provides the generative rules for the other. For Levi-Strauss, too, culture exists in the head, and is the creation of the mind, even as those mental creations are represented tangibly in myth or kinship. The material world provides raw material for the mind to work, but it is the mind which imposes order upon the world—culture upon nature— and not the reverse.

This brief statement oversimplifies the developments it aims to summarize,[2] but it does serve to highlight a salient contrast. For, while materialists and nonmaterialists are equally concerned with the nexus between social structure and culture, each places a different explanatory emphasis upon the *system of action*—the network of personal and group relationships and related processual acts which constitute social structure—and the *system of meaning*— the complex assemblage of concepts, ideas, and understandings which constitute culture. Whereas materialists reduce the interdependence between action and meaning in one direction, culturalists reduce this reflexivity in the other direction.

Recent Marxist theory, in addressing this reductionist problem, has recognized the "relative autonomy of the [ideological] superstructure with respect to the [material] base" (Althusser 1971, p.35), and this view has been represented in anthropological writings as well (e.g., Legros 1977, pp.31-33). Meanwhile, cultural anthropologists like Geertz and Turner, and their intellectual heirs (e.g., Ortner 1978; Moore and Myerhoff 1975), are paying increased attention to the dynamic between ideational and interactional systems. In calling for an increased attention to political culture, this paper starts from a similar middle ground that does not posit either ideas or interests as the prime mover of human events. Rather, the argument is that a polity may be more accurately understood if the now orthodox concern with politics as a system of instrumental action—who gets what, when and how, in Harold Lasswell's paradigm in a phrase—is complemented with an increased, more actor-oriented attention to politics as a system of meanings.

To explain more fully, and thereby preview the material presented, students of politics in rural India are generally agreed that competitions are generated along two main lines of cleavage. The cleavage between castes and tribes defines the vertical axis of politics reflected in competitions between ranked groups, usually over the control of land, women, offices, or the less tangible resource of status. The cleavage between big men defines the horizontal axis of politics reflected in factional competitions between leaders, teamed with supporters from various castes and tribes, over the same kinds of material scarcities as well as recognition as the biggest of big men. Given that the bones of contention which spark caste and factional competitions are much the same, discussions of politics in rural India have focused on processual differences—say, in mobilizing support—between competitions structured around ascriptive, corporate teams like castes and voluntary, non-corporate teams like factions. Yet the significance of caste and factional competitions is in an important sense independent of their structure and process and depends instead on the system of meanings in which they are embedded, something even the most astute observers of Indian rural politics ignore or treat as a given that does not require separate analysis (cf. Bailey 1960; Nicholas 1968; Robinson 1975). To illustrate, Bengalis refer to politics as *sason*, or rule, and then distinguish between village politics *(gramer kaj)* and government politics *(sorkari kaj)*. The contrast is not a matter of teams, leaders and personnel, or even the manner and means of competitions. It rests instead on the broad goal of political acts. Both village politics and government politics are identified behaviorally with rivalries over rank, but in each are rivalries pursued with a different goal and in relation to a different normative framework. Village politics aims to support and maintain a system of inequalities which is considered divinely given, inherent in the nature of society, and thus beyond the capacity of human change. This goal is defined in relation to the religious framework of Hinduism. In the context of government politics, by contrast, rivalries challenge the given system of inequalities in favor of a more egalitarian order presaged in the Indian constitution and legal system, which also establishes politics and religion as formally separate domains in a secular India.

Village politics and government politics are premised on very different understandings of order, and of the relation between politics and other social domains. Elaborating this contrast, and what it implies for processes of political change in rural India today, requires extending past discussions of politics to include such questions as the following: What are the shared understandings of reality which inform political activity? What are the prizes, the goals, the valued ends toward which political activity is aimed? What are the qualities deemed to merit the political prize? Are these shared understandings, prizes and qualities peculiar to the domain of politics, or are they related to those which inform other social activity?

It is a commonplace that the ethnography generated during field work is colored by the questions used to elicit information, and the analytic perspective that both frames the questions and interprets the responses. In this light, to raise the above questions is to do more than fill an ethnographic gap. It is also to redirect the manner in which we approach the mammoth which is politics by adding to the usual questions about political structure and process an attention to political culture that is missing, left unanalyzed, or treated as a given of secondary importance in accounts of politics in rural India as in even the benchmark political studies of Evans-Pritchard, Gluckman, Fallers and Barth. This limitation of past political anthropology has not gone unnoticed (see Winckler 1970, p.334; Nicholas 1973, pp.64-67), and programmatic calls for a reorientation have not been entirely unheeded (e.g. Moore and Myerhoff 1975). There is as yet no consensus about how questions of structure, process, and meaning can be integrated into a single analytical framework.

From the same act or series of political acts can be abstracted a cultural component of meaning embedded in those acts or a behavioral component of action appropriate to given actors in a given context. Both of these components, meaning and action, can be studied in analytic isolation. But as the questions that mainly concern anthropologists are only partly questions about cultures as ideational systems, and only partly questions about societies as action systems, such analytic separation may be of limited value. Political action, like all social action, is in an important sense unintelligible apart from cultural context. Political meaning systems can be usefully explored and mapped in their own terms—as Schneider (1968) and Inden and Nicholas (1977) have done for kinship—but do not in themselves tell us anything about social patterns of support, leadership, disputing or dispute resolution. Moreover, to focus solely on the substantive content of meaning systems overlooks what is probably the essential functional role of culture: its role in directing and justifying action preferences. Systems of action and meaning, in sum, though analytically separable are experienced by actor and observer as a single, intertwined, inexorably related whole. A holistic anthropology is perhaps best concerned with both.

But how can this be done? In examining politics in a West Bengal village, this paper adopts what Garfinkle (1967), following Mannheim (1923), terms "a documentary method of analysis," or what can be identified in more familiar descriptive terms as the analysis of critical acts as social and cultural paradigms. The documentary method is similar to Gluckman's extended case method and Van Velson's situational analysis in its detailed study of actual events within a broadly defined structural context. Yet it differs from both in the use to which case materials are put. For whereas case studies in the hands of British structuralists have mostly been used to detail patterns of choice and strategic action within the constraints of a given social system, the documentary method is intended to highlight politics as two-dimensional—as singular instrumental acts and as an embodiment or paradigmatic example of an underlying pattern of meaning which informs a number of different, ostensibly unrelated acts occurring at discontinuous points in time. Politics, in other words, is viewed instrumentally and symbolically.

In attending to the symbolic nature of singular acts, the documentary method takes into account that meaning is socially authored and not intrinsic to the particulars of a political event; that the meaning attributed to an event may be different for different participants and observers; and that an event may be attributed a different meaning at different points in time, even by the same persons. In this regard, the documentary method is similar to the analysis of action as an "open" text suggested by Ricoeur (1971) and exemplified in Geertz's (1973) study of a Balinese cock fight. Where it differs from the symbolic analysis of acts as text-analogues, at least as presented by Geertz, is in avoiding that form of reading a text which includes psychological interpretations of why individuals act as they do. Like the extended case method and situational analysis of British structuralists, a documentary method restricts interpretation to the significance of observed social behavior as it is understood, perhaps similarly, perhaps differently, by informants and the analyst. The operation by which this is done, left vague by Mannheim and Garfinkle, is here formulated as two-fold.[3] First, a pattern of meaning, or "theme," is derived from the explicit statements of informants asked to interpret specific political events. A theme once uncovered is then used to interpret additional events on the assumption that for actors in a given socio-cultural system both the past and the future are informed by present understandings.[4] This second step of matching theme to events is here called "fitting." Through fitting, the applicability of a theme is tested and, when warranted, can be revised or even discarded. Fitting theme to events, it should be emphasized, suggests only how the reflexivity between meaning and action can be documented as each is used to elaborate the other. It does not imply any determinancy or primacy between them.

Mannheim (1923) described the documentary method as a commonsense empiric by which actors interpret past, present, and future events by locating ostensibly singular acts within a common pattern of meaning. It is used in this paper for much the same purpose and to illustrate by example how social structural and cultural anlyses can be integrated when the smallest unit of study is a certain correspondence between systems of action and meaning.

Political Themes

The village here called Torkotala is located in Midnapore district, West Bengal state. The village is populated today by twelve Hindu castes and, in the outlying hamlets, by tribal Lodhas and Mundas. Out of a total population of slightly more than 700 people in 1971, the village was 46 percent Hindu, 27 percent Lodha, and 27 percent Munda. Aside from a single Brahman family and a single Untouchable *Hari* (leatherworker), all other Torkotala Hindus are of the Sudra varna. There are no castes of the Kshatriya or Vaisya varnas represented in Torkotala, as is generally true throughout West Bengal.[5] For purposes of this paper, two of the Sudra castes are worth mentioning individually. The *Sadgops* are a caste of peasant cultivators who founded Torkotala and are today its most numerous caste and largest landholders. The *Bagdi* are a caste of agricultural laborers who helped clear the village and settle Torkotala alongside their Sadgop employers. The Bagdi are the second most numerous caste and second largest landholders in Torkotala.

Discussions of Indian village life often focus on castes as the elemental social units and rank as the principle by which castes are ordered high and low. In fact, rank as an ordering principle applies more generally to the several worlds of the universe, the six life forms which inhabit those worlds—gods, humans, demonic beings, animals, plants, and objects—and the various social units into which humans are divided. Among these social units are the categories or varnas into which all castes are sorted, the interactional groups we call castes, and the more highly differentiated kinship units of clan, lineage, and family into which castes are divided. All of these social units are birth groups *(jatis)* whose members share by ascription common physical qualities *(gun)*, and a behavioral code *(dharma)* held appropriate to their nature. The manner in which the various life forms and human birth groups are ranked has been discussed elsewhere (Davis 1976a), as has the manner in which individuals can be ranked within and apart from the birth groups in which they are included (Davis 1976b). Those discussions need not be repeated here, but it will clarify the cultural context of Torkotala politics to highlight certain principles of Hindu rank.

1. The various birth groups into which humans are divided are ranked according to their defining physical nature and the moral conduct or behavioral code held appropriate to that nature.
2. The physical nature and behavioral code of a birth group are a single, if duplex criterion of rank. Nature and code are each a reflection and realization of the other.
3. The defining features, and thus the rank, of a birth group are not fixed and unchanging through time, but can be altered for better or worse according to the activities of its members, including their patterns of marriage, diet, food exchange, and occupation.
4. What is true of castes and the various kinship units in which individuals are included is true of individuals as well. Namely, individuals are a unit of rank, can be ordered high and low according to their defining physical nature and behavioral code, and undergo transformations of their defining features and rank in accord with their own activities.

It is the concern, even preoccupation, with rank and the behavior appropriate to ranked social units which defines the context of meaning in which village politics and government politics both are interpreted. That is, both forms of politics are identified behaviorally with rivalries over rank. But whereas village politics aims to support and maintain a system of inequalities deemed divinely given and thus beyond human change, government politics challenges that same system of inequalities in favor of a more equalitarian order deemed the product of human agency and thus continually open to improvement. Informing each form of politics are contrasting premises.

Exegetes of village politics express four consciously held premises. First, village politics aims to uphold and protect *(palana)* dharma, which refers both to the natural and moral order of society writ large, and to the conduct held appropriate to ranked social units and individuals. Second, the means to this moral end should themselves be moral. Third, village politics is the shared responsibility of all in that the head of every social unit—whether of a family, lineage, caste, or village—replicates the ruling functions of a king within a more limited sphere. So do individuals, who rule over themselves in bearing responsibility for adhering to their personal behavioral code *(svadharma)*.

From these three premises is deduced a fourth: that village politics is inseparable from and subordinate to dharma in that it takes its ultimate ground of authority, its definition of goals and its definition of moral means towards those goals from this concept. Specific competitions may be pursued with the hope of material or social gain *(artha)*, but the pursuit of gain must itself be guided by and contribute to natural and moral order.

Consider now those consciously held premises which constitute the theme of government politics. First, government politics aims at progress *(unnoti)*. Whereas village politics assumes a divinely given polity, society, and cosmos not subject to human change, government politics assumes that every social and political order, as well as the world view which accompanies those orders and makes them seem uniquely fitted to the realities of life, is a human construction. Thus, people can create the social and political order of their choice, and in doing so are not bound by that reservoir of behaviors, values, symbols, and meanings which collectively comprise tradition. Second, government politics proceeds ideally through moral activity. Third, government politics is open to all, though it is not expected that all will actively further the work of effecting progress and change in village life, or even that all will be unopposed to such work by others.

Fourth, government politics is separable from and superordinate to dharma—which is equated with religion—in that it takes its ultimate ground of authority from the Indian constitution and legal system, and uses the institutional framework and statutes contained therein to establish politics and religion as discrete, supposedly autonomous domains.[6] Government politics aims to level the inequalities supported by dharma in favor of a more equalitarian social and political order.

An innovative, progressively oriented government politics stands in marked contrast to a conservatively oriented, traditionalist village politics. Yet village politics and government politics are not mutually exclusive forms of rule in Torkotala. Some villagers welcome the innovations associated with government politics. Others find the protective bent of village politics more to their liking. And there are also Torkotala residents who at times variously advance and act in accord with the themes of village politics and government politics. This will become evident in tracing the involvement or lack of involvement of some of the same individuals through several documentary cases of Torkotala politics. So will the role of political themes as ideologies. That is, the themes of village politics and government politics viewed substantively are schematic images of a certain reality which are used by Torkotala residents to type actual competitions, thereby making them intelligible as instances of a more general pattern. They are used as well to justify the interested participation of individuals in specific competitions, and in that sense function as a suasive language of claims. As Bernard Barber (1972, p.246) has pointed out, with notable exceptions like Geertz (1964), the dominant mode among social scientists has been to focus on the substantive content of ideologies. The importance of also attending functionally to the themes of Torkotala politics is that like any ideological statement they are an expression of socially accepted reasons for acting in relation to culturally defined goals; they serve not only to map reality, but to direct and rationalize political activity.

Political Events

The Politics of Caste. Elsewhere (Davis 1976c) the theme of village politics was used to interpret why interpersonal competitions within the Bengal Hindu family are a recurrent feature of village life, and how they sustain a system of ranked inequalities. Here the theme is applied to a second subset of village politics, the politics of caste. In the politics of caste the prize sought is to be recognized as the caste having the more refined features of physical nature and behavioral code, and thus higher rank as well. The politics of caste is thus largely a matter of intercaste competitions, but not exclusively so, for within each caste are occasionally found members whose individual actions threaten the defining features and rank of the entire corporate group. In dealing with such backsliders, the politics of caste also has an intramural face. Both intercaste and intracaste competitions are identified by Torkotala residents as instances of village politics because, while the rank order of a caste in the local hierarchy may be questioned, the principle of ranked inequalities by which castes are ordered is not. Put differently, such competitions affirm and renew caste as a system of ranked inequalities by seeking to insure the proper positioning of castes within that system.

Intercaste competitions focus on attempts by one caste to improve its rank in the local caste hierarchy—to "caste-climb," as Bailey (1968) terms it—and attempts by other castes to block the success of any such climb. "The prosperity of an enemy is a cause for sorrow." By the logic of this Bengali maxim, for one caste to gain in rank is for all others to lose. Those below the climbing caste lose because the relative distance between them in the caste hierarchy is made still greater. Those above the climbing caste lose because the relative distance between them in the caste hierarchy is made smaller. Immediate to the climbing caste in the hierarchy is another which has suffered the direct loss of having its relative rank reversed, so that it is now below a caste it once ranked above. Thus do intercaste competitions involve not only the active competitors, but at least indirectly all other castes in the local hierarchy as well. Village politics is the shared responsibility of all.

The process by which castes climb in a local hierarchy has been described by M.N. Srinivas as *Sanskritization*. In his study of the Coorgs of Mysore, Srinivas found that lower castes sought to improve their position in the caste hierarchy by imitating Brahmans in matters of dress, food, and ritual, while also giving up some of their own customs, like meat-eating and animal sacrifices, which the Brahmans considered inferiorizing. To denote this process, Srinivas first used the term *Brahmanization*. Later the term Sanskritization was substituted to indicate a more general "process by which a 'low' Hindu caste, or tribal or other group, changes its customs, ritual, ideology and way of life in the direction of a 'high,' and frequently, 'twice-born' caste" (Srinivas 1966, p.6). Caste-climbing, in brief, is an imitative process by which lower ranking castes alter their generalized life style to be more like that of higher ranking castes, and then make claim to higher rank on the basis of those changes. The imitative process can persist for generations before arrival is conceded, if at all. A caste of any varna can be the object of imitation, not just Brahmans. In Torkotala, for example, Bagdi efforts to be recognized as Bagra-Khatriyas involved emulating the locally dominant Sadgops, a Sudra caste. A description of those efforts is presented below, and then a processual model for advancing claims to higher rank is suggested.

Until about thirty years ago, Torkotala Bagdis invariably worked as agricultural laborers for landholding Sadgops of the village. Some of this work was done on a daily or short-term basis. More often individual Bagdis were retained by a Sadgop family throughout the year, and did whatever work was required seasonally. This pattern changed when several Bagdi families acquired lands of their own by clearing outlying areas of the village of scrub jungle. Others did the next best thing in arranging to sharecrop lands. Having thus acquired rights to their own land, the Bagdi stopped working in the employ of Sadgops entirely, or combined their work as agricultural laborers with work on their own lands as well.

Sadgop landholders of the village reacted to the new economic independence of the Bagdis by employing in their stead tribal Lodhas and Mundas who had previously worked their fields only as migrant laborers during the peak of the rice harvest. In years past, these Lodhas and Mundas returned to the hilly tracts of western Midnapore when the harvest season ended. Now they were offered permanent employment in Torkotala, and land to settle on as well.

From the early 1940s to the mid-1950s, the Bagdi used their new economic wealth and independence to attract other caste fellows to Torkotala, thereby increasing their numbers. In 1941 there were five Bagdi households; all but one owned their own lands and were at least partially self-employed. By 1951 there were nine Bagdi households; all but two owned their own lands and were at least partially self-employed. By 1971 there were twenty-one households of Bagdi; twelve owned their own land, and nine were entirely self-employed.

As their landholdings and numbers grew, the Bagdi soon were able to employ others to do the kinds of agricultural labor they once did for the Sadgops and later did for themselves. This represented a significant refinement in life style because to refrain from direct physical labor is to refrain from involvement with the more inferiorizing aspects of life. It also created for the Bagdi a number of economic clients and political followers. Still other changes followed. In the late 1950s, Bagdi youth first refused to accept the scholarship aid available to persons of scheduled castes and tribes on the grounds that the Bagdi were not a lowly, disadvantaged scheduled caste. Adult Bagdis also adopted a middle name after the pattern of higher caste persons. Khudi Dolai referred to himself as Khudi Ram Dolai, for example. Satya Dolai referred to himself as Satya Chandra Dolai. In many Bagdi families children were given a middle name at birth. Some Bagdi also substituted the surname Dolopati for Dolai. Dolopati, or "group leader," is held a higher, more sophisticated form of Bengali speech, and therefore a preferred surname.

Accompanying this complex of changes in life-style and naming patterns was the Bagdi claim to be Bagra-Khatriyas, i.e. a caste of the higher ranking Kshatriya (in Bengali, Khatriya) varna. Sadgops of the village pointedly ignored this claim. If the Bagdi wanted to refuse scholarship money from the government by claiming to be what they were not, Sadgops reasoned, that was their choice, and their loss. But the Sadgops would continue to refer to them as they really were, as Bagdis. Neither did the Sadgops recognize other Bagdi claims, like having middle names or the surname Dolopati.

The Bagdi do not admit that they were every without the ritual services of a washerman *(Rajok)*, barber *(Napit)* or Brahman priest. Other evidence suggests that it was not until 1960, or very shortly before, that the Bagdi began to receive the ritual services of the same washerman and barber as serves the Sadgops and other high ranking castes in Torkotala. Soon afterwards, the Bagdi also secured the services of a Brahman priest, though not the same priest that serves Sadgops of the village. To this day, Torkotala Sadgops discredit the importance of these additional changes in Bagdi lifestyle by saying they are the product of a "black arrow," an arrow that travels by indirect, clandestine, morally suspect paths, whereas village politics should proceed through moral means. In support of this argument, Sadgops explain that the village Rajok was forced out of poverty to serve as washerman for Bagdi families at the threat of losing supplemental income as an agricultural laborer for Khudi Dolai. That the Bagdi were able to secure the services of a Brahman is also discredited by Sadgops in terms of the black arrow of wealth. "With money one may procure tigers' eyes," i.e. that which is most unattainable. In addition, the Brahman who serves the Bagdi as priest is labelled as fallen (*potita*), and his services discounted as not being those of a true (*sat*) Brahman. His real work, Sadgops claim, is fixing bicycles under the giant banyan tree along the road to Narayanghar Town.

In spite of all the refinements in life-style the Bagdi had already effected, in 1960 they still had not won recognition from Torkotala Sadgops or others in the village as Bagra-Khatriyas. Recognition was not to come until a matter of government politics of interest to Sadgops was manipulated by Bagdis for their own purposes of village politics.

In 1957 the West Bengal state government, acting under directions from the federal government in New Delhi, passed legislation for the establishment of statutory councils (*panchayats*), including village councils, throughout the rural areas of the state. Participation in these councils would be open to all citizens through free and recurrent elections in which every adult—as political equals—had the right to vote. The actual organization and establishment of *Panchayati Raj* proceeded at a very uneven pace throughout the state, so that in 1960 there still were no statutory councils in the Torkotala area. Councils had been organized, and elections had occurred in other parts of the state, though. Torkotala residents were aware of this, and anticipated the time when a statutory council would be organized in their village, too. Whenever established, it was expected that a Sadgop would be elected as council head, as *Adhyaksa*. Far less certain was which Sadgop would be elected Adhyaksa, as both Atul Mahabarto and Anil Pal wanted the position.

Campaigning for the position of Adhyaksa began well before any government officials ever entered Torkotala to organize the first statutory village council. The Sadgops were divided in their support of Atul and Anil. Both men thus canvassed for decisive support among non-Sadgops of the village, and especially among the Bagdi, the second most populous caste in Torkotala, and also the second most influential caste in the number of economic clients counted within their political following.

While Atul and Anil were trying to win support for their selection as Adhyaksa, Khudi Dolai was making final preparations for the marriage of his daughter. Part of those preparations included indirect soundings as to whether or not certain leading Sadgops of the village, including Atul and Anil, would accept an invitation to his daughter's wedding feast. No Sadgop had ever accepted even drinking water from the hands of a Bagdi. Yet Khudi was now asking if a wedding invitation, which carries an implicit agreement to accept food served as part of the wedding feast, would be accepted. Sadgops who did accept the invitation, it was implied, would receive Bagdi support when the new statutory village council was formed, and the support of all Bagdi clients as well.

To Khudi's soundings, Anil was at first noncommittal. Atul—voicing a goal of government politics—immediately let it be known that he favored breaking down all social barriers separating castes of the village. To do so would contribute to village unity, and was consistent with the equalitarian goal of Panchayati Raj. Not to be outdone, Anil was soon heard making similar statements. Other Sadgops of the village, in response, called a meeting of the caste council to decide whether Anil and Atul should be allowed to accept Khudi's invitation, as they said they would. Should the Sadgops not defend themselves against another of Khudi's black arrows? Those present at the council meeting debated this question for some time, but in the end none remained opposed to Anil or Atul, not even Haripado Bhunai, the traditional head man (*Mukhya*) of the village. It was Haripado, speaking as Mukhya, though, who suggested that Khudi's invitation should only be accepted if he agreed to have the wedding food cooked and served by a true (sat) Brahman, and if he agreed to contribute fifty rupees to the village fund for the honor of having Sadgops attend his daughter's marriage. By this plan the Sadgops could attend a Bagdi wedding feast, as Khudi wanted, without acting in disaccord with Sadgop dharma, as Haripado wanted, for there was no Sadgop injunction against accepting food from a true Brahman. Further, by this plan the Sadgops could attend a Bagdi wedding feast, as Khudi wanted, without violating the established order of ranks between castes of the village, as Haripado wanted, for in agreeing to make a contribution to the village fund the Bagdis were, in effect, honoring Sadgops as a higher caste.

Khudi agreed that the Sadgops could arrange for the service of any Brahman cook they wished. He also agreed to contribute fifty rupees—to be collected piecemeal from all Bagdi families—to the village fund. Sadgops, in return, attended the Bagdi marriage feast as promised, and persuaded persons of other high ranking castes in the village to attend as well. It was during the feast that Atul, for the first time ever, conspicuously addressed several Bagdi men using their middle names. Khudi Dolai was addressed as Khudi Ram; his brother, Satya, was addressed as Satya Chandra. It was also Atul who, for the first time ever, publicly referred to Khudi, Satya and others of their caste as Bagra-Khatriyas. The surname Dolopati never was used by anyone attending the marriage feast, and presently is no longer used even by Bagra-Khatriyas.

Bagdi attempts and eventual success at being recognized as Bagra-Khatriyas are interesting for several reasons. The object of Bagdi imitation, and the principle audience for Bagdi claims, was the locally dominant Sadgop caste, belonging to the Sudra varna, and not the single Brahman family represented in Torkotala. Local Sadgops and then other castes eventually did recognize Bagdi claims to be known as Bagra-Khatriyas, but not, significantly, Bagdi claims to be a caste of the Kshatriya varna. In their eyes the Bagdi remain a Sudra caste, only now they are known by a new (and somewhat misleading) name. Bagdi attempts to caste-climb are also interesting for the length of time and the sequence in which changes in life-style were made and claims advanced before recognition was finally granted by local Sadgops, and then others. Three decades passed before the complex of changes effected by the Bagdi finally resulted in their gaining recognition as Bagra-Khatriyas. At first the Sadgops saw no need to oppose Bagdi efforts to secure rights over their own land by clearing the scrub jungle or by arranging to share crop. They did not object when individual Bagdi stopped working as agricultural laborers on Sadgop lands. Neither did they actively oppose other changes in Bagdi life-style, as when Bagdi took to supervising the work of others rather than doing physical labor themselves, or when individual Bagdi assumed a middle name. Indeed, these changes and any accompanying claim to higher rank were treated so lightly as to be generally ignored. Only when the Bagdi procured the services of the same ritual specialists as served the Sadgops could their claims no longer be ignored. Then they had to be undermined and discredited.

To ignore the claims of a competitor or to try to undermine and discredit and thereby actively oppose those claims are two common strategies in the politics of caste. The former is to avoid a competition by not recognizing the claim maker as a legitimate competitor. The latter is to recognize a claim maker as a legitimate competitor but to oppose the claims made. That the Sadgops first ignored, later actively opposed and ultimately granted recognition to Bagdi claims illustrates that the effects of intercaste rivalries can be cumulative. Small gains at one point in a rivalry provide the basis for larger gains later. Thus the Bagdi used their new landholdings and economic independence to attract increasing numbers of caste fellows to settle in Torkotala; increasing numbers to acquire still more landholdings and economic independence; wealth and numbers to hire others in their employ; having others in their employ to change their working habits; a change in working habits, dress, diet, and so on, to secure the ritual services of a Rajok and Napit; and the services of these ritual specialists to secure the services of a Brahman. In this sequence of changes effected by the Bagdi, each previous change provided the basis for a later one, and taken together all of the changes represented a gradual but progressive refinement of Bagdi life-style. Changes in life-style then provided the basis for claims to higher rank.

The changes in life-style effected by the Bagdi, in conjunction with other accounts of caste-climbing (cf. Gough 1959; Silverberg 1959; Marriott 1968; Bailey 1968), suggest a three-phase processual model for advancing claims to higher rank. Namely, (1) a change in occupation and/or economic independence and wealth, (2) is used to refine caste patterns of dress, diet, food exchanges, service, naming, ritual practices, etc. (3) A refined life-style is then used to claim an appropriately higher rank. In this processual model actual material changes in life-style are critical, but are not themselves explicable apart from the cultural importance given by Hindus to behavior as an outward reflection of inner physical nature, and the fact that nature and code are viewed cognitively as a single, if duplex criterion of rank. The Hindu preoccupation with rank as a cultural value is also critical to this processual model, but higher rank is unattainable apart from material changes in life style. Put differently, because the generalized life-style of a caste is deemed both a reflection and realization of its rank, it is difficult to argue that either the push of an improved life-style or the pull of rank as a cultural value is the prime mover of the politics of caste. Any reductionist account of the material and cultural considerations at issue is additionally problematic because the success of efforts at caste-climbing are also contingent on a certain amount of happenstance. Three decades ago there were ample uncultivated lands surrounding Torkotala for the Bagdi to clear, which they did without impediment from local Sadgops, perhaps because there was an ample number of tribal Lodhas and Mundas to replace the Bagdi as the principal agricultural laborers of the village. Bagdi recognition as Bagra-Khatriyas also depended in part on preparations for the marriage of Khudi Dolai's daughter happening to coincide with the extension of Panchayati Raj into the Torkotala area and the willingness of leading Sadgops to bargain recognition of Bagdi claims for election support as council head.

The processual model suggested identifies the likely phase development of a successful effort at caste-climbing, and the material and cultural considerations at issue. The duration of each phase in the transformation of a caste's defining features is unpredictable, and as with Bagdi efforts to be recognized as Bagra-Khatriyas can be spread over generations. More predictable is that intercaste competitions are timed to redress an actual or perceived inconsistency between the life-style of a caste and its rank. For that reason is it useful to view such competitions, in Moore's (1975, p.234) apt phrase, as "processes of regularization." That is, Bagdi efforts to improve their rank do not challenge the caste system per se; only their position in the local ordering of castes. Indeed, far from challenging the caste system, the cumulative effect of caste-climbing efforts over time is to affirm the principle of ranked inequalities around which castes are organized by dramatizing and seeking to correct an imperfect fit between order culturally perceived and order socially realized. In that sense does caste-climbing evidence how an apparently static caste system is not static at all, but continually renewed through rivalries over rank. Consider now how the temporary disorder of intracaste competitions can also contribute to a lasting sociocultural order.

Though the lead in pressing for recognition as Bagra-Khatriyas was taken by only a few Bagdi families, and especially by Khudi and Satya Dolai, all Bagdi benefited from their activities. It is for this reason that Khudi felt justified in collecting the fifty rupees paid to the village fund from all of the Bagdi families of the village. Simply, it is the nature of castes as political teams to be corporate; what one team member does benefits all. For the same reason, the activities of any member of the team can also cause loss to the entire caste. It is in dealing with backsliders, persons who do not uphold the defining features of the caste, and thereby threaten its rank, that the politics of caste also assumes an intramural face. The Bagdi caste council which met some fifteen years ago to judge an alleged affront against the entire caste provides a documentary case in point.

A young widow of the Bagdi caste returned to Torkotala from the village and house of her recently deceased husband. She stayed with her father for some months, then left to live in Calcutta, where she went alone and without knowing anyone who could help her settle. While in Calcutta the widow did not write to her father, or to anyone else in Torkotala; no one knew where she lived or what work she did. Two years passed. Then the widow returned to the village unexpectedly and again took up residence in her father's house. But whereas she left for Calcutta in poverty, she returned to Torkotala with many new ornaments, fine saris, and other costly objects.

The newly acquired wealth of the widow occasioned much rumor among Torkotala residents, for no one could imagine how the widow acquired such wealth, at least not honestly. Gossip had it that the widow's wealth came through a "loss of character," i.e. through prostitution, and therefore she should be outcasted for not acting like a true Bagdi. But as the widow returned to Torkotala at a time when her father was deathly ill, no one was willing to publicly raise the question of outcasting just then. Shortly after the father's death, a Bagdi council was called for this purpose.

At the council meeting, attended by Bagdi of several villages, it was decided that there was no proof of the widow's activities in Calcutta, only suspicion. Yet suspicion that the widow earned her wealth in ways that violated caste dharma was so strong that it was also decided she should undergo a penance for whatever wrongdoings may have occurred while she was in Calcutta. The widow was informed of this decision before the caste council, and at the same time given a public lecture as to the dharma of the Bagdi caste, of widows, of females, and of Hindus. The widow was also asked to pay a fine to the caste, which she did.

The meeting of the caste council, reported by (the now) Bagra-Khatriyas, was narrated in such a way as to indicate a clear object lesson: that Bagdi behave just like higher ranking Sadgops. Specifically, the Bagdi widow was compared to Jogi Pal, born to the Sadgop caste in Torkotala, but later outcasted for consorting with Lodha females. If the Bagdi widow had prostituted herself, she would have been outcasted like Jogi Pal for not acting in accord with caste dharma. "No one will touch him/her who forsakes the right way for the wrong, not even with a stick," warns a Bengali proverb.

Another case of backsliding that was a focus of intramural caste politics, this time among Torkotala Sadgops, involved Baneshor and Kennaram Dey.

The Dey brothers married into Torkotala. They and their wives—who are sisters—live together in a single compound, but occupy and maintain separate households. When the father of their wives died some thirteen years ago, Baneshor and Kennaram did not feast their caste fellows and others of the village at the close of the death impurity period. And when Baneshor's wife died some two years afterwards, again no feast was given at the end of the death impurity period.

Other Sadgops of the village knew that Baneshor and Kennaram were not well-off economically. The brothers owned no lands of their own, and the lands owned by their wives were minimal. To maintain himself and his family, Baneshor even worked as a day laborer during the plowing season for lower ranking Bagra-Khatriyas, thereby contravening the general pattern of higher ranking caste persons being served by but not serving lower ranking castes with their physical labor. Nonetheless, Sadgops of the village met and decided that the Dey brothers had not acted in accord with caste dharma when they failed to feast their caste fellows and others of the village, following two deaths in the family. As punishment it was also decided that the ritual specialists who served other Sadgops of the village would be prohibited from serving Baneshor and Kennaram.

This situation persisted for almost two years before negotiations began for Baneshor's second marriage. On learning of these negotiations other Sadgops of the village threatened to spoil them by informing the bride's family of Baneshor's past un-Sadgop-like behavior unless the Dey brothers paid a fine of forty rupees and promised to invite all Sadgops of the village to a marriage feast. The Dey brothers agreed. The fine was paid, the marriage held, and also the feast. Not long afterwards Baneshor and Kennaram once more began receiving the services of the Sadgop ritual specialists.

Why were the Sadgops—including Anil and Atul—so upset by not being feasted on two occasions, especially when they knew that Baneshor and Kennaram were truly impoverished? In part this is because poverty is not thought to excuse one from acting in accord with personal or caste dharma. In part this is because of what villagers of other castes said in reprimanding the Dey brothers, and by extension, all Sadgops. Providing a feast at the end of the death impurity period is considered obligatory because the presence of invitees accepting food indicates that the family of the deceased, previously in a state of impurity, is once more able to resume normal social life without restrictions of diet, activities, or social contacts. Not to provide a feast is to fail in one's moral obligations and to act in a way that belies one's defining features and rank. Since village politics is presumed the shared responsibility of all, it also provides an occasion for others in the village to say—as they did—that Sadgops do not know, or worse yet, know but do not follow, Hindu dharma. As the activities of any caste member reflect on the entire caste, Sadgops felt required to respond to such public criticism by censuring Baneshor and Kennaram. Moreover, in the specific means selected for that censure the Sadgops evidenced that they indeed knew what was proper, i.e. moral behavior for all Hindus. Both the denial of ritual specialists and exposing potential marriages as improper are well-established locally as steps toward outcasting in the absence of reform.

The censure of the Dey brothers, like the reprimand of the Bagdi widow, and the refinements in life-style used by Bagdi to claim high rank as Bagra-Khatriyas, all document how village politics takes its definition of goals and the moral means towards those goals from considerations of dharma. Indeed it is the strain to uphold and protect dharma, to realize socially a prescribed cultural order of ranked inequalities, that generates the politics of caste and characterizes such competition as processes of regularization. Specifically, intercaste competitions are generated by actual or perceived inconsistencies between the life style of a caste and its rank. They are resolved when the appropriate rank ordering of castes is resolved. Intracaste competitions are generated by actual or anticipated action by a backsliding member which threatens the corporate whole. They are resolved by rectifying or forestalling acts by individual caste members that would debase the defining features and rank of the entire caste.

Competition can be regarded as the inevitable product of social inequities. Or competition can be regarded as the avoidable result of individual misconduct in a just and moral society. The latter is the view of Torkotala residents of competitions within and between castes. In principle, there would be no politics of caste if each corporate unit and all individual members acted in accord with their own behavioral code. In fact, the politics of caste is an anticipated and recurrent feature of Torkotala life. Thus is a culturally prescribed harmony opposed by the cacophony of day-to-day life. This contradiction is mediated by a language of claims which justifies political competition—however undesirable and potentially disruptive—as a moral means to rectify and forestall errant behavior. An acceptable reason for engaging in village politics, in other words, is the moral claim to be acting to restore or maintain dharma, to ensure a lasting sociocultural order through the temporary disorder of politics.

But are there no competitions which challenge and seek to alter a sociocultural order of ranked inequalities? There are. Torkotala residents do not regard such competitions as negative examples of village politics, though. They are labeled instead as instances of government politics, to which the discussion now turns.

Panchayati Raj

Government politics refers ultimately to the activities of the central government in New Delhi, but also to its more immediate extension in Calcutta, the capital of West Bengal state, Midnapore Town, the district headquarters, and Narayanghar Town, the local site of many district-level offices. But whatever the specific reference, unlike village politics which originates locally, government politics is always identified by Torkotala residents with programs and policies that originate outside the village and seek to alter Torkotala life in accord with the ideals of a modernizing nation-state. Panchayati Raj is a documentary case in point.

Article 40 of the Indian constitution directs the several Indian states to establish village councils (panchayats) and to endow them with such resources and authority as may be necessary to enable them to function as units of self-government. The constitution does not also set forth the organization and function of these panchayats, but guidelines for state legislation on these matters were provided in 1959 by a government-sponsored study team (popularly called the Mehta Committee) set up for that purpose. The Mehta Committee proposed a tiered system of rural self-government consisting of village, area and district-level councils, each having delegated responsibility, powers, and resources for planning and executing development programs in their respective jurisdictions. Through these development programs it was intended that rural India would come to share the political, economic, and social progress already evident in urban centers, thereby reducing, if not completely eliminating, a major barrier to national unity and a major problem concern for national planners—rural poverty and social backwardness.

Panchayati Raj was intended as something more than a new approach to community development, though. On one hand, it was intended to actualize the constitutional commitment expressed in Article 40 to a decentralized economic and political democracy. And on the other hand, it was intended to incorporate local administrative units—village India—into the broader national polity, principally by extending those features of a modern parliamentary democracy which already characterized central government activity into rural areas. In their day-to-day operation, for example, panchayats are to rely on bureaucratic procedures, participation in their activities is to be open to all persons as a right of Indian citizenship, and leadership positions are to be achieved and circulated through open and regularly recurrent elections. Also, associated with Panchayati Raj (though not active in the Torkotala area) are judicial courts which rely on a predominantly secular and impersonal system of coded law and which operate on the premise that all persons have equal rights before the law. In all of these respects does Panchayati Raj aim at extending into rural India those features associated with modern political and legal systems.

The formal organization and stated goals of Panchayati Raj are known by Torkotala residents, not from their own reading of the relevant legislation, but from explanations given them by the block development officer (BDO) and his staff. It was also the BDO, in 1962, who organized the first panchayat election in Torkotala. At his direction Torkotala was divided into three voting wards, a northern ward which includes the tribal Munda hamlets, a southern ward which includes the tribal Lodha hamlets, and a central ward which includes the caste Hindu hamlets. From each ward were to be elected three council members, thereby guaranteeing equal representation to each of the three major social divisions of the village. As part of his efforts to organize the first panchyat, the BDO made it clear that all adult residents, male and female, could stand for election and could vote for the election of others; how the right to vote gave all persons, regardless of caste or tribe, an equal voice; and how persons elected as council members could be held responsible to their electors.

The panchayat election took place several months after the BDO's initial organizing efforts, in August 1962, under his supervision. The assembly of all villagers met as provided for by law to place nominations, three from each voting ward. But no nominations were ever asked for or received from the assembly because prior to the meeting Atul and Anil, with the apparent consent of the BDO, met privately to compose a list of panchayat nominations of their own. Their list included just nine nominees, one for each available council seat, thereby eliminating the need for an actual election. Indeed, none was held. The assembled villagers merely approved by voice vote the list of nominees placed before them.

The Torkotala panchayat was not truly elected, nor did nominations for council membership come from the village assembly as provided for by law. Neither did the council ultimately provide equal representation for each of the major social divisions in Torkotala because the Lodhas, saying their Hindu employers would never pay them heed, decided not to occupy the panchayat seats alloted to them. The same seats were later reassigned to lower-caste Hindus.

Once the panchayat was formed, it remained for its members to elect one of their number as council head. Both Atul Mahabarto and Anil Pal campaigned for the position. Atul won and soon after taking office, ignoring legislation which provides for the assistant council head to be chosen through a separate election, appointed Satya Dolai, a Bagra-Khatriya, as his second. Atul and Satya have led the Torkotala village council in the absence of a second election since 1962. With one exception, the membership of the village council has remained unchanged as well—a lower-caste Hindu left Torkotala in 1968; his seat on the panchayat remains unfilled.

Since its formation, the Torkotala statutory council has met forty-five times in nine years, but not since 1969. Even the relative inactivity of the council does not give an adequate picture of the ineffectiveness of Panchayati Raj in Torkotala, though, for the successful completion of any project in Torkotala requires that Anil Mahabarto, Anil Pal, and Haripado Bhunai, as leaders of the three principal village factions work in cooperation with each other, or at least not in active opposition. Yet, throughout the history of Panchayati Raj in Torkotala, this has never been the case.

Haripado Bhunai never sought membership in the statutory council, arguing from the time when Panchayati Raj legislation was first explained to villagers that the concept of elected authority and the rule of the majority were alien to Torkotala and inherently divisive. Villagers, in his opinion, should continue to follow the established customs of the village which include being led by their Mukhya, himself, and to make all decisions through consensus and unanimity. Haripado is committed to the premises of village politics. He countered whatever importance the BDO and others attributed to a democratic system of rural self-government by labeling it, pejoratively, as an instance of government politics, i.e., a scheme by government officials and other outsiders to alter life within Torkotala. By first refusing to seek panchayat membership and later refusing to involve himself in panchayat affairs, Haripado also undermined the effectiveness of the council by not lending it the legitimation that would accrue from his personal support and that of his factional following.

Anil Pal, for his part, originally sought involvement in this new system of rural self-government through panchayat membership and election as council head. Like Atul, Anil was in sympathy with many of the stated goals of Panchayati Raj. And like Atul, he recognized that the powers invested in the office of council head, as well as the money distributed through that office, could be manipulated and used to personal advantage, even while advancing certain village causes. Anil's involvement in the panchayat was short-lived, though, for not long after losing the election for council head, he withdrew from active participation in council affairs and like Haripado began to speak of the council pejoratively as an instance of government politics. After 1963, the first full year of panchayat activities, in which he attended five out of fifteen meetings, Anil never again attended another meeting of the village council. Moreover, in addition to avoiding panchayat activities, as Haripado did, Anil actively opposed any project which Atul supported.

The Torkotala panchayat continues to exist and to be active even without the support of Haripado and Anil and their respective factional followings. But lacking this support, the Torkotala panchayat has become over the years less a village council than a factional council, a legally constituted and government-funded body through which Atul Mahabarto is able to advance his factional ends. This said, it must be emphasized that the village panchayat nevertheless also advances projects that benefit Torkotala villagers as a whole. And the village panchayat has effected many of the social, economic and political changes envisioned by the national planners of Panchayati Raj. In addition to specific development projects, for example, the extension of voting rights to all adults and the introduction of popular elections have, in combination, allowed previously subordinated but numerically significant groups in the village to gain a say in village affairs. Their votes must be bargained for in any panchayat election. And even in the absence of a second panchayat election, tribals and lower caste Hindus have secured an increased say in village affairs because Atul is aware that he must use the office of council head to advance the well-being and political participation of as many villagers as possible against the day when there is another election. Then, too, because the formal existence, if not the actual effectiveness of any village council is independent of particular men, the mere existence of Panchayati Raj in Torkotala has opened the way for the advance of a new leadership. By their lack of involvement with panchayat affairs established village leaders like Haripado and Anil have allowed others, like Satya Dolai, to seek and gain positions endowed with legal power.

In many ways the activities of the Torkotala village assembly and council do not conform to the provisions of Panchayati Raj legislation. Panchayat members were not truly elected, nor was the assistant council head. The village council does not meet regularly. And the new council members, or even a new council leadership, are not chosen every four years. On all of these accounts is Atul Mahabarto accused of acting outside of the law, of acting immorally, in order to maintain the personal advantages of his present position. Government politics is ideally moral activity, but in this instance the ideal, Anil and Haripado would say, is far from realized. They believe Atul acts out of self-interest rather than commitment to the premises of government politics. In the behavior of Atul and Haripado and their factional supporters is reflected another premise of government politics. Namely, that participation in government politics is open to all, though not all may wish to participate or even welcome the aim of government politics in effecting progress and change. Anil, for one, seems to have no interest in the development projects undertaken by the village council. Haripado does, welcoming those projects deemed to benefit the village as a whole. But his opinion of government politics is not unmixed, for to the extent that panchayat activites are successful, the given social and political orders of the village are likely to change. It is to protect and maintain those same orders for which Haripado, as the traditional headman of Torkotala, is responsible.

Prior to 1962, there was no Torkotala village council in the sense of a formally organized and constituted body. When matters of public importance arose they were discussed in ad hoc village meetings called for that specific purpose. Such meetings were, and still are, held irregularly in Torkotala. They are referred to, significantly, as *des jama,* a gathering *(jama)* of the *des* (place, i.e. village), and not as *panchayats,* a term which villagers recognize as a recent addition to their vocabulary. Participation in such ad hoc village meetings is in principle open to all within the village. In practice, only adult males are likely to attend such meetings, and actual attendance is usually predicated on receiving a direct call to the meeting. Active, effective participation is limited still further to those males who head their own households, and especially to those who head households having substantial landholdings. Both presently and in the past this has meant that effective participation in ad hoc village meetings is limited primarily to persons of the Sadgop caste.

It is not unusual for the village Mukhya to preside over an ad hoc meeting of the village. But neither is it necessary. Any villager can call such a meeting, and preside over it as well. In that sense do *ad hoc* village meetings, unlike meetings of the statutory village assembly or council, lack a formal leadership. Also unlike the statutory assembly or council, ad hoc village meetings have no specified powers or functions apart from those which villagers in attendance are willing and able to give it. All power and authority rests entirely in the personal qualities and resources of the villagers in attendance. Decisions can only be enforced by the common agreement of all present to abide by them—expressed as unanimity—and not by the sanction of any outside government agency or set of codified laws. Another feature of ad hoc village meetings is the differential judgments passed according to the defining features and rank of individuals. In every adjudication of a dispute, or judgment of errant behavior, villagers adjust their decisions and penalties according to what is considered just given the birth group and life stage of the individuals involved. Justice is meted out in accord with the premise of inequality. There is not, as there is meant to be in the judicial councils associated with Panchayati Raj, or in the judicial courts of West Bengal state, an emphasis on the impersonal assessments of evidence and the application of impartial law according to specific events and transactions.

In many ways, then, do the village assembly and village council introduced into Torkotala under the auspices of Panchayati Raj represent significant departures from the system of ad hoc village meetings which existed prior to them, and now coexist with them. If these many specific differences can be summed up at all, it is that Panchayati Raj is intended and is in fact both an instance and an invocation of social and economic, but especially political equality. For that reason does the extension of Panchayati Raj into Torkotala represent what Moore (1975, p.234) terms a "process of situational adjustment" rather than regularization. This is evident behaviorally in the leveling, however gradual and partial, of inequalities between castes in the context of local self-government. It is evident also in the language of claims which accompanies Panchayati Raj. Specifically, unlike village politics which is regarded as the avoidable result of individual misconduct in a just society, the competitions occasioned by instances of government politics are regarded differently as the inevitable product of social inequities. The goal of government politics is not to maintain the given order, which is deemed unjust, but to fashion a new and more equitable order grounded on the fundamental equality of all. The language of claims which accompanies instances of government politics like Panchayati Raj thus rationalizes competition as a conduit of progress and change. From the temporary disorder of politics is to come a new and better order.

Panchayati Raj in Torkotala does serve as a vehicle of community development, and has served to extend into this local administrative unit some of those features of a political democracy which already characterizes higher administrative units of the state. But Panchayati Raj in Torkotala is not an unqualified success and does not operate fully as planned by its national architects. The village panchayat is today only sporadically active, has only limited support among Hindus, no support among Lodhas, and since its formation in 1962 has become progressively less a village council than a factional council. It is avoided by many and has been co-opted by others.

This pattern of avoidance and co-option will probably recur elsewhere in rural India where their coexists two sets of understandings about the right and proper order of village life. Beteille (1965), Bailey (1963) and Epstein (1962), for example, each describe how the avoidance pattern of Haripado Bhunai is repeated where the extension of Panchayati Raj meets resistance from men who already occupy established positions of village leadership, and with the same result as in Torkotala. Namely, the avoidance of established leaders tempers the effectiveness of the local panchayat while opening the way for a new set of leaders advanced by popular vote and willing to capitalize on the concept of elected authority. These new leaders, like Satya Dolai, may not have the personal qualities of a big man, but they come to have the legally defined powers of office in a statutory council. Where established local leaders like Atul Mahabarto do not avoid the new panchayats, they may, nevertheless, co-opt the powers of office to buttress the personal basis of their position as a faction, caste, or village leader. A likely result, as in Torkotala and the Uttar Pradesh village described by Retzlaff (1962), is that the distinction between ad hoc councils and the local statutory council, though never entirely lost, becomes increasingly blurred as the leadership of both is in the same person, who does not often or clearly distinguish when he is acting on his personal powers and when he is acting on his legal powers as panchayat officer.

Order and Change

Village politics and government politics posit very different images of social and political order, each with its own validation. Village politics is essentially protective of the traditional; it aims not to reform but to understand, guard, and maintain a present order viewed as divinely given and inherent in the nature of the universe. Validating this traditionalist politics is a cyclical vision of time, which holds that the creator of the universe generates the phenomenal world out of his cosmic body, sustains it for a time, then causes it to degenerate and be reabsorbed in him, only to later begin the cycle anew. Like the universe at large, human society also passes through an interminable series of long cycles, each consisting of four ages. The Golden Age, when dharma was upheld in its entirely, is quite literally in the past. So are the Silver and Bronze Ages when dharma walked on three and then two feet respectively. What confronts men in their own lifetime is the Iron Age or Kali Yuga, when dharma hobbles along on but one foot. To forestall an even further degeneration of behavioral codes and ultimately the destruction of the known world, it is for men to protect what remains of the rule of dharma. Village politics is aimed towards that end.

Government politics, by contrast, posits that every social and political order is a human construction, and thus subject to continual reshaping and improvement in accord with human efforts. Moreover, in creating a new order, men are not bound by local tradition. Innovation is expected. So is progress, a future better than the past. Validating this image of progressive politics is a vision of time as a forward trajectory, having a single beginning and a single, purposeful end, which in contemporary India is seen as progress in accord with the ideals of a modernizing nation-state. The Golden Age of government politics is in the future, not the past, and is accessible to men through their own efforts at reform.

The premises, images, and validations which inform village politics and government politics bear importantly on the process of political change in Torkotala today. To illustrate, traditionalism in the context of village politics does not entail an unchanging set of acts and institutions which have persisted from time immemorial.

It refers to no set conditions, but to a positive evaluation of the present and past order. As such, traditionalism requires that changes be accommodated in a way that they are regarded not simply as new, but also, paradoxically, as old, as reviving or restoring an original and better state that for some reason has been lost in the Kali Yuga. In practical terms this means that events like the Bagdi claim to a new and higher rank are justified publicly as a corrective to the right order of castes—temporarily disrupted—and not as a challenge to that order. It means also that truly innovative aspects of government politics are often characterized, falsely, as restorationist. During the extension of Panchayati Raj into Torkotala, for example, the theme and language of claims associated with a traditionalist village politics was manipulated for the purposes of a progressive politics.

Government officials regularly depict Panchayati Raj as an elaboration of a historic pattern of rural self-government that is documented in the Vedas and the great epics, Ramayana and Mahabarta, as well as in Kautilya's Arthasastra. As the BDO explained to Torkotala residents, during the Golden Age of ancient India, villages were the basic unit of republican government and councils were the basic instrument of village rule. Rural self-government through councils was lost during the centuries of Muslim and British rule. To restore it became the goal of the preindependent Indian National Congress, prodded by Mahatma Gandhi, who saw self-ruling villages as a necessary first step in preparing for a viable, independent democratic state. After independence, it was this same system of rural self-government through councils which was formalized as national policy with the incorporation of Article 40 into the Indian constitution, and which later became known as Panchayati Raj.

Village councils did exist in ancient India, and in parts of northern India (though not in West Bengal) were known as panchayats. But the councils of ancient India were very different from their supposed modern counterparts. They were ad hoc bodies for dealing with the broadest range of village affairs, not formally organized and constituted bodies with specified functions, powers, revenue sources, etc., which is characteristic of the councils instituted under Panchayati Raj legislation. Also unlike the modern panchayats, councils of ancient India were not popularly elected bodies. Their leadership did not circulate regularly and was not in any real sense open to persons without hereditary rights and/or dominant economic status. Their source of support derived from local custom and the personal influence of their active membership, and not from the political and legal systems of a superordinate power.

Panchayati Raj legislation, in sum, did not restore the historic councils of some past system of rural self-government. It created a new kind of council intended to actualize the premises of government politics and to effect progress and change through the devolution of power, both economic and political. Yet in extending Panchayati Raj into villages like Torkotala, government agents (and partisan villagers) manipulated the premises, images and validations of village politics to ease the accomodation of this political innovation. By associating the modern panchayats with a supposed ancient counterpart, these new councils were given a history and genealogy within the Indian Great Tradition which, in effect, then served to validate their (re)introduction. The same process of validating the new through association with the old also explains why these councils were termed "panchayats"; they would be better understood by this traditional sounding name than by any other technically more accurate neologism.

The use of traditionalism as an instrument of political innovation is not limited to rural contexts in India, and may be a generalized process effective wherever traditional and progressive forms of politics coexist. Consider, for example, the events of summer 1975 which led to a proclamation of national emergency in India. On June 12 the high court of Allahabad judged Prime Minister Indira Gandhi guilty of violating Indian electoral law in her 1971 campaign for parliament, ruling that she had illegally used local police to help organize her campaign appearances and had illegally used a government official as a campaign worker. Because being a member of parliament is a prerequisite for being prime minister, this ruling threatened to end Indira's tenure as head of government. Under the terms of the Allahabad decree, Gandhi was also barred from running for any elective office for six years, thus making it impossible for her to avoid the consequences of the ruling by immediately holding an election to seek a new mandate.

Gandhi sought and won a temporary stay of the Allahabad court order, and filed for appeal before the Indian Supreme Court. She also sought to dissipate growing public opposition against her. Activists calling for her ouster in accord with the rule of law were arrested. The media were censored. And Gandhi took her case to the people through personal appearances, radio and television, arguing that her political opponents were using legal technicalities to gain an office they could not win through election.

The Allahabad ruling was heard on appeal in the Indian Supreme Court on June 25 by Justice Iyer, the lone judge handling cases during the tribunal's summer recess. Iyer barred Gandhi from voting in parliament, thereby compounding doubts about her rightful membership in that body, but did allow her to stay on as prime minister pending a final ruling by the full court. Opponents of the prime minister interpreted this action as a victory for them, and took to the streets in great numbers. More arrests followed, as did even stricter censorship of the media. On June 26, the president of India, at the bidding of Indira Gandhi, also declared a state of national emergency, thus allowing Gandhi to use the army to maintain public order and to suspend fundamental rights guaranteed by the Indian constitution. Among those who opposed these acts, significantly, were members of parliament. Some were arrested for their public statements; others chose to boycott the legislature. Thus when parliament met in early August, there was little effective opposition to legislation which retroactively legalized the electioneering acts for which Indira Gandhi had been convicted.

The events of summer 1975 represent radical political changes in India, moving the government from democratic to increasingly authoritarian rule. Whether those political changes would have facilitated the social and economic reforms promised by Gandhi is an open question. For present purposes of interest is the language of claims in which Indira Gandhi justified her unprecedented actions.

> It was very Indian. Immediately after Prime Minister Indira Gandhi declared an unprecedented state of emergency last month she called on her spiritual guru, the aged sage, Vinoba Bhave, to dip into his ancient Vedic texts and come up with a rationalization that would square her action with Hindu traditionalism.... The fate of nations and societies, he said, was to pass through a cycle of distinct eras, each characterized by a dominant social theme. For India, the era of unbridled freedom had passed; the nation was now entering a time when obedience and order would be the social imperatives (Jenkins 1975, pp.42-43).

Billboards which appeared in New Delhi and elsewhere shortly after Bhave's statement capsulized the same message. One read:

"Emergency, an Era of Discipline." Another pictured Indira Gandhi above the statement "She Who Is Between Order and Chaos." Clearly the language of claims reflected in these statements manipulates certain understandings of a traditionalist politics, especially the cyclical vision of time, with its image of a past Golden Age, and the customary validation for the appearance of kings. Simply, like the kings of old, Indira Gandhi will maintain dharma, prevent anarchy, forestall the ultimate destruction of the known world, where ordinary men cannot.

The manipulation of traditional meanings was probably most effective in winning the support of those Indians, rural or urban, who hold politics subordinate to the broader normative frame of religion. But why did Indira Gandhi also win widespread support, which she did, among other Indians who think of politics as separate from and superordinate to considerations of religion? To this audience the emergency regulations seemed justified, no matter how radical the break with tradition, because Gandhi promised they would result in social stability, economic growth and—stated most broadly—quickened progress towards the ideals of a modernizing nation-state.

The meaning of any political event is not determined by the particularities of the event itself. Meaning is socially authored, and meaning attributed by actors may be manipulated for their own purposes. Referring to the councils introduced under state legislation as "panchayats," or adopting Vinoba Bhave's rationalization of Indira Gandhi's emergency reforms, are both instances of the understandings of a traditionalist politics being manipulated for the purpose of a progressive politics. They also suggest an insight of potential importance to agents and students of change in settings like Torkotala. Political change is not foreign to rural India. But village politics and government politics each have their unique manner of rationalizing change, and whatever the ostensible material benefits to be gained, the success of an innovation depends in part on its accompanying language of claims. More specifically, where politics is held subordinate to dharma, changes which challenge the basic premises, images and validations of order will be accomodated more readily when innovated in the name of traditionalism, for innovation can then be rationalized as not simply new, but also as old, as restorationist, as recapturing a past Golden Age. Where politics is held superordinate to dharma, changes which challenge basic premises, images and validations of order will be accomodated more readily when innovated in the name of progress, for innovation can then be rationalized as hastening the Golden Age of the future.

Summary and Conclusion

In closing, some of the points drawn in this paper will be reviewed briefly, and general comments made as to their implications for the anthropological study of politics. First, though systems of political action and meaning can be distinguished analytically and studied separately, it has been the position of this paper that a holistic anthropology is best concerned with both, not only because patterns of personal and group relationships and related processual acts are in an important sense unintelligible apart from the cultural context in which they are embedded, but also because a strictly cultural analysis begs the question of how those shared ideas, concepts, and understandings which constitute a system of meaning are related to actual patterns of social interaction. In combination, these reasons also suggest why politics is best studied as two dimensional: as a system of instrumental action and symbolic meaning.

Second, the study of politics as two-dimensional can be operationalized via a documentary method which focuses on both the themes which define local conceptions of politics and the manner in which those themes inform specific political events. In fitting themes to events there is no assumption that either systems of action or meaning are primary in some determinative sense. The attempt is only to integrate social structural and cultural analyses by taking into account both the patterns of what people do and the patterns of what people say or otherwise indicate as explanation for why they do what they do.

Third, in the attempt by actors to maintain or alter a certain fit between systems of action and meaning can be discerned the processes which generate political compeition. In discussing the politics of caste, for example, it was seen that both inter- and intracaste competitions are generated by efforts to insure a consistency between an order of ranked castes conceived culturally and realized socially. In that sense do such competitions represent processes of regularization that affirm and renew the caste system even as individual castes may alter their position within a local hierarchy. Instances of government politics like Panchayati Raj, by contrast, represent processes of adjustment in seeking to level, if not completely eliminate, the given system of ranked inequalities in favor of an alternative social and political order founded on the premise and actuality of equality.

Fourth, a two-dimensional study of politics which extends the usual focus on political structure and process to include an attention to political culture can enhance our understanding of politics locally and in cross-cultural perspective. The contrasting premises which inform village politics and government politics, for example, evidence why similarly organized competitions may have a very different goal orientation. A culturally informed understanding of Torkotala politics also bears on two of the definitions of politics most widely accepted by anthropologists. David Easton (1959) defines the political as "those interactions through which values are authoritatively allocated for a society," while Swartz, Turner, and Tuden (1966, p.7) equate politics with those "processes involved in determining and implementing public goals." In the same vein, Ronald Cohen (1973, p.872) writes, "We must operationally define the political system as the widest set of authority relations in society." Such definitions seemingly apply to contemporary nation-states of the West where politics does provide a society-wide normative framework. But do they apply, as intended, cross-culturally? Is politics everywhere the domain of ultimate authority? Is politics everywhere the ultimate arbiter of public goals and values?

Both village politics and government politics are identified behaviorally with rivalries over rank. But in the context of village politics, this conjunction of rank and rivalry belies the primacy of politics as the domain of ultimate authority, or even as a domain discrete from religion. The goal of village politics, the moral means towards that goal, and individual political responsibility are all inseparable from and subordinated to religious considerations of dharma. In the context of government politics, by contrast, the Indian constitution and legal system supplant dharma as the broadest normative framework for politics, and also establish politics and religion as formally separate domains. A comparison of these two forms of rule thus suggests that while politics may always involve the administration of public goals and values, it does not necessarily define those goals and values.[7] That this is so also suggests the utility of political studies that explore the relations between politics and other social domains.

Fifth, in attending to political culture, it is useful to consider not only the substantive content of political themes, but also their functional role in directing and justifying action. The use of political themes to justify the interested participation of individuals in specific competitions can take the form of advancing a language of claims. A language of claims may be a forthright statement of actual motives, as when the censor of the Bagdi widow or the Dey brothers was publicly explained as rectifying a transgression of caste dharma. Or a language of claims may mask actual motives, as when government agents manipulated the understandings of a traditionalist village politics to disguise the truly innovative nature of Panchayati Raj. In either case the importance of attending to the public statements which accompany political events is that they are an expression of socially accepted reasons for particular acts, of legitimate rationalizations for action whatever the actual motivation. As C. Wright Mills (1940) noted long ago, varieties of situated action will each have their characteristic vocabulary of motives.

And sixth, just as it is useful to consider how political themes are used as a language of claims to direct and justify action, it is useful to consider how the action content of political events affirms, or does not affirm, culturally defined themes. Indeed, a view of politics as both instrumental and symbolic action demands that theme and event each be examined in light of the other. In Torkotala it is the concern, even preoccupation, with ranked inequalities which defines the context of meaning in which instances of both village politics and government politics are situated, and in terms of which they are typed and interpreted. It is through village politics that an order of ranked inequalities is both affirmed and realized. It is through government politics that a more equalitarian order is both affirmed and realized. In both contexts are theme and event, rank and rivalry, each intelligible in terms of the other. Put differently, the rivalries over rank which characterize both village politics and government politics have a significance which transcends their nature as instrumental means towards an immediate goal, be it recognition as Bagra-Khatriyas or the election of non-Sadgops to a legally empowered village council. They are also symbolic statements about the right and proper order of things. Individual political competitions reflect broader political themes symbolically. They also realized those themes socially.

Anthropologists have long recognized the symbolic importance of religious rites and other public ceremonies for affirming and renewing an existent set of personal and group relationships, and the world view which makes that set of relationships seem uniquely fitted to the realities of social life. The evidence from

Torkotala suggests the utility of also considering political competitions as public ceremonies which support or challenge, uphold or alter, the given sociocultural order. This is more than to view competition instrumentally as a conduit of stability or change. It is also to view competitions as reflecting and addressing the basic premises of order, as another form of symbolic action.

Notes

* The field work on which this paper is based was carried out in West Bengal, India, from January 1971 through June 1972, under a grant from the Foreign Area Fellowship Foundation and while the author was a Danforth Foundation Graduate Fellow. This paper has benefited from critical readings by Peter Bertocci, Judith T. Irvine, and David Jacobson. It has also benefited from work done jointly with Dr. Bertocci in convening a panel (Culture and Social Structures: Contrasting Approaches to the Study of Meaning and Action) at the 76th Annual Meeting of the American Anthropological Association, in Houston, Texas. An earlier version of this paper was presented at the Xth International Congress of Anthropological and Ethnological Sciences, held in New Delhi, India, in December 1978.

1. Marxist approaches are well represented in the recent volume edited by Maurice Bloch (1975).
2. See Keesing (1974) for a more detailed review of recent cultural approaches in anthropology.
3. This discussion of operationalizing the documentary method is adapted in the main from Mannheim (1923) and Peter McHugh (1968). It may read as a restatement of the obvious to those who already treat systems of action and meaning as mutually interdependent, yet independent systems. But as some cultural analysts choose not to relate ideational and interactional systems (e.g. Schneider 1968; Inden and Nicholas 1977), or are discouraging of verifying systems of meaning once uncovered (e.g. Geertz 1973), a restatement of what may be obvious is risked to suggest how meaning systems can be tested through application to events from which they were not derived.
4. For a general discussion of how present events serve as interpretive guides to past and future events, see Mead (1932).
5. For non-Indianists, it is perhaps worth clarifying that all castes can be sorted into categories commonly known as *varna*, which provide a pan-Indian system of classification and rank. The four *varna* described in an origin myth, the Purusasukta, include in rank order the Brahman or priestly castes, the Kshatriya or kingly castes, the Vaisya or castes concerned with the production of wealth through agriculture, animal husbandry or trade, and the Sudra or service castes. Untouchables are a fifth varna not described in the Purusasukta but recognized popu-

larly as a category of castes which do the most odeous and inferiorizing service tasks. Brahman, Sudra and Untouchable castes are all represented in contemporary Bengali society; Kshatriya and Vaisya castes are not. Bengali villagers are uncertain why this is so. Bengali scholars argue that the Kshatriya and Vaisya castes in Bengal have not been eliminated forever; they have been temporarily degraded to the rank of Sudra for failure to observe their appropriate behavioral codes (see Dutt 1969, pp.78-90).

6. Contained within the Indian constitution is the basis for a clear separation of politics from religion as symbolized in the ideal of India as a secular state. But India is also committed constitutionally to the ideal of a modern welfare state in which the model of social, economic, and political justice is contrary to that supported by considerations of dharma. The Indian state, to illustrate, has expanded its jurisdiction over matters of marriage, divorce, adoption, inheritance, and succession to property, all of which are now covered by statutory codes. It has also undertaken to reform temple administration, to abolish untouchability, and to eliminate communalism. In light of such reformist activities on the part of government, Torkotala residents regard the claimed separation of politics from religion as less than full, as more supposed than real.

7. Louis Dumont (1971) would extend this observation to argue that politics is a primary normative framework only in individualistic societies of the West. In India, as in other holistic societies, Dumont holds, what we call religion provides the normative framework that "encompasses" all social life. The limitation of Dumont's argument is that actual societies, including India, are neither wholly individualistic, nor wholly holistic (cf. Davis 1976b). Actual societies may also include more than one set of relations between politics and religion, as in Torkotala.

References

Althusser, Louis. 1971. Ideology and ideological state apparatuses. In *Lenin and philosophy,* ed. Louis Althusser. N.Y.: Monthly Review Press.

Bailey, F. G. 1960. *Tribe, caste and nation.* Manchester: Manchester University Press.

Bailey, F. G. 1963. *Politics and social change.* Berkeley and Los Angeles: University of California Press.

Bailey, F. G. 1968. Parapolitical system. In *Local level politics,* ed. Marc J. Swartz. Chicago: Aldine.

Barber, Bernard. 1972. Function, variability and change in ideological systems. In *Stability and social change,* ed. Bernard Barber and Alex Inkeles. Boston: Little Brown.

Beteille, Andre. 1965. *Caste, class and power.* Berkeley: University of California Press, 1965.

Bloch, Maurice, ed. 1975. *Marxist analysis and social anthropology.* N. Y.: Wiley and Sons.

Cohen, Ronald. 1973. Political anthropology. In *Handbook of social and*

cultural anthropology, ed. John J. Honigmann. Chicago: Rand McNally.
Davis, Marvin. 1976a. A philosophy of Hindu rank from rural West Bengal. *Journal of Asian Studies*. 36, 1:5-24.
Davis, Marvin. 1976b. The individual among Bengali Hindus. *Man in India*. 56, 3:189-214.
Davis, Marvin. 1976c. The politics of family life in rural West Bengal. *Ethnology* XV. 2:189-200.
Dumont, Louis. 1971. Religion, politics and society in the individualistic universe. Proceedings of the Royal Anthropological Institute. 1970:31-41.
Dutt, N. K. 1969. *Origin and growth of caste in India*, vol. II. Calcutta: Firma K. L. Mukhopadhyay.
Easton, David. 1959. Political anthropology. In *Biennial review of anthropology*, ed. Bernard J. Siegal. Stanford: Stanford University Press.
Epstein, T. Scarlett. 1962. *Economic development and social change in South India*. Manchester: Manchester University Press.
Frake, C.O. 1964. A structural description of Subanun religious behavior. In *Explorations in cultural anthropology*, ed. W.H. Goodenough. New York: McGraw-Hill.
Garfinkle, Harold. 1967. *Studies in ethnomethodology*. New Jersey: Prentice Hall.
Geertz, Clifford. 1964. Ideology as a cultural system. In *Ideology and discontent*, ed. David Apter. New York: Free Press.
Geertz, Clifford. 1973. Deep play: notes on the Balinese cockfight. In *The Interpretation of Cultures*. New York: Basic Books,
Goodenough, W.H. 1957. Cultural anthropology and linguistics. In *Report of the seventh annual round table meeting on linguistics and language study*, ed. P. Garvin. Washington, D.C.: Georgetown University Monograph Series on Language and Linguistics, 9.
Gough, E.K. 1959. Criteria of caste ranking in South India. *Man in India*. 39:115-126.
Husserl, Edmond. 1962. *Ideas*. Trans. by W.R. Boyce Gibson. N.Y.: Collier Books.
Inden, Ronald B. and Nicholas, Ralph W. 1977. *Kinship in Bengali culture*. Chicago: University of Chicago Press.
Jenkins, Loren, 1975. *Newsweek*, August 4.
Keesing, R.M. 1974. Theories of culture. *Annual review of anthropology*. Palo Alto, California: Annual Reviews Inc.
Legros, Dominique. 1977. Chance, necessity, and the mode of production: a Marxist critique of cultural evolutionism. *American Anthropologist*. 79:26-41.
Mannheim, Karl. 1923. On the interpretation of Weltanschauung. In *Essays on the sociology of knowledge*. London: Routledge and Kegan Paul.
Marriott, McKim. 1968. Caste ranking and food transactions: a matrix analysis. In *Structure and change in Indian society*, eds. Milton Singer and Bernard S. Cohn. Chicago: Aldine.
McHugh, Peter. 1968. *Defining the situation*. Indianapolis: Bobbs-Merrill.
Mead, George Herbert. 1932. *The philosophy of the present*. Chicago: Open Court.
Metzger, D. and Williams, G. 1963. A formal ethnographic analysis of Tenejapa Ladino weddings. *American Anthropologist*. 65:1072-1101.

Mills. G. Wright 1940. Situated actions and vocabularies of motive. *American Sociological Review*. 5: 904-913.

Moore, Sally Falk. 1975. Epilogue: uncertainties in situations, indeterminacies in culture. In *Symbol and politics in communal ideology*, eds. Sally Falk Moore and Barbara G. Myerhoff. Ithaca, New York: Cornell University Press.

Moore, Sally Falk and Myerhoff, Barbara G., eds. 1975. *Symbol and politics in communal ideology*. Ithaca, New York: Cornell University Press.

Nicholas, Ralph W. 1968. Structures of politics in the villages of South Asia. In *Structure and change in Indian society*, eds. Milton Singer and Bernard S. Cohn. Chicago: Aldine,

Nicholas, Ralph. 1973. Social and political movements. In *Annual review of anthropology*, eds. Bernard J. Siegal, Alan Beals and Stephen A. Tyler. Palo Alto, California: Annual Reviews, Inc.

Ortner, Sherry B. 1978. *Sherpas through their rituals*. Cambridge: Cambridge University Press.

Retzlaff, Ralph. 1962. *Village government in India: a case study*. New York: Asia Publishing Company.

Ricoeur, Paul. 1971. The model of the text: meaningful action considered as text. *Social Research*. 38, 3:529-562.

Robinson, Marqeurite S. 1975. *Political structure in a changing Sinhalese village*. Cambridge: Cambridge University Press.

Schneider, David. 1968. *American kinship: a cultural account*. Englewood Cliffs, New Jersey: Prentice Hall.

Schutz, Alfred. 1967. The phenomenology of the social world, trans. by George Walsh and Frederick Lehnert. Evanston, Illinois: Northwestern University Press.

Silverberg, James. 1959. Caste ascribed "status" versus caste irrelevant roles. *Man in India*. 39:148-162.

Spradley, James P. 1970. *You owe yourself a drunk: an ethnography of urban nomads*. Boston: Little, Brown.

Srinivas, M.N. 1966. *Social change in modern India*. Berkeley: University of California Press.

Swartz, Marc J., Victor Turner and Arthur Tuden, eds. 1966. *Political anthropology*. Chicago: Aldine.

Winckler, E.A. 1970. Political anthropology. *Biennial review of anthropology*, Bernard J. Siegel, ed. Stanford: Stanford University Press.

Chapter 4

Models of Solidarity, Structures of Power: The Politics of Community in Rural Bangladesh [1]

Peter J. Bertocci

Introduction

This paper seeks to explore the dynamic connections between culture, seen as a system of symbols and ideation whereby human beings meaningfully construct the reality of their lives, and social structure, viewed as a system of human interaction which consists of normatively patterned role relationships, rooted in the material conditions of life. I suggest that the study of politics constitutes one of the foci at which one perceives most clearly the processual linkage between the cultural system of meaning, the "thought of" order of existence, and the social structural system of action, or the "lived in" order of daily life. My discussion of the symbolic bases of politics draws heavily upon ideas advanced by David M. Schneider and his colleagues (Schneider 1968, 1969; Dolgin, Kemnitzer and Schneider 1977), and the programmatic suggestions advocated by Aronoff in this volume will be reflected as well. Certain recent formulations by Adams (1970, 1975) will also be utilized, and the final section of the essay will propose elements of a symbolic interactionist psychological orientation that may be helpful in seeking to unify "idealist" and "materialist" approaches to the study of social and cultural life.

The medium for this discussion will involve attention to a central problem in the political anthropology of rural Bangladesh, where I have conducted field work several times over the past ten years. Specifically, I ask what kinds of groups comprise the peasant community in Bangladesh and how might a study of the political processes which structure and animate them illuminate the manner of their formation. While geographical, ecological, and administrative factors must certainly all be considered in comprehending how Bangladeshi peasants organize their social life, I shall argue here that ideational and symbolic processes provide clues to the way in which the dominant Mulsim population of the country conceives of community as a cultural domain, and, further, that the latter conception critically influences the interactional processes whereby community is actually worked out as a political domain. My effort, then, focuses on how cultural systems—systems of meaning—interact dynamically with politics as one component of the general system of action.[2]

Recent Studies in Symbolic Anthropology

David M. Schneider, and those who have been influenced by his work, define culture as a system of symbols, following Parsons, Kroeber, and other eminent spokespersons for this particular social scientific tradition. Cultural systems are more generally conceived of, following Schneider (1968, p. 1), as consisting of "units (or parts) which are defined in certain ways and which are differentiated according to certain criteria. These units [collectively] define the world or the universe, the way things in it relate to each other, and what these things should be and do." Symbols and their meanings are understood to delineate different cultural domains, or orders of phenomena, which are conceptually distinguished from one another, at some level or in some context in the indigenous ideology, world view or ethos of the people under study. In the study of social life, exponents of this approach focus upon the symbols and their meanings which demarcate the relevant culturally distinct domains, such as kinship, caste and so forth, and these are then analyzed, along with the normative prescriptions or "codes for conduct" specified within each domain, with reference to the type of social solidarity they function to create and support. The analysis of cultural systems from this perspective, it is argued, results in the apprehension of truly indigenous models of solidarity, and thus a composite view of the moral order as perceived by the bearers of the culture themselves.

As will be seen, recent work in South Asian ethnology which has reflected Schneider's (as well as Dumont's 1970) approach to the study of culture (and Indic societies) has been fruitful in laying bare the relevance of indigenous theories of social organization and conceptions of the moral order. While this renewed emphasis upon the study of meaning has been important, some proponents of the approach have rightly recognized that it deals with only "half the problem" (Barnett, Fruzzetti and Ostor 1976, p. 628). The other half, they note, "is the relation of an ideology to other aspects of social life (ecology, mode of production, face-to-face behavior and so on)." This paper will attempt to demonstrate a linkage between these two halves in a discussion of the sociopolitical organization of rural Bangladesh by seeking to show how a cultural model of solidarity informs the expression of community life which is otherwise grounded in ecological, administrative and power structural factors, rooted in class relations.

The Problem of "Village Community" in Bangladesh Studies

Conventionally, local level community research in Bangladesh has adopted the peasant village as its focus, in the time-honored tradition of holistic anthropological studies, only to be confounded by what I myself have characterized as the weakness of the Bangladesh village as a solidary entity of social organization and the elusiveness of its unity as a residential social system (Bertocci 1970, pp. 10-14 et passim; see also Glasse 1966). The enduring boundaries of village-as-community in both space and human action have proved exceedingly difficult to fix, and at one point I have suggested that, at least analytically, village organization slips somehow vaguely into larger socioterritorial units of organization, such as market areas and "micro-regions" (Bertocci 1975). One problem with such categories, however, is that they are the abstractional products of extracultural researchers, regardless of the "heuristic" value they may or may not have as formulations relevant to Western social science research. Even the concept of "village" itself as employed in Bangladesh-oriented rural research may not have adequately reflected the content of the entity, "village," as a native category for Bengalis, but rather may have seemed to imply a certain residential boundedness of Bangladesh communities, tending to result in the conclusion that "disorganization" is present where no such boundaries are readily found.

In fact, few centralized, formal suprakinship institutions are to be found in rural Bangladesh, and its villages are certainly not among them. Most observers have noted, however, the presence of what I shall here consider to be religious corporate groups, which variously coincide with, segment, or crosscut local village units. These have by now been fairly well described in the Bangladesh literature, but few scholars have attributed to them the importance I propose to accord them here as, in fact, the primary units of community among Bengali Muslims, providing the social form which quintessentially expresses community solidarity in their culture.

Part I: A Model of Solidarity

Throughout much of Bangladesh, Mulsim peasants belong to small, localized religious corporate groups of the sort postulated by Weber (1964, pp. 145-157), which appear to figure importantly in peasant social organization in other parts of the world (e.g., Mexico—see Dow 1974). These groups are religious par excellence in that they are the social loci of collective worship and the observance of several important festivals; their memberships commonly coincide with the regular congregation of a mosque, although they need not do so. The groups are corporate in the Weberian sense [3] that they limit admission by self-definitional rules prescribing adherence to Muslim faith and submission to Islamic norms as interpreted by group authority, vested in leadership. As their constitution is entirely local and indigenous, having no formally systemic connection with institutions of higher secular or religious authority, these groups may be seen as autonomous, in Weber's terms, as well as autocephalous, in that their leadership acts by group, and not external, empowerment. These "religious corporations" traditionally perform(ed) important functions of social control and dispute settlement, dealing with a broad range of disputes and delicts. Decisions rendered by the leadership are enforced, as often as not, in what Weber termed a "hierocratic" manner, involving " 'psychic coercion' through the distribution and denial of religious benefits," as well as the control of behavior via threats to honor and the inducement of shame (Weber 1964, p. 154).

It is in such groups, rather than in what is otherwise designated as the village per se, that Bengali Muslims act out what is morally and ritually meaningful as community, celebrating important religious festivals, coming together in prayer on critical days of atonement, and also reinforcing when necessary the normative standards to which all are supposed to adhere. It is noteworthy that these groups are commonly called *samaj*, which is the generic term for "society" in Bengali and other Indo-Aryan languages, and in some parts of Bangladesh they are also known as *reyai* (Bertocci 1970), which connotes "follower" or "citizen" and by extension implies the protection of "those who submit." Religious corporate groups of this sort may take the form of sect-like organization, based upon adherence to one of the several Islamic schools of law (see Islam 1974). Their conceptual roots are, however, deeply seated in Muslim notions of the moral order, as may be seen in a symbolic and philosophical analysis of the underlying ideational framework.

Nearly everywhere in northern South Asia, important group components of social organization are referred to by the word *jati*, which, of course, among Hindus specifically denotes "caste," and connotes "community" in the sense of "racial group." Recent writings on Bengali Hindu society by South Asianists who employ Schneider's approach to symbolic analysis (e.g. Inden 1976; Inden and Nicholas 1977) translate jati as "gennus" (or "birth group"—see Davis 1976), to suggest that for Hindus the different "caste communities" into which their society is divided each comprise generically distinct kinds of human beings, differentiated naturally by birth and sharing a "natural substance" (flesh and blood), in which their group "codes for conduct" (behavioral prescriptions) are thought to be "embedded," as it were. All of these jatis are seen as harmoniously integrated into a larger community, and unified by the actions of each in performing the reciprocal roles which contribute to the maintenance of "proper order" *(dharma)* and thus promote the common good (Inden 1976, p.22-29). Thus, for Hindus, community in its general expression consists of naturally different subgroups of people, brought together in a classically Durkheimian model of organic solidarity.

Bengali Muslim social thought proceeds initially in a diametrically opposed direction. The basic distinction made by Muslims among human beings in all their diversity is according to the criterion of religious belief and worship. Muslims, Hindus, Christians, Jews, and so forth, are each considered to comprise separate human communities, also called jatis, distinguished not by anything in the "natural" order of things, but with primary reference to the god(s) each worships and thus the religiously derived code for conduct each enjoins upon its members. Muslims hold that humans are a single species, the distinctions within which made according to how the human faculties of rational intelligence and will are exercised. Islam is certainly not unique among religions in a placing primacy upon the "saving functions" of intelligence and will, but, as Schuon (1972, p. 15) has stated it, for Muslims these human qualities are "the point of departure in a perspective of salvation and deliverance." Moreover, the proper exercise of intelligence, for Muslims, cannot be divorced from its content, which is "nothing other than the knowledge of Unity, or the Absolute, and of the dependence of all things on it." Similarly, will is nothing other than "conformity to what is willed by God, or the Absolute." For Bengali Muslim peasants, who do not ordinarily engage in these flights of abstraction, the matter is clear, and the most basic discrimination they make among their fellow humans is between those who, as they do, recognize Allah and submit to the code for conduct He has revealed through the message of Muhammed, and those who do not. This is not a matter of ascription by birth, as, indeed, suggested by Islam's historic tendencies of proselytization, but of acceptance of revealed Truth, creating differences among humans of a cultural, not a natural, sort.

For Muslims, then, commonality of belief and adherence to code for conduct transcend the ties of blood, or natural substance, in a model of solidarity emblematic of that which Durkheim characterized as "mechanical," a cohesion born of likeness in ideas, values, and normative commitment. But, while it may be generated in culture, the social bond resultant from commonality of belief and code creates ties whose commanding hold is seen as equivalent to ties of blood, and thus symbolic of relationships engendered by nature. Muslims the world over, of course, conceive of themselves as forming a kind of brotherhood, and in the more localized Bangladesh context, so do the members of a samaj group (see Thorp 1977, who glosses the term samaj as "residential brotherhood"). They address each other, for instance, by kinship terms, even where no ostensible links of consanguinity of affinity, in Western anthropological parlance, obtain. "We are as one lineage," the members of one such group told anthropologist Robert Glasse (1966, p. 203), and I have noted that the norms of female seclusion (*purdah*) are relaxed for male samaj members, much as they are among kinsmen. Whereas for Hindus "shared bodily substance" engenders a caste's (i.e., jati) code for conduct, for Muslims acceptance of code creates community (i.e., jati), whose social bond is considered to have a power akin in cohesiveness to that which otherwise resides in the sharing of natural substance.[4]

Additional Integrative Symbols

These conceptions underlie the formalized expression of community through samaj among Muslims in many parts of Bangladesh, the distinguishing feature of which, as argued above, is code for conduct, and whose central symbol, I submit, is that of worship. The samaj might be thought of as the localized expression of the *umma*, the universal Muslim community, based upon revelation and observance of the law whose establishment is recognized as one of Muhammed's major achievements (see Watt 1961, pp. 143-180). For it required the transformation of a kinship-based, tribal society, in which solidarity flowed, as it were, from blood relationships, into a worldwide community whose foundation was the common acceptance of the Truth and the Way of Islam. Thus, the umma unified and encompassed persons and groups of divergent primordial loyalties, limited theretofore to ties of blood; solidarities arising from shared bodily substance, in Schneider's terms, were superceded by those stemming from unity of belief and normative commitment (Schneider's code for conduct). Following Ortner (1973), one might view the umma as a "summarizing symbol" of community for all Muslims, "summing up, expressing, representing . . . in an emotionally powerful and relatively undifferentiated way" what Islam as a sociocultural system means to them (Ortner 1973, p. 1339). The names for these Bengali Muslim religious corporate groups themselves "symbolically elaborate" (in Ortner's terms) the umma, providing what she calls "root metaphors" (Ornter 1973, p. 1341) for its ideational underpinnings. As we have seen, samaj means "society" writ large, and, of course, Islam admits of no boundary between religious and social life; *reyai*, "those who submit" or "followers," hence "citizens" (in the Arabic original), another term for these groups, clearly suggests the subordination of individual wills to a higher power, be it divine or (as we shall see below) human. Significantly, too, in these religious corporations Bengali Muslims commonly act out several of Islam's classic rituals and holy days' requirements, which evoke what Ortner (1973, p. 1341) has termed "key scenarios," elaborating symbols which highlight "clear-cut modes of action appropriate to correct and successful living in the culture." One example of such is the celebration of Id ul-Azha, commemorating Abraham's willingness to sacrifice his son at God's command; others could be given.

The sort of community spirit to which samaj as a model of solidarity corresponds rather well is what Turner (1969, p. 96) has called *communitas*—"an unstructured and relatively undifferentiated ... community, or even communion of equal individuals who submit to the general authority of ritual elders." Especially on ritual occasions, in which behavior approaches the Islamic egalitarian ideals, itself evocative of Turner's antistructural "liminality," everyday social distinctions are blurred and the faithful are united as one body of equal believers.

Some sense of samaj as communitas, and thus as a model of solidarity, may be understood from this record of reminiscences I reproduce below, those of a dear and devout Bengali Muslim friend, as well as excellent informant, of mine.

> The village I lived in as a child had as leader one man, who was my uncle. He was a *sardar* [village elder] and a *moulvi* [Muslim cleric] and had control over religious matters. There was also a *mandal* [village headman] who looked after the villagers' political affairs. Both men were elected. There were three *para* [village hamlets] in all, each with its own petty sardar, all of them under the authority of my uncle.

> My uncle used to see to it that the village poor were fed. He was in charge of the collection of *zakat* [religious tithe] and of *Id ul-Fitra* [the holiday which ends the month of fasting enjoined upon all Muslims] there was a special tax [i.e., the *fitra*] which was to be given to the poor. No man who was in need was allowed to beg. If my uncle saw a man begging, he would ask him "why are you begging? Go to the sardar and he will see that you get food." Everyone was required to give food to the poor; it was a religious duty.

> In those days everyone would say their prayers. It was a sin not to do so. If a man did not say his prayers regularly, when he died there was a separate system for his burial. Instead of the *janaja* [gathering of mourners] at the time of burial, no one would come to the burial of such a man. Nor would he be buried even, but rather his body would be put into the river, for he was a sinner and could not be treated with the same respect as anyone else who had kept regular *namaz* [prayer]. And in those days, too, no one would smoke to-

bacco, unlike today, for this, too, was a sin. I remember once a man was with his bullock cart when my uncle passed. The man quickly put something behind the cart and then said *salam* [a greeting] to my uncle. It was tobacco and he was ashamed and afraid to show it to my uncle.

All religious disputes were referred to my uncle, and in political affairs, to the mandal. All disputes would be solved in this way. No one would take a case to court. And if there was a particularly violent man, then all the mandals of the adjoining twenty-two villages would meet to decide what to do. The involvement in a case of such twenty-two villages was called a *baisi* [from "twenty-two" in Bengali], and even though it is not found much today, still the word is in common use in our language. After my uncle died another man was elected in his place. At my uncle's burial, people cried out "our sardar is dead! Who is worthy of becoming sardar?" And all agreed then and there that only one man could carry on the sardar's duties, and he was elected on the spot. That man was my father.

But nowadays we have become "civilized." We take cases to court, we have fine clothes and have come into contact with urban life. Who cares these days for the poor? All think only of becoming rich. Perhaps you can see why I hate our "civilization."

It does not matter that this is no doubt an idealized recollection of my friend's childhood community, for his musings reflect Muslim community as a "thought of" order of social life, and bespeak the kinds of solidarity which samaj is supposed to create and sustain. The contrast between this and the "lived in" order of social structure in rural Bangladesh, wherein processes all too often are reflected in what Bangladeshis themselves decry as *hingsha* (greed, malice, envy), *daladali* (factionalism), and *maramari-katakati* (throat-cutting slug-fests), is all too evident.

The Individual in Community Life

Muslim *samaj* groups differ from Anglo-American conceptions of community in that the common good is thought to be brought about as the inevitable consequence of (relatively) free individuals coming together in acceptance of divine will and adherence to a divinely ordained code for conduct. Indeed, an orthodox Muslim would assert that if all men abided in such a community, and thus "obeyed the profound law inscribed in the human condition, there would be no social or even general human problems . . ." (Schuon 1972, p. 35). There is, then, in such communities little in the way of public policy to administer other than in matters connected with religious observance and the regulation of ethical conduct. All that the community demands of its members is that they perform the ritual ceremonies required of all Muslims—and in rural Bangladesh the pressures for outward conformity in this respect can be intense—and otherwise regulate their lives in accordance with Islamic ethical canons.

Such communities do not organize common economic activities as a rule, and in that sphere the individual is left to fend for himself. Little community assistance for one's private material endeavors can be counted on, save, of course, in the case of the deserving poor. In material matters, just as in spiritual ones, the individual is left ultimately responsible for his or her own salvation (see Ellickson 1972). Thus, Muslim concepts also foster a certain individualistic striving in the practical matters of economic and political life, a fact which, incidentally, contradicts the fatalism too frequently assigned by some writers (e.g., Zaidi 1971) to Bangladesh's rural inhabitants. Bangladeshi peasants will, to be sure, often verbalize the belief that their lives are governed by *takdir*, seen as the predestined limits and potentialities bestowed by Allah upon each individual life. But, noteworthy in this belief are not only the limits which Allah in His wisdom has imposed upon the person, but also the potentialities which He has granted to each, failure to attempt the realization of which is regarded as a moral transgression. Thus, the ethical underpinnings of Islam as understood by ordinary Bengali Muslims provide impetus to individual human striving and accomplishment, or tadbir.[5] It is neither inconsistent with ethical belief nor surprising as an aspect of human nature that the attainment of wealth, or at least a certain material well-being, is a desired life end, the realization of which is directly associated with prestige in Bengali Muslim culture. And, in central connection to the discussion that follows, an ability to mobilize other persons in the achievement of one's ends, as well as to establish social ties to the powerful who can be instrumental in reaching one's goals, is regarded as pragmatically essential to the realization of tadbir (see Thorp 1977 for an excellent related discussion).

Part II: A Structure of Power

In densely populated, low-lying Bangladesh, with its dispersed pattern of human settlement, clusters of peasant homesteads form *para* (hamlets), which in turn comprise the first level of community infrastructure above that of the family. The residents of several contiguous hamlets, given a significant degree of interaction, commonly come to see themselves as constituting a socially distinct community, which may or may not correspond geographically to the boundaries of an officially delimited *mauza* (village), and within such loosely adherent groupings the comparatively wealthier families tend to exercise predominant social influence. The unity of such constellations is nearly always expressed with reference to samaj or its equivalent as I have sought to depict it above, as a religious corporate group, symbolically constructed as a vehicle for the expression of Muslim community, concretely organized for the enactment of Islamic worship and ritual observance, and solidarily fortified by watchful efforts to enforce Koranic norms. With respect to its religious and ritual functions, one may speak of a minimal samaj, a concrete worshipping congregation, at least with respect to observance of several importance Islamic holy days, even though the group itself may not have its own mosque. Within the samaj, too, rituals surrounding life cycle rites of passage are carried out; marriage ceremonies and their arrangements are functions of samaj organization, as are funerals, and it may be added that nearly all ritual occasions are ones in which food is shared, an important symbolic feature of samaj activities. As noted above, samaj groups have general social control functions, beginning with the regulation of conduct and the arbitration of disputes within the group membership itself. But in this connection one may also speak of a maximal samaj, for the reason that, if the nature of a dispute requires it, the leaders of discrete but adjoining samaj units may come together to collectively preside over or adjudicate a case. This may occur, say, as among samaj groups within the boundaries of a single mauza, or an effective maximal samaj unit may encompass several smaller ones over a much wider area. Thus, for example, I found in the southeasterly Comilla district that minimal such groups (there called *reyai*) could expand to a maximal one encompassing eight mauzas, covering over a square mile, and containing in its "judicial district" some 1,800 people (at the time). By contrast, in the northwestern Rajshahi district, where

I subsequently worked, custom allows for minimal samaj groups to link up, as necessity dictates, to a maximal such assemblage of leaders of twenty-two mauzas, and so fixed, apparently, is this institutional arrangement that it has its own name, baisi, or "group of twenty-two." Researchers who have done rural community studies elsewhere in Bangladesh report, in varying detail, what I think are essentially variations on this basic organizational theme, even though not all have focused greatly on samaj organization, and some have discovered it to be quite weak and ineffective (the most detailed, outstanding studies are those of Thorp 1977, and Zaman 1977).

Power Domains

The workings of such communities in rural Bangladesh may be understood as dynamically shaped by the shifting "power domains" of samaj leaders and their followers in a political environment characterized by pervasive factionalism. Having earlier employed Schneider's notion of cultural domain, I here draw upon the concept of power domain advanced by Adams (1970, 1975), who intends the expression to mean "any relational set in which there are two or more actors or operating units of unequal relative power with respect to each other," especially applicable to "cases of multiple-party relations, where [one person] has domain over a number of subordinates" (Adams 1975, p. 68). While the complexities of Adams's theoretical schematum will not be explored as throughly as they deserve in this analysis, the point I wish to make is that in rural Bangladesh local level leaders, usually representative of the wealthier sections of the peasantry, control access to the preponderance of material and other resources, and have as a result perennially sought to exercise influence over groups of less well-endowed subordinates, in what may be seen as power domains, the latter constantly shifting in the context of factional politics. They have also, in Adams's terms, performed time-honored "brokerage" roles in linking peasant populations to the institutions of state power (Adams 1970; see also Wolf 1966). Thus, they operate at "levels of articulation" (Adams 1975, pp. 75ff), wherein confrontation (i.e., contact) occurs between subordinate and superordinate sociopolitical entities, and their activities thus accomplish the processual connection between "levels of integration" (Adams 1975, p. 80, following Steward), or culturally conceptualized units of organization. As Adams sees it, levels of articulation "are constructed out of the observation or recording of interactions and transactions among human beings," whereas "levels of integration are constructed out of data on levels of articulation, with some conceptual and cognitive dimensions that are brought to bear on that data *(sic)* from an existing generalized, cognitive map of the world" (Adams 1975, p. 80). Thus, Adams's framework for political analysis calls upon us to focus upon the constant interdigitation between the systems of action and meaning, suggesting that, on the one hand, politics shapes the ways in which people conceive of the organization of their social world, and, on the other, symbolic constructs of the social order exert influence on the shape of politics. In the Bangladesh case, the politics of the "lived in" order of interpersonal, factional and state-peasant power domains excercises formational influence on the composition of samaj as expressed in actual human groups, whereas samaj as a model of solidarity, embedded in the "thought of" order of social life, helps to guide the form in which conflict groups coalesce, divide, and channel legitimate power at the local level.

Samaj Origins: Some Speculations

Villages in East Bengal have probably never been the sort of "closed corporate" peasant communities which have typified other parts of Asia, much of Middle America (Wolf 1957), and even Europe in the postfeudal era (see Blum 1971), with their considerable local autonomy in land regulation, their emphasis upon economic cooperation, and their enforcement of wealth-levelling mechanisms. For one thing, the peopling of the Bengal Delta in the last millennium has gone hand in hand with the gradual shifting of its great river systems, producing myriad, "frontier-like" settlements (Nicholas 1963), in constant flux. Existing historical evidence suggests, for another thing, that development of land revenue administration, with the effective encroachment of state power after the eighteenth century, was critical in structuring the expression of rural communities. With the coming of Mughal power, and the later adaptation of Mughal institutions by the British, there developed the *zamindari* system of land revenue collection, which was a system of tax farming. The zamindari system resulted in complex hierarchies of rights in tax collection and land control, focused ultimately on local level revenue units (mauzas) which, although officially designated as "villages," at least by British times, bore no necessary relationship to the socially relevant residental communities both as "thought of" and "lived in" by rural peasants. I cannot review here the infamous hierarchy of subinfeudation which underlay agrarian relations in Bengal down through British times, but needful of emphasis for my purposes is the recent assessment of historians that the zamindari system was not only highly entrepreneurial in character, but also depended in goodly measure upon the co-optation of elites at the local level (Calkins 1971, Ray 1974, McLane n.d.). These elites, possessed as they were of the knowledge of local conditions and of the coercive abilities to exact payment from ordinary cultivators, constituted the linchpins of the zamindari system, and the sine qua non of its operation at the "rice roots." Thus, they exercised considerable economic power in their bailiwicks by administering revenue collection, enforcing payment, facilitating credit arrangements and, financed by these latter general advantages, ultimately controlling the flow of agricultural commodities as well. Viewed politically, they performed the power broker roles which linked otherwise socially amorphous rural populations to the state, these roles at once emanating from their positions of economic dominance and their activities as minions of state power.

It also seems likely that they had formational influence in the evolution of local samaj communities, for who else but members of these elite groups would play the leadership roles, then as now, in the organization of ritual activities and worship—building mosques, sponsoring feasts, and so forth—and acting as hierocratic enforcers of the peace, as likely arbiters of community disputes. Thus, as the concept of samaj which in all likelihood had a pre-existence in Hindu culture well before the coming of Islam (see Inden 1976, pp. 22-29), took on a Muslim coloration as a model of solidarity, religious corporate groups, led by peasant elite leaders variously called (at least today) sardars, matabbars, paramaniks and mondols, each with different functions, seem to have emerged as moral units of community. In a society in which control of land is the key to success, it would seem inevitable that dominant landholders would perform such roles. Thorp (1977, p. 60), in his discussion of the ideology of farmers in Pabna district of Bangladesh, points out that in their logic a poor man who can barely support his family, and who must work for others, while he may have a right to a voice in community affairs, can hardly be turned to for his leadership.

> Those who can easily meet their families' needs are the brotherhood's [samaj] bigmen *(sic)*. The more land a [man] owns the more masterful . . . he is. If [he] exploits his land

fully, the more skillful he will be considered. In the public affairs of the local brotherhood the landed bigmen are also considered to possess the skill to direct the activities of the brotherhood. . . . Because Allah has destined them to be successful farmers, they have a legitimate claim to be influential [in *samaj* affairs].

The ability to coerce and to reward, to bestow favor and disfavor alike, as well as to confer the status of samaj membership itself, must have figured importantly in the development of a "tradition of the exercise of power through personal relationships" (Dolci 1970, p. 117), as, interestingly, it did elsewhere in the world where tax farming superseded farming as a precursor to modern fiscal administration, such as Sicily, where the Mafia arose under a set of historical conditions remarkably similar in this respect to those of Bengal (see Block 1974). Samaj membership affirmed important patron-client ties, and the centrality of the latter as structural components of East Bengali society is certainly consistent with the notion of tadbir and takdir in Bengali Muslim culture, combining a belief in personal destiny with one which links a person's fortune to connections with the powerful. One important implication of recent studies of Bengal's economic history from the point of view of community formation, is that what existed in Muslim Bengal in the way of peasant community solidarity coincided with the expression of local elite power domains, ritual communities which paradoxically at once proclaim a solidarity of equals, and yet function to legitimate and channel the power of a dominant few—individuals, and the class in general, performing power broker roles mediating between the peasantry and the state.

The Politics of Samaj

Although the zamindari system has long been officially abolished, similar patterns of political economy obtain today in rural Bangladesh. Recent surveys of the tenurial situation have documented a high degree of land concentration, accompanied by growing landlessness (Jannuzi and Peach 1977, 1979), and hence the continued domination of the agrarian scene by members of what researchers have described as "rich peasant" class (see, e.g., Bertocci 1972; Wood 1976). While the latter no longer control the "linch pin" positions in the revenue collection system, they are the principal actors in and beneficiaries from local government bodies established since 1947 (Bertocci 1972) and, as often as not, have coopted the leadership roles in rural development institutions as well (Abdullah, Hossain and Nations, 1976; Hartmann and Boyce 1978). Not surprisingly, then, it is around these elites and their political relations at the local level that samaj groups are formed, and that the politics of samaj may be seen as reflecting the relations of members of the "rich peasant" class and their factional followers (Zaman 1977).

There are several ways in which samaj groups as power domains may be seen to operate at levels of articulation with others. Firstly, of course, they confront official units of administration, law and order, sometimes in resistance, other times in cooperation (Thorp 1977, p. 122; Bertocci 1970, pp. 140-142), and some contact between official agencies of law and government and the indigenous social control system occurs precisely because there is no organization other than the samaj below the lowest tier in the administrative hierarchy of government.

Samaj groups are central to the indigenous judicial system, and minimal samaj units link to maximal ones as their various leaders combine and recombine in the formation of councils for the arbitration of disputes *(salishi)* and the judgment *(bichar)* of offenders of the peace (for a detailed account of different kinds of cases, see Zaman 1977). In some local systems a plaintiff may call a meeting of the maximal samaj group to hear a case. Thus, a leader who dominates his own minimal samaj group may be successfully challenged by a rival within it if the latter can call the broader grouping into play, a situation which corresponds to Adams's (1975, pp. 68-74) "multiple-party domains," in which subordinates have access to several competing actors at a superordinate level in a power system (for an extended case example of this, see Bertocci 1970, pp. 165-177).

The solidarities and segmentations of samaj groups play a role in local government elections as well. In this connection it must be noted that the local government electoral wards commonly crosscut mauza boundaries, and thus samaj memberships as well, which means that local council candidates must often compete from fragmented bases of social and political support. If a ward segments one local samaj, but incorporates most of another, a candidate from the former will be disadvantaged, and my field data record cases where this phenomenon has been evident. By contrast, within a ward, samaj memberships encompassed by it may constitute one of the factors a candidate must manipulate in order to be elected. It is clear, too, that, whether they themselves are candidates or not, samaj leaders exercise direct influence upon the voting patterns of many of their groups' members, often channeling decisive vote blocks in favor of their preferred candidates (see Zaman 1977, p. 127; this source, as well as Islam 1974, provide excellent case study materials).

Samaj groups also commonly provide the social basis for new, local level institutions which the national government has sought to introduce in the countryside, pursuant to its rural development programs. Paradoxically, although, as noted above, samaj groups do not rest upon a basis of economic cooperation, the fact is, as Thorp (1977, p. 143) has noted, "development activities concern, and will be carried out by, farmers who conduct their lives in and through their samaj and family units." Nowhere is this better illustrated than in efforts over the past two decades in Bangladesh to induce farmers to form agricultural cooperatives. My early research in Comilla district in the mid-1960s had as part of its focus the study of rural cooperative formation, such institutions having a supposed "village level" base. I found that cooperative societies did indeed form themselves at the "village level," but also that more often than not they tended to overlap samaj communities whose membership seemed to comprise a "natural" social basis for collective action (Bertocci 1970, 1976). But in instances where a cooperative society had been formed in such a way as to overlap several samaj groups, cooperation-vitiating factionalism would readily ensue, with cleavages usually following factional lines both between and within samaj memberships. For, as *samaj* leaderships tended to dominate the managing committees of cooperatives, a competition for elected leadership positions on these bodies could result in leaders seeking to attract members of their own, and other samaj groups to their factional assemblages in trying to gain control of a local cooperative's decision-making body (see Bertocci 1970, pp. 159-160).

Moreover, the introduction of new agricultural technology could effectuate new cause for factionalism and engender new splits in traditional samaj alignments. During a return visit to my earliest field area in 1973, I discovered that the introduction of a deep tubewell for irrigation in the area of my prior study had resulted in the well's location on the land of the most dominant family, with the irrigation benefits going to that family and all members of homesteads in the well's "command area," resulting in the reordering of previous samaj memberships to fit the residential pattern consistent with the irrigated area. Those left out combined to form a new samaj and, indeed, a new cooperative society, and were seeking on this basis the allocation of a tubewell for themselves. Thus, samaj groups constitute paradoxically both helpmate and hindrance to the introduction of rural development institutions. On the one hand they reflect indigenous solidarities on whose basis new institutions can readily be socially superimposed; on the other, the lines of cleavage which traditional samaj alignments have drawn can *ab initio* vitiate cooperative efforts and even be exacerbated by new technology and new sources of material benefit.

I have been arguing, then, that samaj as a cultural model of solidarity takes concrete shape in rural Bangladesh as the expression of the power domains of the economically and politically dominant families and their members, such groups changing dynamically in membership and territorial specificity with the shifting loyalties which their leaders are in constant effort to assemble. For long the only effective form of rural social organization, religious corporate groups have comprised levels of articulation between peasant community and the organs of state power. Conceptually, too, samaj provides a level of integration which dovetails in complex ways with institutions of government as these have laced the countryside with varying efficacy over the past several centuries. Thus, they have contributed to the gradual cultural unification of the eastern half of the Bengal Delta, amalgamating its dense peasant populations into a regionally distinctive culture within the South Asian civilizational complex, and so creating the basis for what became a national state in the latter half of the twentieth century. Samaj as the cultural expression of community comes alive as it vivifies structures of power, while political competition in the context of the latter forever modifies the concrete expression of samaj itself.

Part III: Models of Solidarity and Structures of Power

This is a certain isomorphism in the way in which Bengali Muslim social ideology overlaps with peasant social structure. As Thorp (1977, p. 39a) has summarized it, "within . . . their residential brotherhoods, . . . the farmers of Daripalla feel that they are all equal sons of Adam, and that they are free to compete with each other for positions of influence." Yet, within these same microcosms of communitas, wherein the faithful are united as one body, it is agreed that the "fundamental criterion of success in this competition is the possession of land," and "the more land a farmer possesses or controls, the greater will be his chances of being influential . . ." Control of land, and skill in making it produce (either with one's own labor or the management of that of others) is regarded as tantamount to having also "the skills needed to make good decisions in public affairs," and so permits a man without undue modesty "to celebrate familial and religious feasts with the proper amount of public display." If a man is literate, "if he has powerful friends, if he is in a position to advance money, his assistance will be sought . . . by his immediate friends and neighbors in his residential brotherhood." For such a man is thought to possess *khomota*, skill and mastery, over the basic tasks and fundamental kinds of relationships which are deemed essential to the attainment of the qualitative and quantitative goods of life. Thus, samaj ideology legitimates time-honored structures of power in rural Bangladesh.

But to speak merely of the "legitimating functions" of an ideology, or to regard it merely as the "superstructural" affirmation of a materially based structure of power often tends to overlook the motivational functions of a system of symbolic meaning, reducing it, as it were, to a mask-like role in social life. To my mind, this is just as erroneous as an exclusive focus on ideology which mistakes a normative system for the actuality of how a given society "works." For a complete account of social structure as well as social process, I would argue, attention must be paid to the psychodynamic connections between a system of meaning and the system of action in which it is reflected. In what ways, we must ask, do ideational, symbolic, and cognitive processes influence the dynamics and diachronics of "on-the-ground" social groups, and concrete actors in ordinary, or even extraordinary, situations? How best can we understand the manner in which these processes motivate actors, and so perceive the operative nexus between symbol, sentiment, idea, and action?

Following C. Wright Mills (1940), I would suggest that the "vocabularies of motive" that actors produce in justification of their doings might provide clues of the sort we need to sense the reflexive junctures between the "thought of" and the "lived in" orders of social life. Influenced by Weber (1964, pp. 98-99), Mills argued for a conception of motives not as "subjective 'springs' of action," but rather as "typical vocabularies having ascertainable functions in delimited societal situations" (Mills 1940, p. 904), occurring in speech when observed or openly proposed conduct is—or is likely to be—questioned. An actor must be able to justify his or her conduct to others, and such justifications must be plausible and meaningful to at least some others whom the conduct affects, or might affect, in some way. As Mills points out, a person might sincerely begin an act out of one motive (or complex thereof), postulating same to others as the reason(s) for the act; and only then, in the discourse and challenge of interaction with others, develop other motives, just as genuine, just as appropriate, either as reinforcements for or alternatives to the original motive(s). "Shifts in the vocabularies of motives that are utilized . . . by an individual disclose an important aspect of various integrations of his actions with concomitantly various groups," Mills (1940, p. 908) tells us. And "motives actually used in justifying or criticizing an act definitely link it to situations, integrate one man's action with another's, and line up conduct with norms."

The functions, then, of vocabularies of motive are to control conduct by providing actors with acceptable rationales for their actions. Motives once expressed can stabilize the resolve of actors and may win new allies for their acts. To be acceptable, or even conceivable by the actor himself/herself, motives must, moreover, always be linked to at least one subset of consensually recognized norms relevant to a situation. Of course, the particular normative subset evoked may clash with others having equal validity in the same situation. Thus, for example, Marvin Davis (1976b), in describing "the politics of the family" in a rural, west Bengal village, has shown how different family members in competition for rank call upon conflicting "reasons" which serve their rival claims to status and deference. His paper points to the use, then, of vocabularies of motive in situations of conflict, linked to consensual themes in the symbolic system underlying the allocation of prestige and rank in a Hindu kinship system. Blustain, in his paper prepared for this volume, provides another excellent case in point, drawn from the caste politics of a Nepalese village.

If the foregoing is accepted, then what I am suggesting is that vocabularies of motive provide us with one clue to the link between culture and social action, much as Mills originally proposed. Going further, however, I would also say that if it is agreed that cultural systems symbolically construct the human social universe, delineating its respective domains and postulating the codes for conduct relevant to each, then from where else do the internalized and verbalized motives for individuals' actions spring? It is not, lest I have implied otherwise, that motives are to be viewed as cynical rationalizations, trotted out by actors merely to mask justificatorily whatever they do (even though often, in politics especially, this may be the case). Rather, in a manner caught by Geertz's (1966) definition of religion as a cultural system, the wellsprings of conduct lie embedded in culture, which, "by formulating conceptions of a general order of existence," itself establishes motivations linked to that "thought of" order. Thus, in the "lived in" order, culture prompts human action in ways which are not only "uniquely" meaningful to individual actors, but are also at least potentially sensible to others. The system of meaning thus provides not only the *ideas upon which* people act, but also it shapes the *emotions from which* they act, and so furnishes the repertoire from which vocabularies of motive are drawn. And, human conduct is always, if only by unconsciously derived source in internalized thought, situated in interactions with others; thus, in the system of action, actual outcomes are constantly negotiated, the terms dependent on the relative power of the actors concerned, however exercised and wherever it may reside, as well as the ability of the actors to employ the power at their disposal.

My own field data from Bangladesh record, and in other writings I have partially reported, cases in which political conflict reflected such links between samaj as a model of solidarity, along with expressed allegiance to its code for conduct, and the factional processes which characterize samaj groups as structures of power. A comparatively wealthy man, for instance (Bertocci 1970, pp. 152-65), challenges the Islamic propriety of his elder half-brother, a samaj leader, who refuses him assistance in providing land to build a mosque. Armed with the evidence of the brother's unfitness as a samaj leader, the same actor presses his case against the latter in a *salishi* (arbitration) council involving all the power broker figures of the entire maximal samaj, calling for dismissal of his half-brother as leader, and the instatement of himself in the latter's place. He succeeds, but at the cost of a factional realignment of the whole maximal samaj, whose "spin-off" fissures affect every single other minimal samaj group in the local system. His expressed motives include every possibility, from that of coveting his half-brother's land, to acting out of spite at the latter's prestigious position, to seeking the position for himself, to genuine indignation that a samaj leader would not give aid in the noble effort to build a mosque. For all their mutual contradiction, such motives are not less real, and each points to culturally postulated trigger of action.

A powerful family, seeing the possibility of getting a tubewell for themselves and their neighbors, actively recruits membership for a newly established agricultural cooperative society, the formation of which is a sine qua non for government allocation of the device to the village. Seeking to dominate the managing committee of the society, they allege (with some apparent truth) that their rivals, all heads of opposing samaj groups, have previously mismanaged cooperative affairs and cheated members out of loan money. Their final coup against one remaining rival group is made possible when a samaj dispute over who may attend the wedding of one of that group's members is resolved in such a way as to bring insult to the honor of the cooperative society's other members who are not adherents of the samaj in question. This ensures the power aspirants of controlling positions on the cooperative's managing committee in the subsequent elections. Once in power, they obtain the tubewell, which is located on their land and benefits their supporters in the factional melee which had occasioned their rise to power. At one point or another, the politics of any situation in rural Bangladesh can become the politics of samaj, and either violation or affirmation of samaj codes for conduct become grist for the factional mill, as vocabularies of motive constantly make evident (this case is detailed in Bertocci 1970, pp. 160-162).

In 1975, I had occasion to observe the efforts of a powerful Awami League politician, the virtual *nawab* (ruler) of all he surveyed in his constituency, buttressed by handpicked, sycophantic "party cadres" who did his bidding there, as well as by the increasingly autocratic and dictatorial national power structure then evolving under the regime of Sheikh Mujibur Rahman. This particular member of parliament (M.P.) for various reasons, desired to install his own henchman at the helm of affairs in the *thana* (county) level board of directors of the central cooperative association. The henchman, armed with a falsified record as cooperative activist, was easily nominated by a cowed membership as a candidate for election to the board at the upcoming annual general meeting. Faced, however, with a host of candidates for only four positions on the board, the M.P. was forced to resort to extraordinary means to ensure his henchman's acquisition of a seat. The M.P. himself, on one of his rare visits to his bailiwick, arrived on the meeting day and addressed the assembled delegates. First effusively expounding on the plight of the peasantry and the need for agricultural cooperatives as the answer to their problems, he went on to note with regret that the electoral atmosphere had engendered all manner of unfortunate back-biting competition, setting village against village, kinsman against kinsman (an exaggerated account of what, in fact, had been the preelectoral scene). He would, the M.P. went on to say, be glad to alleviate this tension-ridden situation by offering his own good offices as mediator among the candidates. Why not, he queried rhetorically, dispense with the formality of elections and have all the candidates meet with him in private, in the manner of the time-honored salishi of samaj, and resolve the matter. While this amazing proposal flew directly in the face of the electoral procedures whereby board members were to be chosen, the assembled delegates, mindful of the M.P.'s power of retribution against opponents, could publically offer not a word of protest. Thus, the salishi was held, and predictably its outcome was that the M.P.'s henchman was installed as chairman of the board. This result was announced to an ever-dwindling number of delegates, many of whom had left in disgust. The M.P., however, did not even grace the remaining audience with his presence at the announcement, but could be seen rushing off to his jeep as it took place. His lame resort to traditional samaj conflict resolution procedures as a putative justification for his act was instructive to me as a witness to the persistence of cultural themes as guides to action, even in a situation of abuse of power. It had, of course, convinced no one; next to me, a gnarled old farmer muttered beneath his breath, "*this* is democracy in Bangladesh!"

The System of Meaning, Class Consciousness, and Peasant Mobilization

There remains, especially in the light of the last example offered above, the question as to how a system of meaning can motivate the comparatively powerless members of a society to seek redress of their plight, just as it serves to legitimate the domination of the powerful. Scott (1975), in a provocative essay, has rightly argued that no study of the process whereby the class consciousness of the exploited is heightened can be meaningful without reference to the cultural framework in which the victims themselves identify what constitutes injustice and exploitation. In that connection, it must be noted that land, access to money, and skill in the management of patron-client and "brokerage" roles are not the only wherewithal a peasant needs to be considered legitimately powerful in rural Bangladesh. As Thorp (1977, p. 139a) has noted, "the kind of influence a person will have within his brotherhood is conditioned by his moral reputation." He continues:

> The virtuous and pious man is held in greater respect than the person with a reputation for being irreligious, disputatious, or corrupt. To possess land, and use it skillfully, will make a person influential within his brotherhood. However, a person's moral reputation colors the acceptance his influence receives from his fellow brotherhood members. The morally upright influential man is listened to more willingly than the rich but reprobate individual.

Jahangir (1978) provides several case instances of poor peasant resistance to exploitative and venal rich peasants' actions, for which no amount of justificatory protest by the latter, with reference to traditional norms of solidarity—kinship and "brotherhood"—would assuage the ire of the complainants. Such instances included the profiteering from food aid in the national rationing system at the expense of the poor, the misallocation of flood-related relief grants, and the effort to shelter cattle-thieves, all of which clearly violated deeply felt senses of basic fairness and justice as well as directly affecting the material interests of the poor. In the cases Jahangir relates, the angry peasants had the good fortune to have strong leaders, and it is of interest, moreover, to note that several of the confrontations took place in the context of samaj-type arbitration courts, referred to as *bichar sabha*, or "councils of judgment." The idioms of protest and solidarity used by the offended peasant groups have not only the sound of colorful analogy and metaphor with which Bangladeshi peasants are wont to express their reactions to social and political events, but seem rooted in concepts of fairness intrinsic to the Muslim moral order, such as to override the claims of legitimacy of the powerful, but ethically corrupt. As Jahangir notes (1978, p. 37), "traditional loyalties are not enough to mobilize support in a village where rivalries between persons of unequal social status gradually take the shape of conflicts between opposing interest groups." To this one may add that when the powerful conduct themselves in manners which betray the traditional bases of their legitimacy as leaders, they expose themselves to resistance which is predicated on that very same moral order, around which deeply held notions, involving justice itself, the powerless may mobilize and formulate a vocabulary of resistance in their own manner. Samaj in Bangladesh is morally grounded, as noted in several points above, in the "likeness of believers," adherence to code, and, ultimately, the equality of the faithful. Under present conditions in Bangladesh, a thrust for equality, and for the right, unimpeded, to realize tadbir, is ever-present. Should samaj-derived notions of solidarity take hold and coalesce around groups pushed by material conditions into heightened class-consciousness, one outcome could be abolition of samaj as an organizational form itself.

Summary and Conclusion

This essay has attempted to describe the ways in which cultural systems of ideation, symbols, and meaning concretely shape the actual expression of a social system of action, attempting to suggest one of the ways in which the dynamic relationship between ideology and social relations may be perceived and analyzed. Utilizing data from rural Bangladesh, it has sought to show how peasant communities in that country are formed with reference to an Islamic model of social solidarity, which in turn coincide in specific manifestation with the power domains of individuals representing the dominant peasant elites. While the core elements of rural social structure are seen as grounded in ecology, mode of production, and economic class relations, a model of community rooted in an Islamic world view and ideological system is viewed as having equal importance in the shaping of everyday political and social life. Finally, it is argued that symbols and normative concepts embedded in Bengali Muslim culture are readily perceptible in the vocabularies of motive utilized by actors in political conflict, thereby reflecting the link between an ideology and the social structure it informs.

The thrust of this essay lands, as it were, between two contrasting conceptual viewpoints in present-day anthropological writing, rejecting the potential for reductionism in exclusive adherence to either "idealist" or "materialist" epistemologies. It is at least in partial keeping with Althusser (1971, pp. 134-136) and other Marxists who argue for a "relative autonomy of superstructure with respect to base" and for the need to focus on "the reciprocal action of the superstructure on the base." And while it accepts Sahlins's (1976) view that culture constitutes the ultimate in "practical reason" whereby humans confront the phenomenon of their "being-in-the-world," and, with Berger and Luckmann (1967), agrees that "reality" is socially constructed, it would argue that material conditions, however subjectively they may be interpreted, not only impose independent constraints upon a social formation, but also contribute to sociocultural change and ideational reformulation itself. Elaboration of these points would require another essay, and I am not sure that contributing to a potentially sterile debate over the relative primacy of "ideas" versus "material reality" would be worthwhile. Suffice it to say here that a holistic account of politics, at least, and a rich analysis of historical processes, require attention to both. Such a perspective is what this paper has attempted to reflect.

Notes

1. My work in Bangladesh over the years has been generously supported by several funding agencies and local host institutions, all of whose support is gratefully acknowledged: NDEA/Fulbright-Hays Fellowship, 1966-67; ACLS-SSRC South Asia Program research grant, 1975; Oakland University sabbatical leave, 1975; Academy for Rural Development, Comilla, 1966-67; Institute for Bangladesh Studies, Rajshahi University, 1975.
2. Davis's essay in the volume contains an extended discussion of the "system of meaning" and "system of action" alluded to herein.
3. For a discussion of the use of the concept of "corporation" in anthropology, and the rationale for application of Weber's notion of "corporation" as used herein, see Dow (1973).
4. Bengali Muslims also, it must be mentioned, may use the term *jati* in the sense of "caste" to denote ranked, occupationally marked, and endogamous subgroups within their own fold, the presence of which has perennially prompted observers to insist that Muslims have a caste system. But for Bengali Muslims the criteria of rank are fundamentally related to adherence to code for conduct, failure to conform to which results in a particular group's low rank and avoidance of it as a source of marital alliances. Importantly, the ideas of permanent states of purity and pollution, so central to Hindus' ideology of rank, are absent in the Muslim one, and for Muslims changes in conduct more in the direction of conformity with Koranic norms and related standards as interpreted in Bengali Muslim culture allow for individuals to change rank. This topic is to be explored in another paper.
5. See Hara (1967, pp. 23-43). *Takdir* refers to the concept of predestination. *Tadbir* means administration in classical Islamic thought, as in, say, government, but even the management of a household. The concept is apparently related to *tadbir al-manzil*, one of the three divisions of Islamic practical philosophy (ethics, economics, and politics, as adapted from Greek thought), and refers, then, to economic life, especially the acquisition, preservation and utilization of wealth and property. See *Encyclopedia of Islam* (first ed.), volume IV, p. 595.

References

Abdullah, Abu, Hossain, Mosharaff, and Nations, Richard. 1976. Agrarian structure and the IRDP—preliminary considerations. *Bangladesh Development Studies*, Dacca, 4:209-266.

Adams, Richard N. 1970. Brokers and career mobility systems in the structure of complex societies. *Southwestern Journal of Anthropology* 26: 315-327.

Adams, Richard N. 1976. *Energy and structure: a theory of social power.* Austin: University of Texas Press.

Althusser, Louis. 1971. Ideology and ideological state apparatuses. In *Lenin and philosophy and other essays*, ed. Louis Althusser, pp. 127-186. New York: Monthly Review Press.

Barnett, Steve, Fruzzetti, Lina and Ostor, Akos. 1976. Hierarchy purified: notes on Dumont and his critics. *Journal of Asian Studies* 35: 627-646.

Berger, Peter L. and Luckmann, Thomas. 1967. *The social construction of reality.* Garden City, NY: Doubleday-Anchor.

Bertocci, Peter J. 1970. Elusive villages: social structure and community organization in rural East Pakistan. Ph.D. dissertation. Michigan State University.

Bertocci, Peter J. 1972. Community structure and social rank in two villages in Bangladesh. *Contributions to Indian Sociology* (New Series) 6:19-52.

Bertocci, Peter J. 1975. Microregion, market area and Muslim community in rural Bangladesh. *Bangladesh Development Studies*, Dacca, 3: 349-366.

Bertocci, Peter J. 1976. Social organization and agricultural development in Bangladesh. In *Rural development in Bangladesh and Pakistan,* eds. Robert D. Stevens, Hamza A. Alavi, and Peter J. Bertocci, pp. 157-184. Honolulu: University of Hawaii Press.

Blok, Anton. 1974. *The Mafia of a Sicilian village.* New York: Harper Torchbooks.

Blum, Jerome. 1971. The European village as community: origins and functions. *Agricultural History* 45, no. 3:157-178.

Calkins, Philip B. 1971. Collecting the revenue in early eighteenth century Bengal: from the cultivator to the zamindar. In *Bengal: change and continuity,* eds. Robert P. and Mary Jane Beech, pp. 3-30. East Lansing, Mich.: Michigan State University Asian Studies Center, occasional paper no. 16, South Asia Series.

Davis, Marvin. 1976a. A philosophy of Hindu rank from rural west Bengal. *Journal of Asian Studies* 36: 5-24.

Davis, Marvin. 1976b. The politics of family life in rural west Bengal. *Ethnology* 15, no. 2: 189-200.

Dolci, Danilo. 1970. *The man who plays alone.* Garden City, NY: Doubleday-Anchor.

Dolgin, Janet L., Kemnitzer, David S., and Schneider, David M. 1977. Introduction: 'as people express their lives, so they are . . .' In *Symbolic anthropology: A reader in the study of symbols and meanings,* eds. Janet L. Dolgin, David S. Kemnitzer, and David M. Schneider, pp. 3-44. New York: Columbia University Press.

Dow, James. 1973. On the muddled concept of corporation in anthropology. *American Anthropologist* 75:904-908.
Dow, James. 1974. *Santos y supervivencias: funciones de la religiòn en una comunidad otomí, México.* Mexico City: Instituto Nacional Indigenista.
Dumont, Louis. 1970. *Homo hierarchicus: the caste system and its implications.* Chicago: University of Chicago Press.
Ellickson, Jean. 1972. A believer among believers: the religious beliefs, practices and meanings in a village in Bangladesh. Ph.D. dissertation, Michigan State University.
Geertz, Clifford. 1966. Religion as a cultural system. In *Anthropological approaches to the study of religion,* ed. Michael Banton, pp. 1-46. London: Tavistock Publications.
Glasse, Robert. 1966. La société Musulmane dans le Pakistan rural de l'est. *Etudes Rurales* 22-23-24:188-205.
Hara, Tadahiko. 1967. Paribar and kinship in a Moslem rural village in East Pakistan. Ph.D. dissertation, Australian National University.
Hartmann, Betsy, and Boyce, James. 1978. Bangladesh: aid to the needy? *International Policy Report,* Washington, D.C., 4.
Inden, Ronald B. 1976. *Marriage and rank in Bengali culture.* Berkeley: University of California Press.
Inden, Ronald B., and Nicholas, Ralph W. 1977. *Kinship in Bengali culture.* Chicago: University of Chicago Press.
Islam, A.K.M. Aminul. 1974. *A Bangladesh village: conflict and cohesion.* Cambridge, Mass.: Schenkman Publishing Company.
Jahangir, B.K. 1978. Peasant mobilisation process: the Bangladesh case. *Journal of Social Studies* 1:25-42.
Jannuzi, F. Tomasson and Peach, James T. 1977. *Report on the hierarchy of interests in land in Bangladesh.* Washington, D.C.: U.S. Agency for International Development.
Jannuzi, F. Tomasson and Peach, James T. 1979. *Bangladesh: a profile of the countryside.* Washington, D.C.: U.S. Agency for International Development.
McLane, John R. n.d. Revenue farming and the zamindari system in 18th century Bengal. Mimeo, draft cited with permission.
Mills, C. Wright. 1940. Situated actions and vocabularies of motive. *American Sociological Review* 5, no. 6:904-913.
Nicholas, Ralph W. 1963. Villages of the Bengal delta: a study of ecology and peasant society. Ph.D. dissertation, University of Chicago.
Ortner, Sherry B. 1973. On key symbols. *American Anthropologist* 75:1338-1346.
Ray, Ratna. 1974. Land transfer and social change under the permanent settlement: a study of two localities. *Indian Economic and Social History Review* 9, no. 1:1-45.
Sahlins, Marshall. 1976. *Culture and practical reason.* Chicago: University of Chicago Press.
Schneider, David M. 1968. *American kinship: a cultural account.* Englewood Cliffs, N.J.: Prentice-Hall.
Schneider, David M. 1969. Kinship, nationality and religion in American culture. In *Forms of symbolic action,* ed. Victor Turner, pp. 116-125.

New Orleans: American Ethnological Society, Tulane University.
Schuon, Frithjof. 1972. *Understanding Islam*. Baltimore: Penguin Books.
Scott, James. 1975. Exploitation in rural class relations: a victim's perspective." *Comparative Politics* 7:489-532.
Thorp, John P. 1977. The world view of the farmers of Daripalla and the rural development of Bangladesh. Dacca: report for the Christian Organization for Relief and Rehabilitation, Bangladesh.
Turner, Victor W. 1969. *The ritual process: structure and anti-structure*. Chicago: Aldine Publishing Company.
Watt, W. Montgomery. 1961. *Islam and the integration of society*. Evanston: Northwestern University Press.
Weber, Max. 1964. *The theory of social and economic organization*. New York: Glencoe-Free Press.
Wolf, Eric R. 1957. Closed corporate peasant communities in Mesoamerica and Java. *Southwestern Journal of Anthropology* 13:1-18.
Wolf, Eric R. 1966. Kinship, friendship and patron-client relations in complex societies. In *The social anthropology of complex societies*, ed. Michael Banton, pp. 1-22. New York: Praeger.
Wood, Geoffrey D. 1976. Class differentiation and power in Bandakgram: the minifundist case. In *Exploitation and the rural poor: a working paper on the rural power structure in Bangladesh*, ed. M. Ameerul Huq, pp. 60-159. Comilla: Bangladesh Academy for Rural Development.
Zaidi, S.M. Hafeez. 1971. *The village culture in transition: a study of East Pakistan rural society*. Honolulu: East-West Center Press.
Zaman, M.Q. 1977. Social conflict and political process in rural Bangladesh: a case study. M. Phil. thesis, Institute of Bangladesh Studies, Rajshahi University (Bangladesh).

Chapter 5

Caste, Ideology, and Power in North-Central Nepal

Harvey S. Blustain

The relationship between ideology and power is one of the persistent problems of South Asian ethnology. In this paper, I will offer an analysis of caste based upon the premise that it is within the context of political and economic relationships that ideologies must be examined. Although the discussion will focus on a Hindu-Muslim village in central Nepal,[1] it is expected that the analysis will yield insights which have applicability to other areas of South Asia. Combined with the other papers in this volume, it will also hopefully lead to a greater understanding of the role of ideology and ritual in political analysis.

There have been at least four major approaches to the study of power and ideology in South Asia. Many writers on caste operate with the assumption that caste status and political power are more or less commensurate. Frederik Barth (1960), for example, refers to this coherence as "status summation" and argues that power and ritual rank are, in the Indian context, mutually supportive. Those castes with power have greater opportunity to raise themselves in the hierarchy (if they are not there already), and high caste status has traditionally provided access to increased wealth through such channels as education, government appointments, and the like.

For Louis Dumont, the "initial postulate . . . [is] that the ideology is *central* with respect to the social reality as a whole" (1970, p.263). The logical opposition of purity/pollution and the subordination of power to status are the ideological principles through which caste society can be comprehended; force, economics, and territory are the "empirical residue" (1970, p.38). By approaching Indian society through its own values, Dumont hopes to eliminate the ethnocentric bias which results from the imposition of Western theoretical concepts.

McKim Marriott, Ronald Inden, and other members of the "Chicago School" also attempt to understand caste in "cognitive and ethnosociological terms" (Marriott and Inden 1977, p.227) which reflect South Asians' own conceptualization of their social system. Every "genus of living beings" (including castes and individuals) possesses "defining coded substances" which are at the same time natural and moral. Through interaction with other castes, these particles are transformed and exchanged. Unlike Dumont's dualism (which they see as a reflection of Judaeo-Christian thought), Marriott and Inden's monism argues that codes for conduct are intrinsic to an individual's physical being.

A fourth approach, and the one to which this paper will primarily address itself, employs a Marxist analysis of caste. Beginning with Beidelman's (1959) study of the *jajmāni* system, many South Asianists have seen exploitation and class relations as the key concepts necessary for an understanding of Indian society. Implicit in this approach is the concept of "dominant ideology," a concept which is expressed most forcefully in Marx and Engels' *The German Ideology:*

> The ideas of the ruling class are in every epoch the ruling ideas, i.e., the class which is the ruling *material* force of society, is at the same time its ruling *intellectual* force. . . . The ruling ideas are nothing more than the ideal expression of the dominant material relationships, the dominant material relationships grasped as ideas. . . . (1970, p.64)

Although questions have been raised about the consistency of Marx's ideas on the subject (Abercrombie and Turner 1978), the underlying premise is that ruling ideas serve the interests of the ruling group by promoting a set of beliefs that legitimize and justify the dominance of that group.

Starting from the premise that ". . . caste has functioned (and continues to function) as a very effective system of economic exploitation," Mencher (1974, p.469) claims that the ideology of hierarchy serves as a dominant ideology, legitimizing the superior social position of the dominant class. What Mencher (and others) find particularly distressing, however, is that anthropologists seem to have fallen for these "rationalizations." Berreman (1971), for example, takes Dumont to task for adopting a view of caste "which conforms rather closely to the high-caste ideal of what the caste system of India ought to be like according to those who value it positively; it conforms well to the theory of caste purveyed in learned Brahmannical tracts" (p. 23). Similarly, Meillassoux (1973, p.90) argues against those who, "steeped in an idealist, conservative ideology . . . , do no more than raise the apologetics of the Brahman ideologists to an apparently scientific level." If one accepts Berreman's and Meillassoux's criticisms as valid, then it is indeed ironic that the self-serving ideologies of the higher castes have claimed as victims a whole generation of anthropologists.

Yet what is even more ironic, according to these writers, is that because social scientists have internalized the dominant ideology, they have been blind to the fact that the lowest castes themselves do not accept this ideology. Berreman (1971, p.17), condemning the "Brahmannical view of caste," argues that "any hierarchy . . . is opposed by those who see its effect upon themselves as disadvantageous, no matter how loudly or piously it is advocated by those who benefit from it." While the lowest castes may publicly proclaim their social position to be the result of karma, one also needs to recognize that they may have other, less publicized, views. The view that the Untouchables *do* have is one based on opposition to the presumed moral imperative of the purity/pollution ideology. "Looked at from the bottom up, the system can be seen as having functioned primarily as one of economic exploitation and not one wherein 'every caste has its special privileges'" (Mencher 1974, p.478).

I will certainly not disagree with Mencher and the others in arguing first, that higher-caste people generally enjoy more wealth and power than do lower-caste people; and second, that the ideology of purity/pollution serves as a legitimizing device for high-caste dominance. Yet the problem of ideology in South Asia consists of more than just the recognition that there are dominant castes in society and that they attempt to impose their ideology on the lower strata of society. As the other contributions in this volume demonstrate, there is no simple correspondence between "social reality" on the one hand, and rituals, symbols, and ideology on the other. Political power may determine the rituals being performed, but the rituals themselves help to define the political position of actors within society. As Professor Olcott shows in this volume, it was through their attempts to reconstruct Kazakh myth that the Soviets hoped to redefine the Kazakh's perception of their own role in a socialist society. And later in this paper I will argue that pollution rules imposed constraints on the behavior of the dominant, high-caste Hindus themselves.

The argument to be presented in this paper rests upon the premise that people's ideas about what society is and what society should be (i.e., their ideologies) are to a great extent a product of their position in that society. In this, my basic assumption differs little from Mencher, Berreman, and, ultimately, from Marx. Yet in most cases, society will consist of several groups, or blocks of groups, whose interests will shift, converge, and differ within the context of specific situations; to understand people's ideologies, it is thus necessary to understand the multiplicity of their social relations.

After presentation of ethnographic data on a village in north-central Nepal, three lines of analysis will be pursued. First, I will show how hierarchy is used by the dominant caste to reflect and enforce its superior status. Second, I will demonstrate that rules of purity and pollution are manipulated by all castes (not just the dominant one) and that the flexibility and inconsistency in the application of those rules play a considerable role in the dynamics of political relationships. Finally, I will suggest that there are, in fact, ideologies other than hierarchy which can be invoked by individuals in a caste society.

Ethnographic Context

The village of Liglig Dumre, located on the western edge of Gorkha District in north-central Nepal, contains within its eighty-six households a population of 146 Muslims and 256 Hindus. Although primarily an agricultural village, additional income for some households is gained through military service, employment in Calcutta, traditional economic exchanges (*bāli*; similar to the Indian *jajmāni* system), and (for the Muslims) involvement in the bangle trade. While the most obvious division is between Hindus and Muslims, there are, in fact, three distinct and recognized groups in the village—the high-caste Hindu Chetris, the low-caste Hindu occupational castes, and the Muslims.

The Chetris (Kshatriyas) are the descendants of the Rajputs who came up from India in the fourteenth century. While there are Brahmans living in nearby villages, the Chetris are ritually the highest caste in Dumre. Of the twenty-one Chetri households, twenty belong to the same clan (*thar*) and worship the same lineage god (*kuldevata*); the other household is a relatively recent arrival and has as yet established no marital tie with the other Chetris.

Included in the low-caste section of the village are three ritually impure occupational castes—Damai (tailors; 15 households, 78 people), Kāmi (ironworkers; 6 households, 24 people), and Sarki (leatherworkers; 11 households, 40 people). While the Damais and Kāmis still maintain their traditional occupation, the Sarkis have given up leatherworking and now gain their livelihood primarily as landless laborers. While there are slight status differences between these three castes (the Damais are lower than the Kāmis or Sarkis), both in their own eyes and in those of the other villagers, these castes are considered to be a "unit" and are often collectively referred to as the *sāno jāt* ("small castes").

Finally, the thirty-three households of Muslims are the largest single caste in Dumre. Evidence suggests that because of their skill in manufacturing glass bangles, some Muslims in northern India were induced in the eighteenth century by local petty rajahs to come and settle in the Himalayan foothills. In return they were given generous land grants, one factor which accounts for the large holdings of some of the Muslims today. Although organized into eight separate patrilineages, the 146 Muslims (aided considerably by cross-cousin marriage) are all related through consanguineal or affinal ties.

Economically, it is the Chetris who are the dominant caste in Dumre. Although only twenty-eight percent of the population, they own fifty-two percent of the irrigated land. Table I illustrates the distribution of population and land holdings in Dumre.

Yet power in the village setting to a great extent depends not only upon control over basic resources, but also upon control over people through situations of economic dependency. The Chetris are powerful not just because they own much of the land, but also because they employ people to work in the fields, give loans, and sell grain. In short, by controlling resources, the Chetris are able to

TABLE 5.1
Land Owned—By Caste—1975

Caste	No. H.H.s	No. People	Irrigated Land (%)	Unirrigated Land (%)
Chetri	21	114	52.0	31.7
Damai	15	78	6.8	18.1
Kāmi	6	24	—	2.4
Sarki	11	40	—	12.0
Muslim	33	146	41.2	35.8
TOTAL	86	402	100.0	100.0

dominate the lower castes. Important, too, however, is the association between the Chetris and the government. One of the Dumre Chetris, the tax collector, is able to use his position to gain influence over many other aspects of village life—inter-caste disputes, domestic quarrels, and controversies over land. Finally, because they can maintain relatively large factions, the Chetris are able to use, or threaten to use, physical force to reinforce their domination over the other castes.

It should not be inferred, however, that Chetri dominance is equally strong vis-à-vis all of the castes in Dumre. Unlike the three impure Hindu castes, the Muslims are in a position of relative strength. First, they own a substantial amount of land in the village—forty-one percent of all irrigated and thirty-six percent of all unirrigated land. Second, the Hindu and Muslim labor pools are for the most part separate—Hindus hire Hindus and Muslims hire Muslims. From the Muslim point of view, several factors account for this: Muslims trust each other more than they do Hindus; Muslims congregate together more often, thereby making it easier to recruit labor; and kinship ties weave all of the Muslims into a single community.

Third, the Muslims in the hills of Nepal have traditionally engaged in the peddling of women's bangles. In fact, *cureto*, a term commonly applied to the hill Muslims, is derived from the word *cura*, or bangle. Almost half of the Muslim household heads have travelled around the countryside selling bangles,[2] and my estimate is that such activity infuses between six and eight thousand rupees a year into the Muslim community. This is clearly an important source of wealth and, because of the presumed pollution attached to this activity by the Hindus, it remains a Muslim monopoly. Fourth, faced with what they perceive as a threat from the surrounding Hindu environment, the Muslims remain united; as much as possible, disputes are resolved without the aid of Chetri mediation.

What all of this adds up to is a situation in which Muslims are economically and politically more independent of the Chetris than are the low-caste Hindus. Looked at from the other perspective, the Chetris are in less of a position to dominate the Muslims than they are to dominate the low-caste Hindus. Thus, although the Muslims are socially and economically integrated into the village system, they nonetheless maintain a certain degree of independence from the Hindus.

There are, therefore, three main blocs within Dumre. The Chetris are the dominant caste, yet they maintain a stronger hold over the low-caste Hindus than over the Muslims. On the other hand, there is relatively little interaction between the low-caste Hindus and the Muslims. The Damais and Kāmis do have Muslim patrons, but aside from this there are few economic links between them: Muslims do not enlist the low-cast Hindus as members of their factions (and vice versa); Muslims rarely hire low-caste Hindus as agricultural laborers; and neither the low-caste Hindus nor the Muslims are dependent upon each other for subsistence.

Yet political and economic ties are not the only bases for intercaste relations in Dumre. Ritual and attitudinal factors are also an integral part of (and, to a great degree, reflect) the political realities, as seen in the following case study.

Intercaste sexual affairs are a routine matter—so routine, in fact, that it is reputed to be common for a whole group of boys to meet a whole group of girls in the forest; after singing, gossiping, and flirting, couples gradually start to wander off in search of some privacy. In early 1973, it seems that a group of Muslim men who were walking to a rendezvous with their Hindu lovers encountered in the forest a group of Hindu men who were on their way to a similar assignation with Muslim women.

The morning after this incident of the path-crossed lovers, the whole village assembled at the teashop in what all informants reported to be a very excited state. Fights broke out and tempers were running high. The Damais, Kāmis, and Sarkis had evidently agreed beforehand that as punishment the Muslims should be forced to rinse their glasses in the teashop. Traditionally (and, until 1963, legally), contact by a Chetri with a Damai, Kāmi, or Sarki required purification by water. Muslims, on the other hand, both customarily and legally, were accorded a rank which was also impure, yet contact with them did not require such purification. In practical terms, this meant that, among other things, the low castes had to rinse out their glasses after drinking in the teashop. The action consists of someone from pure *(chokho)* caste pouring a little water into the soiled glass, after which the low-caste individual swishes it around and spills it out. The Muslims, because of their higher status, were under no such stricture.

The argument of the lower castes was simple: why should they (the low castes) be considered lower than the cow-eating, neck-slicing, beard-growing, circumcised Muslims?[3] Their plea for Hindu unity struck a responsive chord only after the low castes gave the Chetris an ultimatum: either the Muslims be forced to rinse their glasses, or they (the Damais, Kāmis, and Sarkis) would refuse to do it. Chetris, apparently considering the debasement of the Muslims a more palatable alternative than the liberation of the Sarkis, decided that the Muslims would have to adopt the new custom. The Muslims, of course, were unhappy about the turn of events, but given their numerical inferiority, there was little they could do but comply.

The apocryphal accounts of the following months indicate that whatever the truth of the matter, in village memory there was a lot of tension in Dumre during this period. Stories were told of the Muslims uniting in an attempt to overcome the new ruling, but being forced to back down in the face of Hindu numerical dominance.

The next major development occurred in January, 1975, when the Muslims decided to open up their own teashop. There was a small building near the Hindu teashop that was owned by a Muslim. It had remained unoccupied for years because the Hindus, not liking the idea of a Muslim living in a basically Hindu section of town, had threatened to beat up any Muslim who moved into it. That January, however, the Muslims decided to turn the building into a teashop and further, that each man would contribute two rupees towards the purchase of glasses, sugar, and tea. At first, the teashop provided an arena for the display of Muslim solidarity. After a week, however, a shortage of sugar and an unreliable supply of buffalo milk caused some of the more easily disgruntled Muslims to patronize the Hindu shop. From then until my departure, the Muslim teashop operated on an erratic basis. While the building was always open and served as a place for Muslims to congregate, it provided only marginal competition for the Hindu shop.

The Hindu reaction was interesting. The low-caste Hindus, who were particularly upset by the teashop, threatened to make their prediction of quick failure into a self-fulfilling prophecy. The Chetris were much less vocal in their opposition, and after a few weeks I noticed that Chetris were sitting inside the teashop (but not drinking, of course). After a month or two, the Muslim teashop became a major center for Chetri-Muslim card games. The lower castes rarely entered the teashop (due as much to Muslim lack of hospitality as to low-caste hostility); if they were interested in what was happening inside, they stood at the door or window and leaned in.

Being a caste-stratified society, Dumre exhibits many of the features classically associated with the Indian caste system—ritual avoidance, rules of commensality, and the like. But there are several patterns of interaction which are noteworthy for their lack of consistency. Two general areas will be discussed—food exchanges and teashop behavior.

Food Exchanges

If one were to ask informants about the dietary restrictions for each caste, they would have no trouble compiling a fairly complete list of who can eat what. Similarly, they would have no problem in relating which caste can eat the food of which other caste. Chetris, citing caste regulations, are allowed to eat sheep and goats. Forbidden to them are cows, bulls, buffaloes of either sex, pigs, hens, and alcohol. And because of their ritual standing, they claim not to eat cooked food or water thouched by low-caste Hindus or Muslims. The low-caste Hindus are permitted to eat male buffaloes, goats, sheep, and fowl. They will eat the food of Chetris, but not of Muslims. The Muslims for their part, will eat all meat except pigs, provided that it has been slaughtered the correct (*halāl*) way. All Muslims claimed that to eat food cooked by low-caste Hindus would be polluting; and most claimed that they would eat (and did, in fact, eat) food cooked by Chetris—although a few Muslims considered the Chetris to be ritually inferior as well.

As ideal forms of behavior, these rules are fairly clear-cut and unambiguous. For most members of most castes, these rules did, in fact, serve as guidelines for their behavior.

The Chetris deserve notice, however, because, as a group, they deviated the most from their stated ideal behavior. It was hardly a secret in the village that many of the Chetri men drank alcohol. A few Chetris ate cheese and buffalo meat cooked by Muslims and were even known to frequent one Damai's home in the middle of the night to eat pork and get drunk.

Teashop Behavior

The Dumre teashop (which is owned by high-caste Newars of a neighboring village) serves as an arena for interaction between individuals of all castes. Inside the teashop is a small bench and, against the back wall, a low wooden cot upon which the owner sleeps. While only Chetris and Muslims (from among the castes of Dumre) may sit on the cot, men from all castes can sit on the bench.

Physical Contact. When I first arrived in the village, I was fascinated by the way in which men sitting in the teashop would spontaneously rearrange themselves. After having sat relatively still for a while, they would suddenly shift positions; some sitting on the bench would move to the floor, some squatting on the floor would move to the cot, and, if it was crowded, some sitting inside would move just outside the door. What usually precipitated this flurry of activity was the making of tea. Even though contact with the low-caste individual no longer requires purification with water, it would be wrong to assume that the basic principle of purity/pollution has itself been significantly altered. So while it is acceptable for a Chetri and a Sarki to sit together on the bench and talk, it is considered polluting for that Chetri to drink tea while the Sarki is still sitting there. On the other hand, informants maintained (and my observations bear this out) that had the Sarki, not the Chetri, been drinking tea, they could both remain on the bench as long as there was no body contact.

The situation vis-à-vis Muslims is more complicated. Chetris argue that the Muslims occupy the same status as Damais, yet in actual practice the Muslims do not have the same restrictions as Damis—for example, they sit on the cot. Even more inconsistent is the way the Chetris and Muslims interact. At times members from both castes would sit on the cot or bench together and drink tea; at other times the Muslim would voluntarily move himself to the floor; and finally, the Chetri would sometimes order the Muslim off the cot or bench. There are two possible interpretations to this ambiguity. On the one hand, Chetris have different notions about the "pollutability" of Muslims; to a certain extent, this is in itself related to each Chetri's individual ideas and opinions about pollution in general. On the other hand, the fact that a Chetri would allow one Muslim to sit next to him while drinking tea, and then force another Muslim off the bench, indicates that personal bonds of friendship are at least partially responsible.

Another situation in which Hindus and Muslims can be found sitting together is in the playing of cards. As most of the games are held outdoors, the players usually sit on woven straw mats *(gundri)*. Men of all castes can sit together on them until tea is served, at which time the low-caste Hindu men and Muslims have to move off. In this respect, the strictures operate evenly against low-caste Hindus and Muslims. What is interesting, however, is what happens when a card is needed. If the low-caste Hindu squatting off the *gundri* needs a card from the pile, he has to ask a Chetri to pick it up for him and throw it on the ground; for him to reach for it himself would result in contact with the mat and thus pollution for the Chetri. A Muslim needing a card, on the other hand, is often (although not invariably) able to pick up the card without third-party intercession.

A third situation which involves physical contact between castes concerns itself with the ways in which tea is handed to people. After stirring the tea, the high-caste owner passes it to whoever had ordered it. If the recipient is a Chetri, it is placed directly in his hand. If, on the other hand, it is being given to a Damai, Kāmi, or Sarki, it is placed on the floor; at no time are men of a high and a low caste to touch the glass at the same time. In the case of a Muslim, however, the situation is more variable. At times the owner hands the glass directly to him and at times he places the glass on the floor.

In each of these activities—sitting on the bench, sitting on the mats, and the handing over of tea—certain patterns can be discerned. In all cases, physical contact between castes is allowed as long as none of the parties are eating or drinking. Yet as soon as one of the people starts to drink tea, then intercaste barriers are erected. In all cases, contact is clearly avoided between the low-caste individual and the Chetri. One fact which has not been mentioned is that a Muslim observes the same care vis-à-vis the low-caste man as does the Chetri. For example, if a Muslim and a Damai are sitting on the bench, and the Muslim starts to drink tea, the Damai is forced to vacate.

In all three cases, the Muslim occupies a more ambiguous position. In the first instance, he may or may not have to get off the cot. In the second instance, he may or may not be able to reach for the card himself. And in the third instance, he may or may not be handed the glass directly.

Smoking. One of the first points of etiquette learned by a cigarette smoker in Nepal is that it is considered selfish for one person to smoke a cigarette all by himself. After several long drags, the well-socialized smoker is expected to pass it on to someone else. Further, that cigarette can only be given to someone of the same or of lower status in the hierarchy. A Chetri can give his stub to another Chetri or, say, to a Damai; once that Damai has smoked it, it cannot go back to the Chetri.

Taking this universally stated rule—that cigarettes can only go across or down in the hierarchy—and trying to fit it exactly to actual behavior presents something of a problem. Both Chetris and Muslims do not accept the cigarettes of the sāno jāt. The sāno jāt, accepting their low position vis-à-vis the Chetris, smoke Chetri cigarettes. On the other hand, the lower castes, who argue that Muslims are the lowest of all castes, do accept Muslim cigarettes. Finally, the Chetris and the Muslims treat each other as status equals by smoking each others' cigarettes. Brahmans, however, who will smoke a cigarette started by a Chetri, will not smoke one started by a Muslim. Again, it can be seen that the Muslims occupy a more ambiguous position in the caste hierarchy.

Analysis

An examination of the data reveals that there are all kinds of inconsistencies in the expression of the caste hierarchy:

- Chetris claim that Muslims and Damais are equally polluting, yet they smoke Muslim cigarettes and allow them to sit on the cot; the Damais can neither pass their cigarettes to a Chetri nor sit on the cot.
- Chetris impose varying standards of ritual purity on different members of the Muslim community. In terms of rules regarding physical contact—the passing of tea, and the like—Chetri behavior is highly inconsistent; the "some do, some don't" principle is more applicable here.
- The low-caste Hindus, who are more antagonistic to the Muslims, refuse to eat Muslim food because the Muslims are, they claim, ritually inferior to them. Yet they smoke Muslim cigarettes, provide them with occupational services, and eat buffalo meat slaughtered (but not cooked) by the Muslims—all of which indicates a superior or equal Muslim ranking.
- Chetris recognize that the Damais are the lowest caste in Dumre, yet

they consume alcohol and pork (both forbidden to them) in the houses of Damais, not in the homes of Kāmis or Sarkis.

Chetris are of a higher ritual status than the low-caste Hindus, yet it was the latter who were more adamant about lowering the status of the Muslims in the teashop. Similarly, the low-caste Hindus were more upset than the Chetris at the prospect of having a new Muslim teashop— this despite the facts that the Muslim teashop had the potential of decreasing business at a Chetri teashop, and the Muslim teashop would have shared a common wall with a Chetri house. Along the same lines, it might be noted that one of the low-caste leaders told me that because the Muslims were polluting, I should not go to the Muslim section of the village before going over to the low-caste Hindu section. The Chetris offered no similar injunction and were, on the whole, quite blasé about my friendly relations with the Muslims.

To explain these apparent anomalies, it will be necessary to consider three important aspects of the role of ideology in society. First, I will contend that the imposition of rules of purity and pollution is a reflection of, and an instrument for, political domination. Second, I will argue that the multiplicity and the ambiguity of the expressions and symbols of the ideology of purity and pollution play an important role in village politics. Third, I will show that there are other ideologies invoked by villagers which help to explain some of the inconsistencies of the villagers' behavior.

Power and Ideology

When Chetris make Sarkis wash their glasses, they are doing more than removing pollution; they are also quite clearly making a statement about the relative distribution of power in the village. The same could be said about rules for sitting on the bench; or about cigarette smoking; or about any of the other expressions of pollution which the Chetris impose upon the lower castes.

By viewing pollution rules in terms of power, one could also conceivably explain the nonobservance of those rules by a few Chetris. By eating pork and drinking alcohol in Damai homes without paying, they are demonstrating more than just that they are powerful enough to coerce the Damais into providing them with an evening's entertainment; they are stating, in effect, that they are so powerful that they can violate with impunity the same rules regarding pollution which they force others to observe.

Yet why are such reminders not directed so consistently at the Muslims? As I indicated earlier, the Muslims stand somewhat outside of the village economic community. First, Muslims tend to hire other Muslims as agricultural laborers, and only rarely do they employ low-caste Hindus. In contrast, the Chetris are quite dependent upon the labor of the Damais, Kāmis, and Sarkis, especially at peak agricultural seasons. Where Chetris and Muslims work for each other, it is often on an exchange *(parma)* basis. Second, Muslims earn extra income through the bangle trade, an activity traditionally closed to Chetris.

Muslims, therefore, do not intrude greatly upon the Chetri economic niche. While they do compete for land, they do not compete for labor. Neither do they compete for cash income. This, plus the fact that the Chetris are not dependent upon Muslims for labor, means that the Chetris do not need to ritually remind the Muslims of their subservient position. Indeed, in economic terms, it is questionable whether the Muslims are, in fact, in a subservient position vis-à-vis the Chetris.

This is not to say, of course, that there is no competition or enmity between the two groups. What I am suggesting, however, is that pollution rules are imposed most rigorously upon those groups over which it is most necessary to express dominance. In this sense, purity and pollution operates as a fairly effective means of social control.

In important ways, too, the ideology serves as a constraint on Chetri behavior as well. Only a few Chetris violate the taboos so flagrantly, and their actions meet with widespread disapproval. That more Chetris do not break the rules indicates the strong hold which the ideology has on caste members. Even the actions of the dominant caste are constrained by the ideology which is aimed at promoting their self-interests.

The Manipulation of Symbols

Thus far, it might be inferred that purity and pollution are nothing more than the ideological epiphenomenon of the power structure, and that, therefore, it is only the Chetris who are in a position to manipulate the rituals and symbolic expressions of that structure. Yet to let the argument rest there would leave unexplained some of the other ambiguities of caste ranking—that is, why the hierarchy derived from the acceptance of cigarettes is different from that derived from the acceptance of food.

Srinivas (1975, p.73) has argued that such ambiguity in caste ranking "was not only a function of the flexibility of the system, but also facilitated its acceptance." Unquestionably, people in Dumre draw attention to those expressions of hierarchy which enhance their status. Muslims cite the fact that Chetris smoke their cigarettes. The lower-caste Hindus call attention to the fact that they do not eat Muslim food—conveniently ignoring, of course, that Muslims do not eat theirs. Chetris, for their part, talk about how their purity precludes their having to wash their glasses in the teashop. Both Muslims and low-caste Hindus respond by indicating that the Chetris consume forbidden pork and alcohol and thus are not as pure as they would like to believe. In sum, people do indeed invoke those symbols which enhance their status and this probably does make acceptance of the system easier.

The variable nature of caste ranking, however, can be better understood through an appreciation of the political domain. Marriott (1968) argues that each "medium" of intercaste transaction (such as the giving and taking of food and services), while independent and discrete, can be added up to yield a total score "by which every caste may be ranked in relation to every other caste" (1968, p.155). What is of particular relevance here is not so much the matrices by which one can arrive at a net ranking of all castes, but rather Marriott's appreciation of the role of political and economic factors in the patterns of these transactions.

In the case of Dumre, it was shown earlier that the imposition of pollution rules should be considered as an expression of Chetri dominance. At the same time, however, not all political relationships occur dyadically between Chetris and one other caste; there are many different types of interactions happening between all of the castes in the village. What I am suggesting is that the multiplicity of expressions for hierarchical ranking allows for symbolic readjustments of the distribution of power.

Take, for example, the incident in the teashop. The successful attempt by the low-caste Hindus to debase the status of the Muslims was not prompted by a sudden re-evaluation of Muslim *karma*. Rather, it was a political action stemming from dissatisfaction with their position vis-à-vis the Muslims. The immediate cause of their action was their outrage at the insolence of those Muslims who had dared to have relations with Hindu women. There were, however, more long-standing sources of discontent— relative Muslim wealth and frustration over the lax imposition of pollution rules among the Muslims. Awareness of communal antagonism in India (often expressed through third-hand stories of Muslim atrocities committed upon Hindus) also should not be overlooked as a contributing factor in their attitude toward the local Muslims.

For the low-caste Hindus, then, the ability to force the Muslims into rinsing their glasses represented a significant political victory. The fact must not be overlooked, of course, that it was the power of the Chetris which really proved effective. Still, for the lower castes to mobilize the Chetris on their behalf was in itself an accomplishment. One Muslim summed it up when, in the course of describing the events, he said, "The Hindus got together and made us small (sāno)."

The important point here is that were all of the symbols of hierarchy consistent, there would have had to have been a major reordering of intercaste patterns of interaction; one could imagine the result if the low-caste Hindus had had to change all the rules pertaining to bench-sitting, tea-passing, cigarette-smoking, and eating. The system would have been so unwieldy as to be useless. Instead, the manipulation of just one of the symbols and rituals of hierarchy was enough to make a statement about the relative distribution of power.

Further, the independent nature of these rituals ensure that contradictions are not obvious; glass-rinsing and bench-sitting may be performed at the same time, but the actors do not interpret these actions within a single, larger framework. As Professor Aronoff states in the introduction to this volume, such rituals occur in "controlled and bracketed social settings" in which "the participants agree to sustain for a time a single focus of cognitive and visual attention."

The multiple symbols thus do not merely provide for the "acceptance" of the system. More importantly, they are themselves an important component of the political system. In a caste society, these symbols (or, to use Marriott's term, "media")—and the way in which they are manipulated—serve as potent features of the political sphere.

Alternate Ideologies

Thus far, two arguments have been advanced about the role of ideology in society: first, that ideologies serve as a reflection of, and instrument for, political domination; and second, that the ideology (and its symbols and rituals) can be manipulated in the political process. The final point to be explored concerns the multiplicity of ideologies that can operate within the context of political and economic relationships.

In Dumre, there were three general ideologies which were invoked—hierarchy, egalitarianism, and religious solidarity. Yet here a caveat is in order. When one speaks of "an ideology," there is the implication of a coherent, consistent, and integrated philosophy. When people utilize ideologies, however, they only utilize those pieces and fragments of it that are relevant to the particular situation in which they are operating. Inconsistencies are avoided, contradictions are not noticed, and coherence of argument is not necessary.

When I speak of alternate ideologies, therefore, I refer not to models of social organization as they were described to me by informants, but rather to ideal types (constructed from villagers' statements and actions) which express a logic about the structuring of social relationships. When informants expressed their opinions on intercaste behavior, they utilized only that portion of the ideology which was appropriate to the situation.

Hierarchy. By hierarchy, I mean the values of purity and pollution which provide the basis for much of the interaction between individuals in Dumre. As the vast amount of literature on the subject of commensality and pollution should be familiar to most readers, little will be said about it here. Simply stated, however, it is based upon the premise that there is an innate inequality between men which necessitates the maintenance of ritual barriers between castes.

Egalitarianism. From the way the ideology of egalitarianism is invoked in Dumre, one might easily get the impression that it is an anticaste reaction which does nothing more than deny the moral basis of purity and pollution. In fact, however, when villagers reject the moral imperative of caste hierarchy, they are drawing (some people more than others) from at least two traditions. First, there is the Nepalese Legal Code of 1963 which bars discrimination on the basis of caste. While the impact of this law on actual social relations in Dumre is questionable, most villagers are aware of government policy in this regard.

In the case of the Muslims, there is a second set of concepts which serve as a tradition for egalitarianism—the Koran. The thirteenth verse of the forty-ninth sura states that submission to the will of Allah is the choice of each individual; the implication is that there can be no inevitable ranking of men on the basis of presumed intrinsic qualities. While much has been written on the caste system among Muslims in south Asia, it must be pointed out that all Muslims in Dumre were either Sheikhs or Pathans and were thus able to interdine and intermarry freely; the absence of any low Muslim castes in Dumre turned the ideal of Muslim egalitarianism into a reality.

In addition to the religious mandate for egalitarianism, the Dumre Muslims during this period were becoming increasingly conscious of Islamic movements in the other countries of South Asia. A Muslim from Kathmandu had spent some time in the village establishing an Islamic school in which Arabic and Urdu were taught, and several young men from Dumre had studied at a Muslim school in northern India. This outside influence also contributed to the Muslims' awareness of the Islamic ideal of egalitarianism and to their assertiveness in the village.

Yet, despite these two rather formidable systematizations of the egalitarian philosophy, the people of Dumre, especially the Hindus, could not elaborate on just what a village society based on egalitarian principles would be like. In this sense, egalitarianism remains something of a "counter-ideology"; its precepts are based less on a positive vision of a new society than on a rejection of the current social order.

Religious solidarity. Along with cleavages based on caste, there is in Dumre a split along religious lines. Both Hindus and Muslims were very much aware of the communal problem in India, and religious sentiment played an important part in Dumre politics.

For the Muslims, implicit in the ideology of egalitarianism is the recognition of the need for solidarity in the face of Hindu political, economic, and numerical dominance. Were intra-Muslim exploitation to occur to a significant degree, the probable result would be the splintering and weakening of the community. This does not mean, of course, that Muslims are free from factionalism or petty in-fighting. What it does mean is that they must find some means of overcoming these centrifugal forces. And to a large extent, expressions of egalitarianism, such as common prayer and intermarriage, serve to ensure that the Muslims band together as a unified group. There are other, more infrequent, ceremonies designed to evoke a sense of solidarity. *Bakra-Id,* the festival commemorating the Koranic story of Ivrahim, requires that five or seven households get together and sacrifice a buffalo. It is noteworthy that the cooperating households are usually those with only minimal kinship ties, thus creating a stronger bond between more distant kin. The Muslims also maintained their social distance from the Hindus through appeals to religious unity. They refused to cooperate in a village drinking water project which had been co-opted by the Chetris; they not only avoided sending their children to the government school, but they opened up their own school in which Urdu and Arabic were taught; and there was an (unsuccessful) attempt to prevent Muslim teenagers from participating in the secular activities (such as singing and dancing) associated with Hindu festivals.

The Hindus, for their part, also invoke religious solidarity. In the teashop incident, the guiding force behind the movement to make the Muslims wash their glasses was the low-caste Hindus. While their aim may have been the hierarchical debasement of the Muslims (prompted, no doubt, by political discontent), their most effective strategy was the invocation of Hindu solidarity. The questions they asked were quite simple: Why should we, as fellow Hindus, be forced to do something which the Muslims do not have to do? Should not our common religion unite us against the Muslims rather than create division among ourselves? While the threat to stop rinsing glasses was also responsible for the Chetri decision to side with the lower castes, there can be little doubt that the idea of Hindu unity struck a responsive chord. When I asked a Chetri who they had supported in this incident, he replied, "We sided with the Damais. We are all Hindus."

As should have been apparent, these three ideologies are not mutually exclusive. Egalitarianism can be invoked along with religious solidarity, and similarly, religious solidarity can be invoked with hierarchy. What is important to note is that each of the three caste groupings in the village invoke, within different contexts, all three ideologies.

Chetris almost invariably invoke the ideology of hierarchy. Being politically and economically dominant, it is to their advantage to espouse an ideology which also renders them ritually dominant. Their reason for invoking religious solidarity against the Muslims is more difficult to reduce to one factor. First, it allowed them to avoid a confrontation with the Damais, Kāmis, and Sarkis. Second, it gave them one of their few opportunities to express their dominance over the Muslims. Both of these explanations rest on political and economic considerations. Yet at the same time, there can be little doubt but that Chetris do believe in Hindu solidarity. One Chetri, in explaining to me why I should never lend money to a Muslim, claimed that inherent in a loan is *dhan dharma* ("wealth duty"): if you lend money to a person of your own religion, he has an obligation to pay you back; if you lend to someone of another religion, there is no such obligation. Finally, when Chetris invoke the ideology of egalitarianism, it seems to be more of a rationale for anticaste behavior than a clear commitment to the restructuring of social relations.

The Damis, Kāmis, and Sarkis also invoke all three ideologies. Vis-à-vis the Chetris, they decry the fact that they are forced to rinse their glasses, squat on the floor, and engage in other demeaning behavior. At the same time, however, they invoke the ideology of hierarchy by claiming that the Muslims are ritually inferior to themselves and should be subject to all sorts of pollution taboos. In the teashop episode, they also manipulated the third ideology, and by doing so, they achieved two goals: they not only succeeded in lowering the status of the Muslims, but they also managed to solidify their relationships with the Chetris.

Finally, the Muslims as well utilize all three ideologies. They, like the low-caste Hindus, claim that the concepts of pollution and caste ranking are instruments of Chetri domination. Their egalitarianism, however, constitutes more than just a complaint against the present system. On the one hand, their belief that all men are innately equal is a component of the larger Islamic tradition. On the other hand, this ideology, coupled with that of religious solidarity, provides an important mechanism for the cohesion and continuity of the Muslim community. Yet if religious solidarity implies egalitarianism among themselves, it implies hierarchy vis-à-vis the low-caste Hindus, who the Muslims argue, are deservedly low-caste. Chetris are also viewed as being lower-caste in their behavior, as evidenced by the fact that they eat pork and get drunk. What is interesting, however, is that these same Muslims who criticize the Chetris for being degenerate also try to associate with them by citing with pride the fact that they all sit on the same bench and that they smoke each others' cigarettes. Muslims were also constantly reminding me that their light skin color results in their being mistaken by strangers for Brahmans and Chetris.

Conclusions

If there are two principles which emerge from the foregoing analysis, it is these: first, that ideologies are embedded within—not independent of—power relationships; and second, that different power relationships will result in the invocation of different ideologies. Far from being "located in a framework of ideas and values," as Dumont (1970, p.153) would have it, political relations provide the context within which those ideas and values are played out and given meaning. To divorce hierarchy from its political milieu, as Dumont suggests, is to isolate it from the very features which give it its form and expression.

The materialist approach to the interplay between ideology and power—which, as has been shown, has been taken by Berreman, Mencher, and others—is, in my view, a very fruitful one. Ideologies *are* rooted in social action and they do reflect (and, to a not unimportant extent, influence) activity in the political sphere. What I have suggested, however, is that the relationship between the two can be "fine-tuned" so that a greater appreciation of the dynamism and complexity of the social system can be realized.

While it is necessary to view ideologies as embedded in social relations, one should not view those social relationships in terms of consistent and unchanging class interests which result in the invocation of coherent and systematic ideologies. Instead, ideologies and symbols can be manipulated by all actors (with varying degrees of success) as part of the political process. A group which rejects hierarchy as a social principle in one situation can invoke it when, in another situation, it is to their advantage to do so. There is thus more ambiguity, inconsistency, and (in the long run) vitality to the interplay between power and ideology than would be allowed under the premise either that all individuals in a caste society believe in the moral validity of hierarchy (Dumont) or that one's ideology is simply a function of one's economic class (the Marxist approach).

By arguing that the people of Dumre invoke three ideologies, I am not suggesting that this represents an exhaustive typology of ideological options. Wadley (1977) has demonstrated that power *(shakti)* is itself "an ordering principle of social action" (p. 146) which mediates interactions between people. In an analysis of cultural norms in Sri Lanka, David (1977) recognizes three "normative schemata relevant to intercaste relations"—the hierarchic priestly schemata, the hierarchic arsitocratic schemata, and the nonhierarchic mercantile schemata (pp. 192-93, 208-209). Further, he relates these normative codes to particular sets of social relationships—the first two to "bound" *(jajmāni)* relations, the third to "unbound" (voluntary, symmetrical) relations.

Whatever the categories he sets up, the anthropologist has the task of relating these various ideologies to the political, economic, and social behavior he observes between villagers. Among the questions which must be asked are: What is the content of the ideology? By what group, under what circumstances, and vis-à-vis whom is it being invoked? What are the political and economic ties between these groups? What other ideologies are being invoked? What is the effect of the ideology on behavior? There are, of course, many other questions that could be posed. My intention, however, has been to indicate that one cannot speak of "the" ideology of a social system in terms of a single enduring and unchanging philosophy: the analyst must instead examine the relationship between different sets of ideas and their utilization by people in day-to-day social interaction.

There are two additional problems which must be confronted when discussing multiple ideologies. The first concerns the questions of the "manipulation" of ideology. One should not infer from my analysis that people devote a great deal of time and energy to thinking of ways to manipulate ideologies and symbols. In many cases, such as the incident in the teashop, there is certainly a conscious attempt to employ ideologies for the maximization of one's interests. I would argue, however, that much of the time there is no such awareness of the ideology's political implications. A Sarki rinses his glass because he has always done so; he may at times reflect on the social system that requires him to do so (at which time he would be acutely aware of Chetri dominance), but I would certainly not argue that such thoughts constantly remain high in his consciousness. The degree to which people consciously manipulate or unquestioningly accept ideologies is, to a great degree, dependent on particular circumstances.

Second, although my analysis was at the village level, it is important to realize, as Professor Pettigrew in this volume maintains, that the scope of investigation must ultimately be broadened to include such wider factors as national politics, regional and local history, and the Hindu Great Tradition. Chetris did not become dominant just because they ended up owning much of the land in Dumre. Historical factors relating to migration, the development of kingship in Nepal, and South Asian political structures must be recognized as well. Similarly, ideologies such as hierarchy and egalitarianism did not arise solely out of the fertile imaginations of the people of Dumre. While it is certainly true that the villagers adapt these ideologies to their own social situation, one must again take the broader perspective and consider national legal codes, the dissemination of national values to the village, and the Hindu and Islamic religious traditions.

Notes

1. Fieldwork in Nepal was conducted over a twenty-four month period between 1973 and 1977. I am grateful to the Society of the Sigma XI

and to the National Science Foundation for their generous financial support. Much appreciation also goes out to those friends and colleagues who read and commented upon an earlier draft of this paper: Susan Bean, Dennis McGilvrey, Leopold Pospisil, and Barbara Wright, as well as the other contributors to this volume.
2. Selling expeditions can range from several days to several months, and may involve trips to neighboring villages, to the southern plains of Nepal, or even to Kathmandu.
3. When asked to point out the differences between Hindus and Muslims, informants invariably ignored matters of theology in favor of more visible "badges" of religious affiliation. Thus, the two most often cited distinctions involve circumcision and the way in which animals are slaughtered (the Muslims slice through the jugular vein, while the Hindus cut off the head from the rear with one quick blow). Other distinctions include: disposal of the dead (the Hindus cremate, the Muslims bury); sacred direction (for the Hindus it is east, while from Nepal, Mecca lies to the west); and beard-growing (the Hindus do not and the Muslims do). From the Hindus point of view, the Muslims are constantly doing everything backward and upside-down *(ulto)*. One day a Muslim man came into the teashop wearing his t-shirt inside out, and this was taken gleefully by the Hindus to be representative of the whole Muslim gestalt.

References

Abercrombie, Nicholas and Turner, Bryan S., 1978. The dominant ideology thesis. *British Journal of Sociology* 29 (2): 149-70.
Barth, Frederik. 1960. The system of social stratification in Swat, North Pakistan. In E.R. Leach, ed. *Aspects of caste in South India, Ceylon, and North-West Pakistan.* Cambridge: University Press, pp. 113-46.
Beidelman, T.O. 1959. *A comparative analysis of the jajmani system.* Monograph of the Association for Asian Studies, VIII. Locust Valley, N.J.: J. J. Augustin.
Berreman, Gerald. 1971. The Brahmannical view of caste. *Contributions to Indian Sociology.* New Series, 5:16-23.
David, Kenneth. 1977. Hierarchy and equivalence in Jaffna, North Sri Lanka Normative Codes as Mediator. In Kenneth David, ed. *The new wind: changing identities in South Asia.* The Hague: Mouton, pp. 179-226.
Dumont, Louis. 1970. *Homo hierarchicus.* Chicago: University of Chicago Press.
Marriott, McKim. 1968. Caste ranking and food transactions: a matrix analysis. In M. Singer and B. Cohn, eds. *Structure and change in Indian society.* Chicago: Aldine, pp. 133-71.
Marriott, McKim and Inden, Ronald. 1977. Toward an ethnosociology of South Asian caste systems. In Kenneth David, ed. *The new wind: changing identities in South Asia.* The Hague: Mouton, pp. 227-38.
Marx, Karl and Engels, Frederick. 1970 (orig. 1844). *The German ideology.* New York: International Publishers.

Meillassoux, Claude. 1973. Are there castes in India? *Economy and Society* 2(1), pp.89-111.
Mencher, Joan. 1974. The caste system upside down, or the not-so-mysterious East. *Current Anthropology* 15 (4):469-78.
Srinivas, M. N. 1975. The Indian village: myth and reality. In J.H.M. Beattie and R.G. Lienhardt, eds. *Studies in social anthropology.* Oxford: Clarendon Press, pp. 41-85.
Wadley, Susan. 1977. Power in Hindu ideology and practice. In Kenneth David, ed. *The new wind: changing identities in South Asia.* The Hague: Mouton, pp. 133-55.

Chapter 6

A Description of the Discrepancy Between Sikh Political Ideals and Sikh Political Practice

Joyce Pettigrew

Dramatis Personae

Harbans Singh Gujral, M.A., LL.B. Refugee (Potohar area). Urbanite. Legal adviser to Master Tara Singh, Advocate, High Court of Punjab.
Lachman Singh Gill. Landlord, district Ferozepur, chief minister of the Punjab (Nov. 1967-Aug. 1968). Executive member of the Shiromani Gurudwara Parbhandhak Committee (SGPC), the governing body of the Sikh shrines which also funds the Akali Dal. Government contractor.
Harcharan Singh Hudiara. Refugee (District Lahore) smallholder. Junior vice-president of the Akali Dal. Taught at school by Tara Singh.
Jiwan Singh Umralnangal. Member of the Akali Dal working committee. Smallholder from district Amritsar.
Uttam Singh Duggal. Refugee. Urbanite. Government contractor and transporter.
Jai Inder Singh. President of the Amritsar district Congress Committee (Urban). Nonlandowning.
Satbir Singh Professor. Urbanite. Refugee (District Campbellpore).
Sarup Singh, M.A., LL.B. Formerly leader of a breakaway group of the Akali Party in the State Assembly, founder and founder president of the All-India Sikh Students Federation, (AISSF), chairman (1965) of the Gurudwara Judicial Tribunal and chairman Teachers' Recruitment Board. Nonlandowning.

Bhan Singh. Lawyer. Urbanite. Curator of the Sikh Museum and legal adviser to the SGPC. Refugee.
Ajit Singh Sarhadi. Lawyer. Urbanite. Refugee (Frontier Province). Former M.P. sessions Judge. Akali member of the Muslim League Ministry in N.W.F.P. (North West Frontier Province). Friend and intimate of Sir Sikander Hayat Khan and Master Tara Singh. New Advocate General, Punjab (1977).
Ravel Singh, Refugee. Urbanite. Lawyer.
Amar Singh Ambalvi. Smallholder. General secretary of the Akali Dal 1946-47 and 1948. Advocate, high court of Punjab. A member of the defense panel for Sheikh Abdullah, Premier of Kashmir.
Malik Mukhbain Singh. Refugee. Urbanite. Lawyer. Close friend of Tara Singh. First cousin of Malik Hardit Singh, India's ambassador to China and to France.
His Highness the late Yadavindra Singh, the Maharajah of Patiala.
Gurcharan Singh Taura. Smallholder. District Patiala. One-time junior vice-president of the Akali Dal. A one-time member of the Upper House of Parliament and now president of the SGPC.
Chief Justice Gurnam Singh. High Court Judge. Farmer, District Ludhiana. Chief minister of the Punjab (Feb.-Nov. 1967). India's ambassador to Australia.
MS Bhattia. Refugee. Urbanite. Long-standing friend of Tara Singh. Newspaper editor.
Sant Fateh Singh. Originally from the Gangangar district of Rajasthan, senior vice-president of the Akali Dal. Died 1972.
Information was gathered from the above persons with the exception of Satbir Singh and Ajit Singh Sarhadi. The persons listed below also contributed to the information contained in this paper:
Ajaib Singh Sandhu. M.L.A. Morinda Constituency, later to become deputy leader of the Akali Dal.
Ishar Singh Majhail. One-time president of the SGPC and close associate of Udham Singh and Mohan Singh Nagoke, two important Akali leaders in the partition and immediate postpartition period. Smallholders from District Amritsar; closely acquainted with Partap Singh Kairon, Chief Minister, (C.M.) the Punjab.
Giani Bhupinder Singh. Refugee, urbanite. President of the SGPC (1966).
Jathedar Santokh Singh. President of the Delhi Gurudwara Parbhandak Committee. Refugee.
Hukam Singh. Refugee. Urbanite. Former president of the Akali Dal. Lawyer. Speaker of the Lok Sabha (Lower House of Parliament).
Bhagwat Dayal Sharma. President of the Punjab Provincial Congress Committee.
Pandit Mohan Lal. Former home minister. Member of the Legislative Council. Originally a small industrialist from Batala.
Sant Singh Sekhon. Professor and college principal. Member of the Communist Party. Writer.
Professor Ganda Singh. Eminent Sikh historian.
Sohan Singh Josh. Leader of the Punjab Communist Party (CPI).
Kapur Singh. Jat refugee. (District Lyallpur). Former MLA, MP, and ICS officer. Presently national professor of Sikhism.

Sikh Political Ideals and Sikh Political Practice 153

Diary of Events
May 1960-October 1961

1960

May 22nd	Morcha begins.
May 24th	Tara Singh arrested under the Preventive Detention Act.
June 12th	Chandni Chowk procession after which the movement accelerates.
October	Chief Minister Kairon attempts to undercut the movement by recognizing Punjabi as the official language at district level.
December 31st	Nehru's offer of talks.

1961

January 4th	Master Tara Singh released.
January 9th	Sant Fateh Singh gives up fast.
February-May	Nehru-Fateh Singh talks.
August 15th	Master's fast begins.
September	Tara Singh attempts to get UN arbitration and the intervention of prominent Indian political figures. Appeals by Sikhs using "secular" phraseology to end the fast.
October	Tara Singh ends his fast.

Introduction

The data in this paper illustrate that anthropological study cannot contain itself within units confined to the discrete universes of particular peoples, even though these units may be state systems, and suggest that the Sikh account of their political activities cannot be accorded the status of an explanation. It does so in the process of discussing the discrepancy between political ideals and political reality at a specific period in recent Sikh history. This is an issue which has been raised theoretically by, among others, Moore and Myerhoff (1975).[1].

My own interest is partially a response to these past discussions within anthropology, but does not arise out of any particular interest in certain philosophical viewpoints. My concern with the divergence between political ideals and community political activity within the Sikh community stems principally from the fact that it was a preoccupation of the Sikhs themselves witnessing as they did the frequent deviation of their leaders from the ideals they had been elected to fulfil. As they posed the question—why did so many Sikh leaders engage in activities which sabotaged their avowed intent to achieve some measure of sovereignty? The empirical data clearly indicate that this question cannot be answered within a community context and also that political activity is more likely to respond to interests than to community tradition. I have stated this in the following words:

> The nature of the relationships and consequent interests established in the intercommunal, secular realm explain deviation from community ideals.

and again

> Ideals are given by culture and history but actions toward their realisation do not develop in the same contextual realm but in that of trans-contextual circumstance.

The Sikh explanation for the lack of symmetry between their community's stated cultural ideals and their leaders' tactics is that their leaders are corrupt and corruptible. For example, it is common to hear these leaders and their supporters criticized in words such as the following: "The Sikh character is lacking. This situation can be rectified by someone with experience and self-confidence and a fire burning in his heart for the *Guru's* (God's) cause." A specific personality who is religious and prepared for self-sacrifice is seen as providing the community with its will and resolve.

As I shall show, the lack of ethics in particular individuals does not explain political defections from the Akali Dal to the Congress Party in the period under discussion. In saying this I clearly locate the Sikh account of their political activity as being part of culture (and therefore not an analysis).[2] Bauman (1973) describes culture as giving orientation and as being operative solely within the society where its premises are relevant. And attitudes stemming from cultural orientation in the Sikh case may be said to be that the community was united and that the display of individual bravery was enough for it to win in any confrontation situation. The philosophy of "ik Sikh sava lakh" reigned, i.e., a single Sikh endowed with spiritual devotion to God can by God-given heroism overcome a *lakh* (100,000) and a quarter of his foes. Sikhs were in possession not of knowledge about their political system but of attitudes and beliefs about that system stemming from cultural orientation. Nothing illustrates this better than the Sikh leadership's customary captivation with matters relating to their own history and to their religion—both of which they see as being the twin bases for community identification. This captivation took their eyes away from Sikh interests in the area from New Delhi to the Iranian border and the implications for those interests of their own community's structure. The reference here being to the opposing alignments or factions [3] which render the Sikh community organizationally incapable of acting as one (in the same way, incidentally, as it inhibits class formation in Pakistan, see Alavi, 1973). These vertical alignments tended to rupture planned, concerted action. In addition, a man who was a family man rather than a community member and citizen of the state, and who was operating in a society where benefits and losses were personally received and not bureaucratically allocated, could not be expected to promote any ideological aim if that happened to be opposed to interests of a more concrete nature. Inadequate control over intelligence information by a single source and the resultant responsibility of those who gather it to diverse political patrons and alliances also meant that information pertaining to Sikh interests in areas beyond the east Punjab is nonutilizable by the community qua community. It is instead used by individuals in internal disputes and rivalries and to eliminate opponents. And thus with respect to the political alternatives that may face the Sikhs in the coming five to ten years respectively the following: retention of the status quo, federation between Sikh Punjab and Muslim Punjab, a united Punjab with economic colonization of Sind, North West Frontier Province (NWFP) and Baluchistan, Sikh autonomy leaving Pakistan as it is but maintaining good relations—stances would be taken on each of these alternatives on the basis of internal political and intra-administration rivalries. Thus factionalism consequently could come to be foreign linked. Such developments cannot be handled by studying cultural traditions which take us only to the boundaries of their world of shared meanings, to the edge of their respective symbolic universes and no further. We—actor and analyst alike—are left landlocked there, unable to see problems except as the problems of this or that ethnic group, whereas we know from the structuralist and Marxist tradition in the social sciences, organizational forms, and structures are not particular to any one community or to any one culture. My old teacher and intellectual father—Max Gluckman—foresaw the politically reactionary nature of those developments which recognized the status of culture as a central component in any theoretical analysis. In an article entitled "Anthropology and Apartheid: the Work of South African Anthropologists" (*Studies in African Social Anthropology*, ed. Fortes and Patterson) he remarked:

> Some recent trends in social anthropology appear to me to lead their practitioners to positions not very different from those adopted by South African adherents of segregation and apartheid—a stress on the uniqueness of culture (1975, p.23).

But earlier, Lukacs had accused the entire Western intellectual class of making a fetish out of culture by emphasizing the sharp differences between cultures rather than the types of system in which they perhaps existed.

The events described in the paper show it to be impossible to answer the question Sikhs asked—how could leaders who supported any measure of Sikh autonomy collaborate with a Congress government—from within the Sikh tradition and that the problem of explaining the discrepancy between Sikh ideology and Sikh political practice is not one that can be solved within community confines. Any analysis of the Punjab political system has to take into account extensive central influence in community and state affairs. It is this interrelationship between smaller and larger centers of power which determines the course of Sikh politics, not Sikh tradition. The empirical data guide us to this appreciation as also Lukacs' principle:

> The moment the point of view of totality [4] is abandoned then you have the wrong starting point, goals and assumptions (1971, p.29).

The Sikh community's geopolitical position as a minority community on the border between two majorities, their presence in a multicommunal state, the degree of their institutional assimilation into Hindustan and their cultural links to the countries and peoples of western Asia constitutes the total situation in which the community is placed. If we, as anthropologists, fail to accept the challenge this poses to our traditional methods and are unable to see the Punjab political system as being part of a totality inclusive of the political interests in the Iran-New Delhi area, we will be misguided. Political interconnections within the community relate to the activities and policies of sovereign governments within that area. In consequence, it may be methodologically inappropriate to adopt a view of political anthropology which leads us to see the structure of any given community from within the community (see conclusion). Such is present in any community's folk-model. It is also present in Cohen's definition of political anthropology as the dialectical relation between symbolic action and power relations (1974, pp.13, 21). This definition would not be particularly useful in a situation such as the one described in the paper where there is little integration between community symbols and community political practice. In an all-India context, any community's symbols are quite unrelated to the domain of secular power, that domain being one which stretches beyond community boundaries and to which community symbols therefore cannot relate. It thus becomes a most disturbing element in Cohen's theory that it may be unsuited for studying the intercommunal sphere in complex plural societies.[5] This theory gives a new lease of life to small-scale studies in social anthropology, and if accepted would result in us adopting a view of power inconsistent with present economic and political reality in the Indian subcontinent. Distinct as they are, symbols are necessarily isolating phenomena, performing a separating function between groups, but not exclusively. Hence, a consideration of the dialectical relationship between symbols and power relationships involves also a restriction to the specific groups and specific communities whose property they are. Therefore such a theory would require us to turn inward into these small arenas.

In 1960 and 1961, Sikhs put their full vigor behind the achievement of a Punjabi-speaking state (Punjabi Suba). The events of these two years present a web of intrigue in which personalities, their material gains and losses, figure significantly, as also does central interference in Sikh and Punjab affairs. However, the latter element is not seen by the Sikhs themselves as being part of the structure of a situation that might be permanent but as occurring at all, only because of the machinations and conspiring of those who are personally corrupt. In other words, although a key variable has been identified, its role has been inadequately perceived. In addition, the Sikh model of their political situation leaves the material interests of certain socioeconomic groupings unaccounted for, or, at best, understressed. To these I now turn.

The demand for a Punjabi-speaking state emerged from one particular section of the Sikh community, namely from lower-middle-class urbanite refugee Sikhs from west Punjab, now Pakistan. It was raised to aid those among them who had lost all their assets and who, not being landowners or farmers, could not get an allocation of land in east Punjab. No longer having their monopoly of trade, suffering severely from Hindu competition, small shopkeepers were seeking to maintain their position through the education of all their family members. The political claim by the Akali Dal that Sikhs were underrepresented in the civil administration due to discriminatory laws, related itself to the temporary economic disadvantage of this group, which it did not intend to perpetuate into the future. Urbanite intellectuals—chiefly lawyers, but also a few doctors and professors whose parents or other relatives belonged to this particular class—could camouflage the economic interest behind the demand for a Punjabi-speaking state by exploiting the fact that Punjabi in the Gurumukhi script had not been given the formal status of official language of the Punjab, and that this should be the concern of Sikhs as such since the Sikh scriptures were written in Gurumukhi. They coupled this approach of concern for tradition with allegations that certain Sikh army officers were not prompted simply because they were Sikh. From an economic point of view this, as well as the reduction of jobs available to Sikhs in the officer corps of the armed forces due to the implementation of secular laws governing recruitment, primarily affected the Jats. However, it was the urbanites who took a concerted political stand on these matters. Thereby a middle-class urbanite minority actually created an ambience for unity with landowning Sikhs in the rural areas. Jats within the countryside of the Akali Dal only had the support of some large landowning families, and especially those among them with no outside assets that could be confiscated. They were not necessarily orthodox from a religious point of view but were attached to the Sikh tradition through long inheritance, having perhaps played an important historical role in community affairs. Owing to their economic position they were free to support the movement out of loyalty to an honorable past. Other landowners with factory assets in the Indian union could only give support compatible with the retention of their resources and, as with the Sikh urbanite businessman, their position was compromised. In addition, Sikh urbanite industrialists had previously intermarried with Hindus and continued to mix with them socially due to business connections. And it was convenient for any movement for Sikh autonomy, however limited, to express itself through the language and religion not only because these belonged to every Sikh but because it was in the economic interests of those with business assets to keep the demand contained within the realm of the legitimate and constitutional. In the rural areas the economic impact of central government laws—the Hindu Succession Act, the various land-ceiling laws— and the reduced percentage of Sikhs recruited to the army kept the Jat interest in the movement alive. And this rural base was eventually to be used in securing ministerships for non-Jats which were needed to safeguard Sikh (predominantly non-Jat) business interests throughout the subcontinent.

So at the period the paper describes, the movement emanated from a minority within the Sikh community. Subsequently, it was to develop a more popular, in the sense of more representative, base. On the conclusion of the 1965 war with Pakistan, various high-ranking Sikh army officers indicated to the central government that the grant of a Sikh majority area would be a gesture of goodwill to the community for its sacrifices during the war. That the central government was at all prone to listen was due to the extent of the discontent in the Punjabi ranks of the army who had witnessed the poor fighting capacity of certain non-Punjabi units, though the disaffection included high-ranking Sikh officers angry at what they claimed to be Hindu duplicity. Information had come to light that, when Pakistan had planned to cut the Grand Truck Road at Jandiala Guru and to capture two vital bridges at Beas and Harlike, the then G.O.C. General Chaudhuri had suggested on September 10 to Lt. General Harbaksh Singh, commander of the western front, that he withdraw his forces to the banks of the Beas River. The said commander refused and in a subsequent report to the government criticized senior army leaders (see Nayar 1971). Had he agreed he would have abandoned sixty miles of territory, all of it fertile farmland populated principally by Sikhs and including their holy city of Amritsar.

The implication was clear, the Sikhs thought. They, the Hindus, proclaimed their interest in national unity, yet freely laid plans to abandon a part of the Punjab to Pakistan, and, therefore, also the Sikhs who lived there. Faced with such facts, the Sikh army leadership thought it right to test the central government leaders on who is loyal to India. This forced the government's capitulation on the Punjabi-Suba issue. Simultaneously the Akali Dal leadership concluded a deal with rural interests in the predominantly Hindu area between Ambala and Delhi that a new state—Haryana—be created in return for support for a Punjabi-speaking state which would then be a Sikh majority area. With this move the Hindu opposition to a Punjabi-speaking state was divided, now remaining confined to the industrialists of Punjab's major cities.

Empirical Background: Minority-Majority Relationships

The Punjab had been a multicommunal state prior to its partition in 1947. With the partition, two nation states came into existence on the basis of religious community. The Sikh community's struggle to achieve a unity of its own, also on the basis of religion during the period 1947-66 has therefore to be seen within the context of developments within the area among the two majority communities. The achievement of a Sikh majority area in the east Punjab in 1966 can be explained historically: in terms of the scheme for separate electorates for Punjab's three major communities—Hindus, Muslims, and Sikhs—introduced by the British; the initially loose political cohesion among Sikhs due to the presence of two separate traditions and their associated interests—one around the land, civil and military service and the second around business; and the partition plan (culminating in the formation of the religious state of Pakistan) which considered only Muslim and non-Muslim majority areas. This article does not deal with the historical considerations crucial to the rise of community consciousness among the Sikhs but uses empirical data drawn from the contemporary scene. The movement for a Punjabi-speaking state which would be a Sikh majority area was expressive of the economic interests of certain clearly defined social groups within the Sikh community. From the Sikh point of view, the movement also represented a reaction to Hindu chauvinism as evidenced by the Punjabi Hindus denial of Punjabi as their mother tongue (see Pettigrew 1978) and to the central government of India's refusal to give Punjabi in the Gurumukhi script the status of official language of the east Punjab simply because it was the request of one community alone. As will be in evidence, the movement's leadership operated with respect to two realities, both intimately related to minority survival: the political and economic reality of the Indian Union and the cultural reality of their own community. Loyalty to their cultural tradition and historical heritage was successfully balanced by an awareness of the requirements of present economic and political circumstance.

I had indicated (Pettigrew 1978) that what was decisive in the struggle between the community and the government was the extensive control exercised by both the Punjab and central governments over an influential section of the Sikh community through the employment structure and through the distribution of industrial quotas, permits, and licenses. Emerging from this fact, it seemed that the divisive effects of state and central government patronage on the Punjabi Suba movement would be a suitable ethnographic topic of inquiry which would also allow us to explore the theoretical ideas outlined in the introduction. The patronage in evidence is of the type mentioned by Weingrod (1967, pp.377-400), i.e. it is political party-directed patronage, in this case of the ruling Congress party. Congress party resources in India were directed at increasing the degree of centralization, a process which they saw as being synonymous with the integration of India's various regions. Here I will document the actual governmental manipulations involved in the defeat of the Punjabi Suba movement at its most crucial juncture when two Sikh leaders—Master Tara Singh and Sant Fateh Singh—undertook fasts unto death, ostensibly to fulfil the movement's aspirations. A chronological history of the relationships between the Akali Dal, the political party which campaigned for Punjabi Suba and successive Congress ministries in the Punjab and at the Center, is not given. The topic is instead discussed with reference to a series of events between May 1960 and October 1961. First, however, a preliminary discussion is necessary of certain aspects in the relationship pattern between the Sikh minority and the Hindu majority.

One such aspect concerns relevant comments on the interconnection between the communal and secular traditions within the Sikh community. Succinct expression of the communal tradition is contained in a statement of S. Sarup Singh on October 21, 1945:

> Unlike the past the modern attack is not on our persons but on our ideology. We are told for example that religion is a private matter for an individual. This one single, innocent-looking sentence has done more harm to Sikhism and the *Khalsa* (Sikh community as a collective deriving its sovereignty from God, also referred to as *Panth*) than can be easily realized [6]. . . . Except in corporate existence and soli-

darity the Khalsa, based as it is on Sikhism, has no meaning.
. . . Our *ardas* (prayer offered to the deity) is not the work of
any one man or any one time. The whole Sikh nation has
been one with it over the centuries. Sikhism is the common
possession of a rich heritage of memories . . . It is clear that
the Sikh is a member of an organization which embraces all
aspects of his life including the political. Now the point is
such that he cannot individually become a member of some
other organization which poaches on its sphere without violating his loyalty to Panth . . . We are told that since religion
is a private matter for an individual, and since all are Indians,
we should join and strengthen this national organization (a
reference to the Congress) . . . (but) Is Indianism not a by-product of British rule in India?

The secular tradition was advanced by the Congress party then ruling at both state and center. In the period we are discussing, the chief minister was a Sikh, there were many Sikh ministers, and still more Sikhs associated with the governmental process. Noncommunalism—as indicated by attitudes that would regard community loyalties as reactionary, community traditions as old-fashioned, and secularism as progressive, and as evidenced by a willingness to participate in the legislative and administrative activities of a government deeming itself to be secular—was the test imposed on members of a minority for admission to the ruling congress elite.[7] The strength of the Indian government's commitment to secularism was related to India's need for political unity and rapid economic development. When describing Indian government policy towards minorities it is useful to keep in mind Anthony Smith's words:

> We are not dealing purely with a centralizing tendency but with an interventionist role of the State on the grounds that it can raise living standards, educate, unify and achieve (1972, p. 231).

The state Congress party indeed countered the Akali Dal's demands by slogans directing attention to Punjab's economic problems and by raising slogans for higher wheat yields, roads, poultry farms, piggeries, and fruit orchards.[8] It also tried to confuse the issue by saying that in the event of the formation of a Punjabi Suba, Punjabi Hindus would be forced to migrate.

For those in the Sikh community who wished to rule, noncommunalism was one of a number of ideological poses pragmatically adopted and they made use of both political parties: congress for material benefit; the Akali Dal to safeguard Sikh heritage. Both were used for careerist purpose in the interests of something more sacred than either—the family. In this respect both parties were regarded as legitimate avenues for political advancement irrespective of past political commitments. Religious persons could be found in Congress as well as the Akali Dal, interior allegiances most commonly exteriorizing themselves when government ministerships were involved. The consequence is that the secular ideal and the communal ideal are present only as tendencies within the community and are not the basis for any firm division within it. The absence of any political institutionalization of communal identity may be taken as an indication that that is so. The Akali Dal is not supported by all Sikhs, and neither is the Punjab Congress a purely Hindu body.

A second point for preliminary discussion on the topic of minority-majority relationships concerns the proposition that government patronage alone cannot explain the Sikh failure to achieve Punjabi Suba in 1960-61 and that an equally important factor was the lack of consensus within the Sikh leadership and between these leaders and the mass of Sikh voters on the operative concepts which should govern the conduct of the struggle. Certain Akali leaders operated with respect to two realities and two sets of interests: their own community's cultural reality and the economic and political reality of the wider unit of which they were a part—India. Fundamental to their collaboration with the Congress party was the awareness of their own community interests in India, especially northern India. Tactics crystallized from information related to those interests rather than being in congruence with community tradition. Appropriately so!—since it would be the politics of the macrounit that would largely determine the fate of the movement. In the postpartition years, but particularly at the height of the Punjabi Suba struggle in 1960-61 there appeared to be a persistent concession to political and economic circumstances resulting from their incorporation in the Indian union, some Akali leaders presenting the Sikh case in a manner allowed by the constitution but not accepted by Sikh tradition. For example, since the concept of a Sikh homeland, as too eventually that of a Punjabi-speaking state (since that too would have been a Sikh majority area) was thought of by the central government as subversive, the concept of a unilingual Punjab-speaking state was evolved which would involve no division of the province. And while the *morcha* (mass movement) was in progress, Akali Dal leaders engaged in talks with government representatives.

Sikh Ideology

The impact of the Sikh position between two larger religious communities has reflected itself in modifications of orthodox Sikh tradition. As I have written recently, "The doctrine of Sikhism as synthesis was one calculated to blur communal boundaries and as such one acceptable to the multi communal secular state" (Pettigrew 1978). Likewise, an emphasis on the tradition of inner spirituality of the first guru (prophet), Nanak, detached from the need for its protection and material realization stressed by the tenth and last guru, Govind Singh, served similar purposes. However, the spiritual values stressed by Nanak and the means to defend them emphasized by Govind Singh were in fact part of a unified tradition. Hence, orthodox Sikhs regarded the activities of one Sikh leader—Fateh Singh, supported by the Punjab Congress Ministry of Partap Singh Kairon—as exploiting one part of that tradition, for political reasons, as heresy.

Sikh tradition on matters concerning the community as a body of believers in special relation to God (variously referred to as Khalsa and Panth) favored no negotiation and direct confrontation. The most important element of the ideology that need concern us here is the view that religion cannot be defended without political sovereignty and that political rule in turn must be guided by the principles of religion. Hence, the demand for a Sikh state was in accordance with religious principle and was not a matter for negotiation, and hence, also, the view that in being loyal to the secular state Sikhs were serving, as Kapur Singh, ex-M.P. put it, a "godless centre of power and command" (Gur Rattan Pal Singh, 1979:117). The Sikh prayers recited each evening in congregation in the *gurudwara* (a place of Sikh worship) shortly before ardas begins record that the Khalsa was founded in compliance with the will of God and shortly after the ardas closes they state that the Khalsa will rule.

From the Sikh community point of view, an important question has always been: whether such accommodation to empirical reality in the shape of economic and political pressures and interests represented the capitulation of principle? The Sikh masses from whom these leaders won their electoral mandate deemed that to be so, and those among them who negotiated with the Congresses eventually lost their position one by one and were not re-elected. That they were not re-elected was because they claimed to represent the community. The community is a religious entity and is one with a God corelated with truth. Hence, if actions were factious and dishonest their perpetrators were automatically discredited by the very nature of that in whose name they fought.

In the Sikh community's cultural tradition there is a close interdependence between values and power. In Sikh ideology these are linked in almost isomorphic fashion and their close relationship (as noted by Kapur Singh) is supposed to be given overt, public expression.

> There is a firm tradition in Sikh history of individuals and groups of Sikhs making a resolve to die fighting against a tyrant who interferes in their way of life. . . . There is no turning back in this Sikh tradition on any pretext whatsoever.

Thus, when leaders such as Sant Fateh Singh and Master Tara Singh abandoned their fasts on the advice of Sikh leaders who had talked with Nehru or collaborated with then Chief Minister, Kairon, they stood condemned for using methods incompatible with the end they sought to attain, and their behavior was deemed to be corrupt and cowardly. The ethic of no surrender was one applying only to those who fought in the community's name and who were required to raise the quality of their actions so as not to devalue that for which they fought. The Congress, unlike the Dal, was not hampered by the same restraints, having no connection to the Sikh community and its traditions, but to the secular polity. Inherent in the structure of the situation there was scope for misunderstanding, an additional difficulty for the Akali leaders being that the Sikh masses had no access to the motivations of those among them campaigning in a constitutional manner for an unconstitutional demand.

Sikh Ideology and Central Government Policy

Relationships between Sikhs and Hindus were governed by the sphere in which both operated—namely the political and economic sphere, which was under majority control. Under these circumstances, Sikh tactics were more in accordance with practical possibility than they were in congruence with community cultural aims. I argue that the nature of the relationships and consequent interests established in the intercommunal secular realm explain the deviation from community ideals. Sikh community leaders operating in both the national and community arenas developed in the process, an awareness that the concepts and interests to which they would have to relate political activities must in fact have a dual reference—adaptive, incorporating as much of the facts of the actual concrete situation as they could know about; and cultural, relating to community tradition. Concepts utilized by minority leaders in situations such as I will describe would themselves appear to be dual—being either concepts with roots in specific cultural traditions or concepts that are adapted to the legal, political, and ideological framework of the state.

The concept of a state based on the Punjabi language was an exception in that it was supposed to be both consistent with Sikh ideology and acceptable to the central government. Acceptable to the latter because all states in the Indian union had been created on a language basis, and acceptable to the Sikh community since this political measure would allow them continued access to their religious tradition in that the Sikh scriptures were written in Gurumukhi. However, the central government eventually branded the demand as communal since it was one emanating from a particular community alone. The matter then came to be decided on criteria which had little to do with language: whether it would heighten communal tension in the state as such and render precarious India's "emotional integration." But, the chief consideration appeared to be that Punjab was a border state. Quoting a former union home minister: "Punjab was situated on a sensitive border area of the country. Anyone who creates dissension in this region and thus makes it weak must be held to be disloyal to the country." In these terms the Punjabi Suba movement became antinational.[10]

It was in this context that the concept of a unilingual state, earlier referred to, was one more in line with interests than with ideology, and compatible with the Sikh community's then geo-political position between two larger ethnic groups.[11] This did not mean that community ideals are not valued, for "it is not inconceivable that a particular society may strongly believe in one set of values and actually practice, out of material considerations, values which are totally different" (Faiz 1975).

Values are shielded in the ghetto of the mind, in the sanctuary of the gurudwara. They are given by culture and history, but actions toward their realization do not develop in the same contextual realm, but in that of transcontextual circumstance. Rather than recognize this to be the explanation as to why tactics of the leadership were rarely in accordance with cultural aims, the mass of Sikh voters categorized any lack of symmetry between the two as discrepancy, and saw the discrepancy as brought about by the corruptibility of individual leaders.

The question asked by Sikhs themselves—"How is it possible for leaders committed to a Sikh majority area to collaborate with the Congress?"—has its answer in the structure of majority/minority relationships and not in the character of particular personalities. Cultural ideals cannot be made politically operational in the environment of the multicommunal federal state. Of great importance for minority leaders whose communities are encapsulated in secular states, is the task of unlearning cultural habit in their dealings with the majority community and in defeating their own history, so that present tactics are in no way determined by past happenings and traditions (hence becoming predictable and known to those with an interest in the collapse of community boundaries), and the nature of present conditions thereby concealed by narrow interpretations.

Case Study

In the preceding pages I have provided a tentative, theoretical outline explaining the political defection from cultural intent. I now begin with the material scenario for these innumerable defections from the Akali Dal to the Congress in the early sixties.

Prior to 1960-61, the Congress had made many attempts to control the Akali Dal. Most of these had the rationale that "the religious platforms of these sacred shrines should not be used for political purposes" (interview with Ishar S. Majhail, January 1966).

The real reason for such infiltration was that the Akali Dal was financed by the SGPC and the latter had large financial resources.[12] In 1960, when the morcha was at its height, the Congress-dominated state ministry evolved a plan to divide the Dal. The disturbed communal atmosphere elsewhere in India perhaps explains the seriousness with which this task was undertaken. However, the urgency was also a product of the tenuous community unity that had been forged on a religious basis (and described in Pettigrew 1978) under Tara Singh's leadership. The Akali Dal, and not any one particular faction of it, obtained the support of those who were religious among both ruralite and urbanite Sikhs and, as perceived by the central government, Sikh unity had explosive consequences for Hindu-Sikh relations. In addition, Punjab's close neighbor, Pakistan, was still an integrated nation and a certain amount of suspicion fell on Tara Singh, who had a close relationship with certain members of the government of that country.

The morcha had begun on May 22, 1960. On May 24, Tara Singh was arrested under the Preventive Detention Act. The movement accelerated after the June 12 procession in Chandni Chowk [13] (a main thoroughfare of Old Delhi on which is located the historic Cis Ganj gurudwara). On July 29 the Government forced two Akali newspapers—Jathedar and Prbat—to close down, and on August 3 it banned meetings and processions and prohibited the printing of posters and pamphlets regarding the morcha. By mid-December, a total of fifty thousand were in jail, according to an Akali Dal estimate.

Tara Singh being in jail, Sant Fateh Singh (as senior vice-president of the Dal) was responsible for the morcha's conduct along with a thirteen man committee, at least eight of whose members collaborated with the state Congress Ministry led by Kairon. I shall show that the morcha committee directed matters in accordance with state government requirements. Thus, instead of speaking of Akali infiltrational strategy, as does Nayar (1966, pp.212-33), I argue that it is more appropriate to speak of Congress party infiltrational activities. For example, it was not a matter of chance that control of the morcha fell into the Sant's hands. The Sant was a Sikh of Nanak rather than of Govind, i.e. stressing Sikhism as a religion rather than Sikhs as a people. As such, he could unite both Sikh and Hindu in terms of religious principles respected by both and contained in the doctrine of Nanak. This suited the Congress party's own non-communal emphasis. Satbir Singh, a professor at Khalsa College, Jullundur, attempted to consolidate the Sant's hold over the Sikh masses,[14] giving Sant Fateh Singh the honorific and holy title of Baba. One close colleague of Tara Singh described the situation thus:

> Satbir Singh gave him the title of Sant Baba Fateh Singh. This is a very holy title since Baba was attached to the name of a son of Guru Govind Singh and is usually given to those of younger age who perform heroic deeds. Satbir Singh played on illiterate minds, inventing stories of how Fateh

Singh moved singing shabds (hymns) but that no one ever caught sight of him. He was all the time reciting shabds from Ganganagar to Amritsar but the police could not see him (interview with Mohinder Singh Bhattia).

In its day-to-day tactics, the state government relied on those members of the morcha committee whom it had purchased. The central government also utilized the services of certain persons as liaison officers between itself, the state government, and the Akali Dal. These were Lachman Singh Gill, a government contractor and future chief minister of the Punjab, and Uttam Singh Duggal [15], a transporter who came from the same area of west Punjab as Tara Singh, and who was engaged with Gill in joint business contracts. As will be seen throughout the text, various others—usually either intellectuals or industrialists or otherwise prominent figures—were co-opted as occasion demanded to perform the same function at different stages of the struggle. In the city area of Amritsar, where the Akali Dal offices, the SGPC and Darbar Sahib (the Golden Temple, the principal religious shrine of the Sikhs) were situated, there were two CID (Criminal Investigation Department) networks operating, one part of the official police structure, and the other directly responsible to the chief minister through the then head of the Amritsar urban district Congress Committee, Jai Inder Singh. It was on his orders that the Amritsar CID telephone office was attached to that of the Akali Dal and tapped. Stated Jai Inder: "Even the DIG (Deputy Inspector General) CID didn't know that. And so when the CID people go to Sirdar Partap Singh Kairon, they always explain to him something which he already knows."

While Jai Inder was handling the matter in Amritsar, the headquarters of the Akali Dal, Partap Singh Kairon in Chandigarh, the state capital and Nehru at national level, the public relations department, government of Punjab was shaping opinion throughout the state. Key statements against Tara Singh and the Punjabi Suba movement were arranged at relevant moments from leading politicians. These were published in pamphlet form and distributed. Nehru's correspondence with the Akali Dal leaders was extensively circulated, as were the chief minister's own views. Press comments from all over India on the agitation were published. The Home Ministry also arranged that money be given to certain persons, not for direct information but for speaking in terms favorable to the Congress.

The events leading to Tara Singh's fast, and which bring into focus the specific questions raised in the earlier part of the paper, begin with the fast unto death of Sant Fateh Singh to secure Punjabi Suba on December 18, 1960. By the ninth day of the fast, there was no sign of the government yielding, and by the fifteenth day of the fast the Dal therefore nominated three others to succeed him: Harcharan Singh Hudiara, the then junior vice-president of the Dal, Jiwan Singh Umralnangal, a smallholder from District Amritsar and a member of the SGPC, and Professor Satbir Singh. As Jai Inder remarks,

> Naturally we could rely on Hudiara and capture his support as he was the next to have to fast.

He recalled Hudiara coming to him and warning him that Fateh Singh's fast was genuine. Cash payment was indirectly arranged for Hudiara through the then home minister, while Umralnangal's son was offered promotion in government service. ("To Umralnangal we said 'If you help us we'll help your son with promotion.'" These are Jai Inder's exact words.) According to Ravel Singh, the government had had little idea of the rifts among leading Akalis until then.[16] It was at this point that the government began to arrange the details of a conspiracy which would completely divide the Dal. Again quoting Jai Inder:

> I said to Hudiara, we will do like this—for a permanent rift between Tara Singh and the Sant we will release the former and you then ask Tara Singh on his release to go and immediately sit by the side of the Sant and die together with him. If Master does not agree it will be easy for the Sant to also leave the fast. He will have the pretext that Master did not want him to continue. Master's image will also then be damaged. So Master did not know the cause of his own release.

He was used as a tool in Congress policy. The account given below of the activities of the state Congress Ministry in defeating the morcha is related by Jai Inder Singh but has been confirmed from a number of other sources:

> We helped Sant Fateh Singh in order to oust Master Tara Singh. It was Congress policy to divide the Sikhs! Twenty-five members attached to Master Tara Singh we detached from him and attached to Sant. We could do it! We were in power! Out of twenty-one members of the working committee (of the Akali Dal) we had ten with us. S. Sarup Singh, MLA, used to

go for negotiations on behalf of the Akali Dal but with our money and under our instructions he did what we wanted. Nehru and Partap Singh Kairon were both responsible for splitting the Dal. . . . After his release Master Tara Singh wanted to go home but we arranged that the SSP (Senior Superintendent of Police), S. Ranjit Singh (a close relative of Kairon's), deposit him in the Golden Temple and not at his home. Two pressmen were at the gate. "Masterji," they asked, "are you going to start your fast now with Sant Fateh Singh or not?" Tara Singh replied that this decision would be taken by the working committee, not by himself. They repeated their question but he refused to answer and returned home after seeing the Sant. It was at this point Sant gained credibility in the eyes of the Sikh masses. The next day in the working committee we spent over a lakh rupees so that some members should put forward the motion that Tara Singh should sit with Fateh Singh and die. On the second day of the working committee meeting Sarup Singh was sent on Congress expenses to meet Nehru, who was attending an All-India Congress Committee (AICC) session. From there he telephoned the Akali Dal, saying that if Master is prepared to talk with Nehru, Nehru is ready to talk with him, and urging Master to come by air. On the strength of this the working committee decided that Master Tara Singh should go to meet Nehru at Bhavnagar. A special plane was arranged by Uttam S. Duggal. Then Master Tara Singh said, "It is a golden opportunity for me." He ran away to Delhi by special plane with the permission of the working committee. Duggal paid for the plane.[17]

The Government and those Sikhs cooperating with it had placed Tara Singh in an unenviable position. Gurcharan Singh Taura, the present president of the SGPC, remarks that, "Master Tara Singh blundered when he took the responsibility to save Sant's life. But he was not acquainted with all that was going on" (interview, 1966). This is certainly an understatement. Had Tara Singh not gone to Bhavnagar, as Ravel Singh noted, he would have been accused of wishing the Sant's death. Sarup Singh suggests that Tara Singh acted as he did because

> it was his plan to make Sant a failure, fast himself then settle with the government. . . . We (a reference to himself, Bhan Singh, Satbir Singh and Ajit Singh Sarhadi)[18] built up Sant

not to get rid of Tara Singh but to bypass him and solve the problem. It was necessary to forget about communal percentages and concentrate solely on language. Nehru was bogged down in the narrowness of Tara Singh where every Sikh speaks Punjabi and every Hindu speaks Hindi and he had to be got out of this.

Therefore to say, as does Jai Inder Singh, "Sarup Singh we captured with money and through Sarup Singh got all the others," a view corroborated by Ravel Singh, who mentions that "Sarup Singh and Satbir Singh were paid agents of Kairon to raise the position of the Sant." While this states the reward the existing system gave to the above persons, it does not explain their practical positions. For one may note with respect to the All-India Sikh Students Federation (AISSF), with which these persons had long-standing association, that it was a body that had come into existence to counter the influence of the pro-Congress group among the Sikhs. One may also note with respect to Sarup Singh that, in the words of Bhan Singh:

> He had nineteen years of service to Panth brushed aside. As founder and founder-president of the AISSF he had stood for the separate entity of Panth and was the Dal's vice-president for twelve years. Since he'd even been to prison for Panth he was dissatisfied he was never offered anything.

Those who promoted the idea of a unilingual Punjab-speaking state were alleged to have accepted money from the Congress. A connection was hence assumed between these two events by their political rivals, i.e. that they changed the demand in response to financial inducement. However, as indicated above, Sarup Singh had not forfeited his ideals. Perhaps only one perspective is presented if we discuss the political events of this period on the level of day-to-day maneuver and compromise, neglectful of the vision which certain leaders in the Akali Dal merely did or did not work for according to circumstance. For there was nothing to indicate that Sarup Singh's views had changed since 1945 when he supported an independent Sikh state. And he was, in fact, never substantially benefited by the Congress Ministry of Partap Singh Kairon.[19]

I had interrupted Jai Inder's narrative at the point where Sarup Singh telephoned the Akali Dal office urging Tara Singh to come to the AICC session at Bhavnagar to meet the Prime Minister. In the period between the telephone call and that meeting, Professor Satbir Singh sent a telegram to Nehru, the principal content of which was that Tara Singh was coming for a reiteration of the Prime Minister's statement of December 31 that Punjabi was the dominating language of the Punjab. In fact, he had been authorized by the Akali Dal to use the word clarification. The telegram was therefore intended to sabotage the talks.[20] Besides, Sarup Singh had already informed Nehru before Tara Singh's arrival in Bhavnagar that Sant Fateh Singh had agreed to his statement that the entire Punjab is a Punjabi Suba, the clear implication being that it did not matter whether an agreement was reached with Tara Singh or not as they had signed up another alternative leader with whom the Congress party could reach a compromise solution. Taura, in an interview, corroborated this. Thus, when Tara Singh arrived in Bhavnagar and requested Nehru to make a public statement of trust in the Sikhs, Nehru initially did not agree. Tara Singh then gave a statement that he was dissatisfied with the talks, and after meeting Nehru and before leaving Bhavnagar for New Delhi, he stated his intention to fast unto death if the Sant dies, on the advice of Harbans Singh Gujral. The news was flashed to the press. However, while Masterji was enroute for Delhi, Nehru, over the radio the same evening, made the statement Masterji had earlier requested. It was said the Prime Minister acted thus on the advice of Gulab S. Sethi, close to Partap Singh Kairon, and chairman of the All-India Motor Spare Parts Union, Malik Mukhbain Singh and Malik Hardit Singh, three urbanites whose interests lay outside the Punjab.[21] On arrival in Delhi, then, Masterji was therefore to find that he had been out-maneuvered. He, however, was still left with his promise to fast unto death.

The reiteration Tara Singh had allegedly requested was made by the Prime Minister on January 8. The substance was as follows:

> I have already stated in my speech of December 31 what our views are about the Punjab and the Punjabi language. Punjab itself is broadly speaking a Punjabi Suba with Punjabi as the dominating language there. It is true that some parts of the Punjab have Hindi but essentially Punjabi is the dominant language and should be encouraged in every way.[22]

Nehru stressed that this was not a constitutional statement on his part but a broad approach to the problem which he had earlier stated in a letter to Sarup Singh on December 23, 1960.

To continue with the next part of the drama, again using Jai Inder's crucial information,

> Sant Fateh Singh was to break his fast only with Tara Singh's permission because Sant wants to use the weapon that Master asked him to break his fast. "Santji is not Sant" was once a very true remark made by Panditji,

said Jai Inder, laughing.

> Twice Sant refused to break the fast and told Master to come personally and request him. In the meantime, I arranged pro-Fateh Singh, Tara Singh demonstration at the Golden Temple gates chanting death to Tara Singh. On the same day, on Tara Singh's personal request Sant broke his fast, issuing a statement whose wording was that of S. Sarup Singh: "I firmly grasp the hand of friendship and goodwill extended by Pandit Nehru. I am prepared to discuss all the matters arising out of the Punjabi Suba agitation if Panditji paves the way for it." The next day I arranged the same type of demonstration and told Lachman S. Gill to bring a vote of no-confidence against Tara Singh in the SGPC. After one month (i.e. on February 8) Sant met Nehru, *but serious talks had to be postponed for a year because we needed one year to create a clear rift.* In the meantime, we made Sant agree with Nehru over the language issue. And just before the talks broke (on May 12) we arranged that only Master Tara Singh stood for Punjabi Suba and not the Sant, thus giving the impression that Sant is willing to settle with Nehru but not so Master Tara Singh.[23] This was how we sought to present it. Sant Fateh Singh then took a stand in a working committee meeting that if he is to break his talks Master will then definitely have to go on fast. And he then met Nehru and broke his talks without a compromise being achieved.

This account by Jai Inder Singh, which is now ended, would have us believe that it was primarily the Congress party that maneuvered Tara Singh into his fast, an impasse against which he had been warned by influential and rich urbanites among the Potoharis (urbanite refugees formerly from the districts of Rawalpindi, East Jhelum Attock). As Sarup Singh assessed, "The Potoharis financed him only so long as by so doing they maintained his leadership.

Otherwise his politics of Sikh homeland (financed by them, no doubt) does not suit their business interests."

That the fast was indeed a political pose, a gesture, and had no reality of intention, is indicated by Gujral advising him to go on fast after the failure of the Bhavnagar meeting. Later, when it came to the point when Tara Singh had to fast, Gujral was bothered only about Sikh property elsewhere in India that would be liable to be attacked on the death of Tara Singh. Aside from the activities and pressure from the state and central Congress Ministries, urbanites with business and other interests in India rather than the Punjab, probably caused the abandonment of the fast, aided by Tara Singh's own family. Taura, for example, noted that

> It was decided that members of the working committee should sit with him continuously and recite Sukhmani Sahib (Prayer of Peace) continuously, one by one. This only went on for ten to twelve hours when Master Tara Singh asked them to go. Then custody was taken of him by his wife and his family members. Even on the forty-sixth day he was sitting and talking firmly.

Mohinder Singh Bhattia, Tara Singh's old friend, sadly reflects that "it was the personal weakness of Masterji and of his followers to save him." And Sarup Singh noted, "Master himself was not prepared to die. All the compromising moves are evidence of this."

According to Taura, the working committee of the Akali Dal objected to any effort made towards compromise—of which there were many—during the course of the fast. For example, at the beginning of September, Masterji spoke to representatives of the foreign press, communicating to them that if the matter of discrimination against the Sikhs in the form of a denial of a Sikh majority area is taken to the United Nations he will abandon the fast. He named the intermediaries acceptable to him in talks with the Indian government. He wished the government to appoint Jenkins (a former governor of the Punjab, Sir Penderel Moon (a former deputy commissioner Amritsar) and Major Billy Short [24] as arbitrators.[25] According to Gurcharan Singh Taura this made the working committee think that

> Tara Singh was slipping away from an otherwise bold stand. The working committee took the view that it was up to the government to find some way out of the deadlock. The cause

for any press statement was to lie with the working committee. But after another week passed, Tara Singh announced independently that if the Punjabi Suba question is entrusted to Rajagopalacharia of the Swatantara Party, Ajoy Ghosh (the general secretary of the Communist party of India) and Ashoka Mehta of the Praja Socialist party, he would give up his fast. Masterji's men got the Maharajah of Patiala to become mediator between the Akali Dal and the government,[26] but the working committee appointed S. Gurnam Singh. The Maharajah of Patiala advised S. Gurnam Singh that he should inform working committee members to suggest to Master to break his fast. But S. Gurnam Singh informed the working committee that the government had not accepted the Punjabi Suba demand and that it was useless talking to them. In his experience, further talks would be futile. Following on this Harghunath Singh, the then general secretary of the Akali Dal, said that as the general elections are fast approaching and the Jan Sangh (a Hindu communal party) in Delhi has equipped Hindus to deal with Sikhs along Muslim League lines, therefore in the event of Tara Singh's death, the community will be leaderless and exposed, in addition to losing the elections. It is better Tara Singh give up his fast on the advice of the working committee, he argued. In the meantime, Malik Hardit Singh, Ambassador to France, flew to Amritsar on September 30, talked with Tara Singh and with the Sant, and the next day met the working committee. He brought a piece of paper into the meeting which said that all persons arrested will be released, all cases withdrawn and pensions and positions restored. The government will set up a commission to look into the question of discrimination against the Sikhs. This piece of paper was said to have come from Nehru but it was unsigned. One of Master's friends (this was Mohinder S. Bhattia) then said that were he not saved in twenty-four hours he would die. All sorts of pressures were placed on working committee members. But since they considered that the mediators were self-appointed and that therefore no promises could be taken from them (he means no assurances given by them) since they were not sent for by us, we passed the buck back to Masterji. Meanwhile, however, the Sant delivered a speech that the government had agreed to Sikh demands and the Maharajah of Patiala announced the same in public.

Tara Singh made a statement to the same effect.[27]

It thus appears that one very important dimension to Tara Singh's defeat is located in the larger resources of the state government. Distrust was sown in Tara Singh's honesty and that of other Akali Dal leaders by a government that acted as a rumor control center.

Tara Singh's supporters stressed the innumerable private reasons the intermediaries had for cooperating with the government to end his fast. But aside from governmental influence, exerted in the form of fear of loss of favor or expectation of future favor the onus for Tara Singh's decision not to die lay with capitalist Sikhs who feared substantial economic loss to the Sikh community outside Punjab. The same mixture of personal ambition, genuine concern for the community's welfare, and governmental pressure caused a rupture in the group around Tara Singh, all of whom alike, but separately, had participated in complicity with the Congress Ministry.

Division within this group around Tara Singh, whose members had been close to each other previously and who indeed had played a unitary role in community life at partition as members of the AISSF, was the result of government activity and of separate private bargaining with each, so much so that each regarded the other as compromised and to a certain extent each was!

But in any case, Tara Singh had alienated the religious. Once ardas is said the deed promised beforehand—which in this instance was a pledge to die if a political end was not secured—has to be undertaken. The saying of ardas is a seal in advance for the completion of any deed. For the religious, the noncompletion of the vow was expiated by a tankhaah, or fine being imposed whereby he was to clean the shoes and utensils of pilgrims visiting the Golden Temple and make *prshad* (holy food). This punishment implied no disgrace but was the just penalty for wrong action. "We punish Master Tara Singh and by doing so restore his honour," one leader commented.

Sikh leaders pointed out that even Maharajah Ranjit Singh had been forced to be responsible to the community and to the community alone. It remained that the community stood betrayed, however, in terms of its cultural norms, which were Jat norms, and Sant's rise as a leader is associated with that fact. But most importantly it is associated, as we have seen, with the Congress party's sponsorship of him and its manipulative politics in the institutions of the SGPC and the working committee of the Akali Dal. Because of the esteem in which Tara Singh was held (even after the fast debacle, he was elected president of the SGPC in November 1961), the government also attempted to defeat him noninstitutionally.

Such differences as existed between urbanite and ruralite Sikhs, and between the areas of Majha and Malwa were magnified.[28] Regarding the first, Tara Singh's vacillatory leadership and his lack of resolve were attributed to his urban origins.[29] This point of view was put across particularly by a Malwai landlord, Lachman Singh Gill, an aspirant for higher office of some kind, who later became chief minister for a short period. With respect to the second point, it may be said that, Tara Singh having offended the Sikh religious code, this then became an occasion for an ambitious person such as Gill with strong support in Malwa to alter the balance of power in its favor as an economically disadvantaged area. By whipping up an intensity of rural feeling behind the Sant in Malwai villages, he served the area by drawing attention to its needs, served his own political ends, while also, as Kairon wished, shifting support away from Tara Singh to the Sant. Malwai villagers supported the Sant because he came from a village. For a long time Chief Minister Kairon had, similarly, the goodwill of Punjab's rural population for the same reason—that he too came from a village. Kairon endeavored to give ordinary rural people a new dignity vis-à-vis the police and civil administration and the rise of Sant as a leader specifically with the support of Malwai farmers has to be seen as yet another indication of the rise of village Punjab, a fact that had already been reflected in the organization of the state government, the Punjab Congress, and was now about to occur also with respect to the leadership of the Dal. Though rural versus urban, or indeed Majha versus Malwa, never became a distinct pattern, it never overtook the predominantly factional nature of the support coming from the rural areas.

The backing of Malwa's farmers for the Sant was also a product of the insularity and parochiality of certain of its districts, most notably Bhatinda, Sangrur and Ferozepur. Until recent times, the area had been under princely rule and was an area of larger landholdings whose farmers and tenants were predominantly illiterate. It had not contributed to the growth of the realm of Maharajah Ranjit Singh and had less participation for exclusively Sikh interests due to being under British protection. In addition, there was a Sant tradition in the area and this reverence for Sants—including Hindu Sants—in Malwai villages allowed Fateh Singh to take a stand whose focus was Hindu-Sikh unity rather than Sikh unity—

without disturbing Sikh farmers, and as already noted, this faciliated his being used by Partap Singh Kairon as an exponent of a noncommunal point of view.

But that the ruralite/urbanite and the Majha/Malwa issue could have been raised at all, if only for a brief period, was, as Giani Kartar Singh, former secretary of the Akali Dal expressed it to me, only because

> Master Tara Singh did not achieve his objective during seventeen years. This is what is responsible for Jat desertions. The Jats are not against Master Tara Singh on account of his being non-Jat, but what has been achieved by the partition of the subcontinent? Sikhs merely went from under a Muslim majority to under a Hindu majority. The Jats took the view that what we have done for Master Tara Singh's leadership, he has not done for the Sikhs.

Shifting loyalty away from Tara Singh was one means of continuing one's loyalty to Panth. The incorruptible community standards were affirmed as against the failing leadership of a person.

Conclusion

It is said of John Locke that he "did not hesitate to sacrifice theoretical consistency for the sake of arriving at practical compromises and ideological combinations that gained his ends." As explained by Novack, who makes this comment (1971, p.26), this was not Locke's own individual characteristic. Likewise, I would argue, neither could the actions of Akali leaders be given such a reference, that is in terms of the corruptibility of individual character. Their decisions were not private matters, but were related to the socio-political situation of Sikhs as a community. Statements such as that would appear to reflect that while, on the human level, these can be attributed to the immediate political advantage then expected through affiliation with the Congress party, structurally they express the ambiguity of the Sikh position. That same ambiguity is illustrated on another level by the various ideological presentations of historical fact. These have appeared to bear some relation to the relative political strength of the Sikhs vis-à-vis Muslims and Hindus. At one stage in history, Guru Govind Singh was stated to be an avatar, (personal incarnation of the deity), thereby bringing him within the Hindu tradition. But in the period under consideration different facts were brought to the fore: that it was a Muslim who saved the Guru's life; and that he encountered his main opposition from the Hindu Rajas. The different emphases reflect no confusion over or lack of continuity with a tradition, but rather are a response of that tradition to external circumstance. I believe that the structural position of the Sikhs between two communal majorities and their position within a state dominated by one of these explains any alleged inconsistency between ideal and practice, as too does their dilemma (faced by many other minorities) of being faithful to the tradition which distinguishes them, but which yet must not be allowed to reduce their capability for participation in social groupings beyond the community. The story of the Sikh Punjab is the story of border country—of economic integration into Hindustan coupled with cultural affinity to the people of west Punjab.

In my introduction I had stated that the methods at the disposal of Akali leaders during the period in question to keep their promises to a tradition and to the masses believing in that tradition were not evolved within the context of the tradition itself but within the intercommunal, national sphere.

> This was necessarily so because a policy cannot be grounded in principle, it must also comprehend the facts of the situation (Merleau-Ponty, XXXV, 1969).

The result was that the cultural framework could not comprehend the action of the Akali leaders. Sikh political practice was the epitome of the Kantian view of politics as the mere technical expertise in a utilitarian doctrine of prudence. But Sikh ideology would not abandon the notion that politics ought to be guided by ethics. The latter conviction indeed was not sacrificed for the sake of consistency with the community's material condition in the years under consideration. In this respect, community values remained unaffected by the community's absorption into the secular state and by formal community acceptance of secularism as a scientifically grounded philosophy operating independent of time, place, and circumstance, and which, within the polity of India, would provide for enduring relationships to be founded between communal groups on a noncommunal principle. Community values remained values even though no action was taken that materially accorded with them. Tara Singh, for example, never sacrificed the principle fundamental to Sikhism and to the continued existence of the Sikh community—namely that of the indivisibility of religion and culture on the one hand with politics and the state on the other—despite doing little to further its end. Cultural concepts were thus completely separated from compulsions in the sphere of strategic action, empirical circumstances affecting tactics alone but not touching the structure of community ideals. Thus if we are to agree with Kafka that "every value—material as well as spiritual—involves a risk. For every value demands protection" (Janouch, 1968, p.67), equally we have to acknowledge the power of ideas protected from the profanity of practice. Ideals so secluded are removed from the sphere of political life which is the arena of conflict between minority and majority. At least, thereby, the autonomy of community values is preserved to form the basis for future independent political action. During the period 1947-66, the exclusion of minority cultural concepts from the political realm pertained simultaneously to the minority's positional interest while, too, preserving its undefeated integrity.

The evidence presented in the paper would provide the foundation for a plea to the Sikhs not to use their own culturally based version of reality as an analytical tool. And with this in mind, I have been concerned to show the practical inadequacy of the folk-model for the Sikhs themselves, from an operational point of view. It is no doubt the case that one of the means of safeguarding the integrity and survival of community life is present in the strict adherence to cultural values. But when a community is located in a strategic area, the international political arena is then not on its borders but frequently in its midst. This situation demands of any community placed in such a structural position—even in terms of its own avowed political purposes—a loss of cultural perspective when operating in the international scene; a recognition that its own traditional model is not enough with which to work. This is why we need, in this instance, an explanation other than Sikh explanation. As I have sought to show in the paper, two kinds of action are required of the Sikh political leadership; one allowing the community to preserve the style of its past into the future, and the other ensuring not only its survival but its place in the world community. For, as the Urdu proverb has it, "the elephant must have two sets of teeth, one for eating, the other for show." As has been suggested, the unrelatedness of Sikh political practice to Sikh cultural ideals secured the community's survival as a cultural entity with considerable political power at this particular stage. The seeming segregation of political action from cultural and religious belief was a position particularly suited to the time in question, namely 1947-66, when the Sikhs were seeking to consolidate their identity on a communal basis but within the boundaries of a national state—India—the principles of whose constitution were secular. I have been arguing that such a separation did not imply disloyalty to community ideals, but was simply an appropriate accommodation with the material situation of their position.

With the achievement of a Punjabi-speaking state, the Sikh community came to be concretely associated with a distinct territory, and community affairs became firmly entwined with the material interests of the Punjab state. After April 1966, community and territory were one and the same and the Sikh people now had a common referent independent of the intangibles of religion, language, and history which were their common heritage. A favorable alteration in the material condition of the Punjab state in the ensuing years was then to totally alter the picture of its encapsulation into the Indian union in all but a formal sense.

In the four years from 1966 to 1977, ninety percent of the total cropped area was covered in the new, high-yielding varieties of wheat. The Punjab was already surplus in wheat and a wheat exporter and diffusion of the new agricultural propserity was aided by the land tenure pattern. By 1969-70, 88.3 percent of its cropped area was under self-cultivation. Punjab wheat was sold to India at half the cost of American wheat, Punjab thereby saving the country annually valuable amounts of foreign exchange. The profitability of farming and of industries associated with its development generated more investable surplus. These found their way to other parts of India. In 1977, an official source close to the Chief Minister mentioned to me that only one-third of the total number of deposits (to be precise thirty-five in each one hundred) invested in Punjab's banks remained within the Punjab. In 1977, measures were under way to control this movement of capital by encouraging Punjabis to invest their money in the cooperative banks which would keep their money within the Punjab. In 1978, demands for financial autonomy were made to secure assistance from the central government for the development of heavy industry in the state. In a speech before the working committee of the National Development Council in early 1979, the Chief Minister of Punjab threatened to finance his own budget. Speaking on the sixth five-year-plan, he commented,

> Ninety-five percent of Punjab's plan in the next four years would be required to be financed by the state from its own

resources. At the same time I find that there would be many states in India whose plan would be financed by the center to the extent of thirty to forty percent and in some cases to the extent of nearly ninety to ninety-five percent. Mr. Chairman, if in a federal system of government, Punjab, as one of the constituents of the union of India, is going to find itself so grossly discriminated against, we might as well turn 'round and say "Thank you very much." If we can find ninety-five percent of our plan requirements ourselves we might as well find the remaining five percent also. We will raise our plan resources ourselves, formulate our plan schemes . . . according to our own best wisdom and priorities (Government of Punjab, 1979, p.8).

One of the contexts for central assistance for industrialization was that the high productivity of agricultural raw material such as cotton, potatoes, and sugar cane had no industrial outlets. In March 1979, in his presentation of the budget to the Punjab Assembly, the Finance Minister made reference to this and to the fact that "it is equally essential that we expose our agriculture to international markets in order to provide additional marketing for our agricultural surpluses" (1979, p.6).

In the early postindependence years, the east Punjab had been in process of transition from a feudal to a capitalist society. Much earlier than 1979 it had succeeded in developing a capitalist farming base. Indeed from 1971, with capitalist relations steadily in the ascendancy, Punjab was in an increasingly strong economic position as has been indicated in the two preceding paragraphs. Certainly, within a purely Indian context, a material base now exists allowing the Sikh leadership to be theoretically guided by the principles of their own culture, and this might indeed have occurred had the area not bordered and been in close proximity to several Islamic states represented a pocket of egalitarian prosperity between the feudal Islamic lands of western Asia and the sea of poverty of inegalitarian Hindustan. And still more significant, as is indicated in the finance minister's speech, is that the market transcends the limits of the Punjab state and of India and is bent on extending itself into the international sphere. Hence, both the place and position of the province and the development of economic relations which draw the state into the world market to sell its commodities are unlikely to allow its leadership to retreat into cultural inwardness and are likely to guarantee during this phase a continuing disparity between community cultural ideals and political practice as a characteristic operating feature of the system.

The late prime minister of Pakistan, Zufilqar Ali Butto is quoted as saying that "Pakistan's foreign relations can be divided into two segments. The pragmatic where the country is compelled to react to changing world currents, and the sentimental which ties it to a peculiar value system and hence fixed perceptions and preferences" (Ziring, *Journal of Asian and African Studies*, 1973).

This undoubtedly describes the Sikh situation in practice. But in theory such disparities between political practice and cultural belief are interrelated and connected. For as Habermas (1974, p.236) stresses, "interests as well as ideas are but dialectical moments of the same totality."

Notes

The data contained in this paper were gathered over a two year period in the east Punjab of the middle sixties and during August 1977 and January 1978. Those who gave information, as can be seen from the list of the dramatis personae, were nearly all politicians affiliated with the Akali Dal and the Punjab Congress party. I did consult newspaper reports regarding the events described, and took into account the views expressed in various written documents produced by the Akali Dal and the ruling Congress Party. From an ethnographic point of view, the core of the paper is the information provided by Jai Inder Singh who was then the President of the Amritsar District Congress Committee (urban). Giani Ajmer Singh, Secretary Shiromani Akali Dal, the late Master Tara Singh, and S. Birinder Singh (advocate New Delhi) significantly added to the wealth of intrigue only part of which is reported in this paper. The present Finance Minister, government of Punjab, S. Balwant Singh, read the paper and made some useful comments and suggestions.

Drafts of the paper were read at the Institute of Social Anthropology, University of Bergen in 1977, and in the Department of History of the Indological Institute of the Rijks University, Leiden 1978. I wish to cordially thank Harold Tambs-Lyche, Julian Kramer, Professor Reidar Grönhaug, Professor Dr. Jan C. Heesterman and Dr. Schott for their comments.

1. "What happens when a community that idealizes communal harmony is faced with internal conflicts and contradictions? .... What kind of analytic framework can be used to consider the congruities and the discrepancies between ideology and action in social situations?"
2. See in this connection: Mannheim (1960)—no partial standpoint has validity; Marcuse (1972)—analysis involves critical knowledge, knowledge of one's own deformation by society.
3. Factions control the allocation and distribution of economic resources

and political power. Their members usually have diverse occupations and are linked by reciprocal patronage. For further information see Pettigrew (1975, 1976).
4. The concept of totality was one which was later rejected. Previously Hegel had used the concept to attack Kant's notion of a duality between mind and the outside world, denying the existence of such duality. In this paper I am using the concept somewhat more pragmatically, to assert the domination of the whole over the parts, and to draw attention to the fact that anthropology has a need for concepts which allow it to operate at a macrolevel.
5. In my conclusion, it is also implied that it is not only multicommunal federal units to which Cohen's theory cannot be applied, but that the theory is also inappropriate when powerful local minorities adjoin international boundaries and deal directly with the international market.
6. Sarup Singh hints here at the existence of conditions which are very normally imposed on minorities by the state in which they are encapsulated, namely that the latter will accept individuals from these groups but not the corporate character of the minority to which they belong. In all instances, the minority fear is of progressive atomization as a community.
7. Thorstein Veblen (1919) in an essay "The Intellectual Preminence of Jews in Modern Europe," observed that such distinctions were always purchased by Jewish thinkers by extracting themselves from their own heritage. Likewise in this instance, political and civil power could be retained only by being somewhat ambiguous about one's traditions and sacrificing some definiteness in that regard.
8. Kairon's policies implied commitment to a different vision, (though some would argue a different pathway to the same vision) whose focus was primarily on rural development with respect to the entire territory of the Punjab. Irrigation facilities were dramatically extended, which meant larger acreage in crops and higher yields per acre. Schemes for the development of new mandis (markets) were planned and each block (containing 100 villages) was to have a seed farm so that improved varieties of seed would be available near the farmer. Large loans were set aside for the purchase of fertilizer and insecticides. Attention was also paid to horticulture and dairying, and the Fruit Development Board was revived in 1959. The setting up of Punjabi University was the Chief Minister's response to Tara Singh's concern for Sikhs and the Sikh language, as was his active interest in and promotion of Agricultural University, Ludhiana.
9. For a fuller description, see Pettigrew 1978.
10. I may add here that instructions posted to all Sikhs in the Akali newspaper, *The Spokesman* September 13, 1965) under the heading of "Our Duty" do not seem to be antinational: "Help defend the motherland. Join the armed forces. Contribute to the Defense Fund. Donate blood for the jawans (troops). Don't spread rumors. Don't believe enemy broadcasts. Cooperate with the authorities." There had been many official precursors to Nanda's statement reflected in the resolutions on States Re-Organization of the All-India Congress Committee

(AICC). For example, the working committee at the Hyderabad session in January 1953 mentioned with respect to the report of the Linguistic Provinces Committee that "while confirming that policy, the Congress would draw special attention to the other factors which must be taken into consideration in any reorganization of the present states in India, such as the unity of India, national security and defense, financial considerations and economic progress. . . . The successful implementation of the Five-Year Plan must always be kept in view."

The Working Committee in 1955 reaffirmed that they had "always laid stress on national unity and solidarity as overriding considerations to be borne in mind in determining the constitutional structure in India," and in November of the same year added that "they noted with deep regret that disruptive forces were at work in the name of linguistic provinces."

The fullest statement was that contained in the Amritsar session of February 1956: "More than thirty years ago, the Congress encouraged the formation of linguistic provinces . . . to encourage the growth of the Indian languages and cultures associated with them . . . but language cannot be the dominating factor in the demarcation of states . . . If language is allowed to encourage separatist tendencies then it does unity to the basic concept of the unity of India."

11. Uncertainty as to Pakistan's intentions should the Sikhs get into a major conflict with the government was a consideration always, while with respect to the Congress Government, Professor Sant Singh Sekhon notes, "The Sikh feels the government is not his and that the government will give him no quarter if he comes down to violence."
12. These were far in excess of the amount officially stated.
13. The scene was one of an indiscriminate lathi charge by the police—"It was the automatic assumption that all bearded men were Akalis" (Professor Sant Singh Sekhon, 1966).
14. Gulati (1974, p.170) notes that the Sant was a nonentity. The credit for his meteoric rise went to his advisors. Sarup Singh mentioned to me in an interview in 1966 that both he and Bhan Singh "had persuaded the Sant to accept a unilingual state." My account differs on some details from Gulati's. These differences center on his evaluation of the character of Sant Fateh Singh who is variously described as soft-spoken (145) and of transparent sincerity (170). On a more serious level, Gulati mentions (172) that Tara Singh was released from jail as a result of Jai Parkash Narain's intercession with the Prime Minister. Whether or not this is so (my data present a different view), the certain consequence was that the chief minister and the Congress party profited from the release. I think Gulati also fails to bring out that the rise of the Sant as a leader owed a considerable amount to the collaboration in which he himself was unwillingly or willingly an accomplice.
15. It was said that Uttam Singh Duggal hoped to get elected to a Rajha Sabha seat. He was rewarded for his efforts as mediator by having his income tax arrears neglected. Harbans Singh Gujral also gives yet another reflection on his allegiance. He reports that Duggal had a grudge against Tara Singh. In prepartition days Tara Singh had re-

fused him an Akali ticket while also contesting a seat against his cousin, Jaswant S. Duggal.
16. "Then it emerged that there was a group around the Sant—Umralhangal, Hudiara, Satbir Singh—who would rather see the death of the Punjabi Suba demand than the death of the Sant."
17. The conspiracy element contained in Jai Inder's account is confirmed by Amar Singh Ambalvi:

> Certain people in the Congress or allied to it were urging Masterji to persuade Sant to give up his fast (for example, Satbir Singh, according to Gujral, said that Sant should not be allowed to die). Immediately after he complied with their request he was criticized for it—he wants to fast himself and get the glory, it was said. Later when Masterji went on to fast, the same group of people put up the argument— it is against religion, it is antinational. Then when he gave up they said it was betrayal. The same group of people all the time were saying these things.

18. Bhan Singh, Sarup Singh, Ajit Singh Sarhadi, and Amar Singh Ambalvi had long been associated with each other as members of the AISSF. Sarhadi, Ambalvi and Sarup Singh at the time of partition had tried together to get Tara Singh to meet Jinnah, who had told them he was prepared to discuss an independent Sikh state. On the day of the meeting Tara Singh went into hiding. Along with S. Hukam Singh, Sarup Singh and Bhan Singh had been planning to oust Tara Singh from the leadership ostensibly because of his lack of support for intellectuals. Hukam Singh's view, stated in a letter to Nehru who was abroad at the time, was that "Master Tara Singh should not die in his fast because he will be worshipped by the Sikh community in their ardas."
19. Sarup Singh incurred Tara Singh's dislike (according to Bhan Singh) by bringing Nehru around to the view of a unilingual state and Kairon's dislike by acting independently. Lachman Singh Gill, for example, mentioned that he often met Nehru without the chief minister's prior permission. Bhan Singh confirms this and says that the chief minister was against Sarup Singh because he was becoming too close to Nehru and was going to make a compromise which would have deprived Kairon of some of his fame for solving the Akali problem. It was rivalry that was purely personal because Kairon himself supported a unilingual state.
20. For, to quote one member (this member was Lachman Singh Gill and the extract below is from a letter to the Akali Dal dated May 11, 1961),

> The majority of persons were then of the view that the Prime Minister's statement (on December 31) did not satisfy the conditions under which Sant Fateh Singh had started his fast.

The Akali Dal held an enquiry into Satbir Singh's action during which Harghunath Singh MLA issued the following affidavit:

>I accompanied Master Tara Singh to Bhavnagar to see the Prime Minister. When we reached Delhi I read the telegram in question. All were of the opinion that the telegram was meant to torpedo our mission at Bhavnagar. At the aerodrome (at Bhavnagar) Balwinder Singh, younger brother of Professor Satbir Singh, met me. . . . he reached Bhavnagar by air a day previous to our arrival there.

21. This was also confirmed by Lachman Singh Gill who, as an intermediary, should know.
22. The full text is as follows:

No Ground for Fateh Singh to Continue Fast
Nehru's Statement at Sardarnagar
Division of Punjab Harmful

Sardarnagar, January 8. Mr. Nehru said here today that his declarations at Delhi and here on the Punjabi language clearly met "the substance" of what Sant Fateh Singh had said and the latter should, therefore, have no difficulty in giving up his fast.

The Prime Minister, who was addressing a mammoth public meeting at Sardarnagar this evening, referred to his talks with Master Tara Singh last night and said: "Punjab itself, broadly speaking, is a Punjabi Suba and Punjabi is the dominant language there.

"It is true that some parts of Punjab have Hindi but essentially Punjabi is the dominant language there and it should be encouraged in every way. Thus there is no linguistic difficulty at all. It is not right for such questions to be considered from a communal point of view. I would like to repeat that there is no question of discrimination against Punjab or against Sikhs.

"Master Tara Singh, the Prime Minister declared, had told him that he was equally anxious that Sant Fateh Singh should give up his fast. If so, there could be no difficulty at all. I have said previously I am prepared to discuss any matter afterwards."

Referring to Master Tara Singh's statement to him that Sant Fateh Singh had taken an oath (regarding Punjabi Suba) and should not be asked to break it, Mr. Nehru said that oaths were taken not in regard to legal aspects or statutory way of doing things but about the substance of things. "And, therefore, what I have said should be quite enough for Sant Fateh Singh to meet this difficulty and give up his fast."

Mr. Nehru spoke in Hindi and explained the background to the Punjabi Suba problem and then said that for the benefit of the pressmen he would repeat it in English. He then read out in English from a prepared text his reactions to Master Tara Singh's public statement today.

Text

The following is the full text of Mr. Nehru's prepared statement:
"I met Master Tara Singh last night and had a long talk with him.

It is known that there is a basic diference of approach between him and me in a number of matters. I shall not enter into these matters, but there is one thing which I should like to clear up so that there might be no misunderstanding.

"Master Tara Singh has said to the press that he wanted me to declare that it was not out of any discrimination against Punjab or distrust of Sikhs that the process of forming linguistic states was not possible after applying it elsewhere. I told him that there could be no question of discrimination against Punjab or distrust of Sikhs in any matter. Punjab is happily a prosperous state, and we want it to prosper more and more. It would be absurd to discriminate against it. As for the Sikhs also, they are, as I have said often, a brave and vital part of our nation whom we respect and whose progress we should like to encourage in every way.

"Thus the question of discrimination does not and cannot arise. Indeed, I am surprised at such a suggestion.

"As for the formation of states, many matters have to be taken into consideration for each area. Among these matters is certainly language. But language is not the sole consideration. I could not accept a proposal that I should accept as a principle the formation of purely linguistic states.

Division Harmful

"So far as Punjab is concerned I am convinced that any kind of division of the state would be very harmful to Punjab, to Sikhs as well as to Hindus and to the whole of India. One of our leading and progressive states would fall back and get entangled in new problems.

"I have already clearly stated in my Delhi speech on December 31 what our views are about Punjab and about the Punjabi language. Punjab itself is, broadly speaking, a Punjabi Suba with Punjabi as the dominant language there. It is true that some parts of Punjab have Hindi, but essentially Punjabi is the dominant language and it should be encouraged in every way.

"Thus, there is no linguistic difficulty at all. It is not right for such questions to be considered from a communal point of view.

"I would like to repeat that there is no question of discrimination against Punjab or against Sikhs.

"We are anxious that Sant Fateh Singh should give up his fast and return to health. Master Tara Singh told me that he was equally anxious about this. If so, there should be no difficulty at all. I have said previously that I am prepared to discuss any matter afterwards."

Mr. Nehru then added the following to his written text:

"Now to add one more word to this, because Master Tara Singh mentioned it to me about Sant Fateh Singh having taken an oath and he should not be asked to break it.

"I do not like asking any person to break his solemn oath and it is difficult for me to advise in such matters. But I am convinced that what I have stated in my Delhi speech and what I am stating today and the facts that I have placed before the country in regard to the Punjabi language clearly meets the substance of what Sant Fateh Singh has said. Oaths are not taken in regard to some legal aspects or statutory way of looking at things, but about the substance of things. And therefore, what I have said should be enough for Sant Fateh Singh to meet this difficulty and give up his fast."

P.T.I.
The Tribune
Monday, January 9, 1961.

23. In the first meeting, Sant and Nehru are in agreement that the population percentage of any one community in a Punjabi speaking state is irrelevant, and Nehru stresses that if the Akali Dal gives up looking at the issue on a religious basis and takes it up on a linguistic basis only, then he will consider the matter. Before Sant goes to the second meeting Tara Singh takes an extreme stand that Punjabi Suba is a religious demand to protect Sikhism.
24. The Major of the 11th Sikh regiment was trusted by Tara Singh. At partition, he had done valuable liaison work on behalf of the British government to restore Muslim-Sikh amity and hence prevent the division of the Punjab.
25. Short and Moon tried to get the Sikhs to throw in their lot wih Pakistan since, to quote Moon (1961, p.84), "it was in accord with the real interests of the Sikh community which lay with N.W. India rather than with Hindustan."
26. Another version is that the Maharjah of Patiala and Malik Hardit Singh, acting on government auspices, gave assurances to Tara Singh that there would be an appointment of a commission to investigate Sikh grievances, consisting of Tara Singh's nominees knowing that the government is not going to be true to its assurances with respect to these. Gujral said that the Maharajah was pro-government, while Hardit Singh, he claimed, was worried that Sikhs would be left in a vacuum. He states that the majority of the working committee were of the view that Tara Singh's death ought to be avoided. This contradicts the information given by Gurcharan Singh Taura.
27. "I have been assured by responsible friends Malik Hardit Singh and his Highness the Maharaja of Patiala that the government of India at the instance of the Prime Minister has issued a communique assuring us of appointing immediately High Power Commission consisting of men of the highest integrity to examine the grievances and differential treatment to the Sikhs which led me to my fast. As the only grievance that led me to my fast is the nonapplication of the linguistic principle to the Punjabi-speaking area, resulting in discrimination on a social plane, the said commission is going to examine this question, that is the question regarding the formation of a Punjabi-speaking state.

"As the Akali Dal had earlier asked for these two assurances vis-à-vis the High Power Commission, i.e. the consideration of the question regarding the formation of the Punjabi-speaking state and acceptable personnel thereof, the said assurance by our basic requirements. As advised by the Working Committee of the Shiromani Akali Dal and other friends, believing it to be in the larger interests of our cause and the country which are so dear to my heart, I have decided to end my fast today the 48th day of the fast.

"I thank the conscientious citizens the world over for their love, prayer, and sympathies and assure the government that every fair approach would be fully reciprocated with warmth and love by the Sikhs."

Dated January 10, 1961   Tara Singh—Master

28. Had these been significant social divides they would also have been reflected in the organization of the Punjab Congress which, they were not.

Malwa covers districts Ludhiana, Ferozepur, Bhatinda, Sangrur, and Patiala. Majha, for the Sikhs was the area between the Beas river and the Pakistan border.

29. It was extensively propagated at this time that urbanites were controlling the affairs of the Akali Dal. Figures do not support this. Of the Presidents of the SGPC, from 1926 to 1962, four out of fourteen have been urbanite. The four urbanites—Master Tara Singh, Gopal S. Quami, Baba Kharak Singh, and Bawa Harkishen Singh were from west Punjab and hence refugees. They occupied a total of twenty-one years ten months in office, as Master Tara Singh was elected several times in the period from 1933 to 1962. With respect to working committee members for the years 1955-6, the combined refugee and urbanite number out of twenty-one was usually small:

1955-57	9
1957-58	8
1958-59	6
1959-60	5
1960	6

References

Alavi, H. 1973. Peasant classes and primordial loyalties. *Journal of Peasant Studies,* vol. I, no. I, pp. 23-62.

Bauman, Z. 1973. *Culture as praxis.* Routledge and Kegan Paul, London.

Cohen, Abner. 1974. *Two-dimensional man.*

Faiz, Ahmed Faiz. 1975. *Problems of national art and culture.* Extracts from a report of the Standing Committee on Art and Culture, 1968, Lahore, Pakistan.

Fortes, M. and Patterson, S. ed. 1975. *Studies in African social anthropology.* Academic Press.

Government of Punjab. 1979. January 1975. Text of speech of Sardar Parkash Singh Badal, Chief Minister, Punjab, at the meeting of the working group of the Committee of the National Development Council, New Delhi.

Government of Punjab. 1979. March. Speech of Sardar Balwant Singh, Finance Minister presenting the budget for the year 1979-80, Chandigarh.

Government of Punjab, Public Relations Department. Press comments on

the Punjabi Suba agitation, Chandigarh, 1960. Authoritative documents leading to the end of Master Tara Singh's fast, 1961. Resolving the fast issue. Prime Minister's correspondence with Akali leaders, 1961.
Gulati, K.C. 1974. *The Akalis past and present.* Ashajanak, New Delhi.
Habermas, J. 1974. *Theory and practice,* Heineman.
India National Congress. Undated. *Resolutions on states re-organization 1920-1956.* All-India Congress Committee, New Delhi.
Lukacs, G. 1971. *History and class consciousness.* Merlin Press, London.
Lukacs, G. 1973. *Marxism and human liberation.* Delta Publishing Co.
Mannheim, K. 1960. *Ideology and utopia.* Routledge and Kegan Paul.
Marcuse, H. 1972. *Studies in critical philosophy.* New Left Books.
Merleau Ponty, M. 1969. *Humanism and terror.* Beacon Press, Boston.
Moon, Penderel. 1961. *Divide and quit.* Chatto and Windus.
Moore, S. and Myerhoff, B. 1975. *Symbol and politics in communal ideology.*
Nayar, B.R. 1966. *Minority politics in the Punjab.* Princeton University Press.
Nayar, K. 1971. *India, the critical years.* Vikas, New Delhi.
Novack. G. 1971. *Empiricism and its evolution.* Pathfinder Press, New York.
Pettigrew, J. 1978. The influence of urban Sikhs on the development of the movement for a Punjabi-speaking state. *Journal of Sikh Studies,* vol. 5, no. I, pp. 152-175.
Pettigrew, J. 1975. *Robber noblemen.* Routledge and Kegan Paul.
Pettigrew, J. 1976. Conflict escalation in the Punjab. *Freedom and Constraint* ed. Aronoff, M. Van Gorcum. Assem.
Shiromani Akali Dal. 1961. Synopsis of the Nehru-Fateh Singh talks on the issue of the formation of a Punjabi-speaking state. Amritsar.
Singh, Gur Rattan Pal. 1979. *Illustrated history of the Sikhs.* Chandigarh.
Smith, Anthony, D. 1972. *Theories of nationalism.* Harper Torchbooks.
Weingrod, A. 1967-68. Patrons, patronage and political parties. *Comparative Studies in Society and History.* vol. 10: 377-400.
Ziring, L. 1973. Bhutto's foreign policy. *Journal of Asian and African Studies.* vol. 8, 3-4.

Chapter 7

The Fabrication of a Social Past: The Kazakhs of Central Asia

Martha B. Olcott

My paper considers the attempt by the Soviet Union to create a Kazakh Soviet culture, nationalist in form and socialist in content. It analyzes how the Soviets took the prerevolutionary Kazakh culture and its rituals which were integrated with the Kazakh tribal and nomadic past, and attempted to recast them to provide cultural support for the social and economic changes that the regime sought to introduce. In large part this reinterpretation of the past was designed to elevate secular reformers to national heroes, and to secularize religious ritual through merging customary practices with Soviet introduced social and political structures. The question then is whether the politicization of myth was sufficient first to change the content of myth and then, through the creation of new myths, to alter the nature of the Kazakh political belief system itself.

* * *

One of the avowed goals of the nationality policy of the Soviet regime was the creation of new national cultures for each of the constituent nationalities of the Soviet Union. These new cultures were to be national in form and socialist in content, and were expected to educate the masses in the practice of socialism and proletarian internationalism.[1] This formula dominated the Soviet cultural policies through the 1920s and 1930s and influenced the nascent Kazakh national culture.

The regime went to great lengths to explain what was meant by both "nationalist in form" and "socialist in content." The "nationalist in form" related to the structure of culture or how the culture was presented to the population—the language, the historical and literary traditions of the culture and the "realia"[2] of the culture, the morés, customs and geographical specifics of the culture. Under "socialist in content" were grouped the new international aspects of culture—the teachings of Marxist Leninism, the friendship and cooperation with other peoples (most importantly the Russians) and the communist attitudes.[3] Because ideology has changed over time, the meaning of "socialist in content" has also been altered, causing changes in the acceptability of different facets of a national culture.

Stalin himself, in an early formulation of this policy, distinguished between two cultural streams, the national proletarian culture (i.e., a culture which was national in form and socialist in content) and national bourgeois culture. The former eliminated all the reactionary elements from the national culture while retaining the national forms and symbols which were to be the vehicles for the new Soviet content. The national bourgeois stream was heretical as it accepted the national heritage in its entirety and failed to recognize the inherent nature of the class struggle in national historical development.

This distinction between the "progressive" and "reactionary" aspects of national culture has survived the demise of Stalin and the eclipse of many of his teachings. It remains basic to the Soviet concept of nationalism as witnessed by its inclusion in a recent history of Central Asia and Kazakhstan:

> It took the peoples of Central Asia and Kazakhstan thousands of years to create the cultural values inherited by socialism. This heritage contains democratic elements, which are used in the formation of socialist culture, and also elements of the culture of the ruling classes, which are alien to the masses ...
>
> To regard the artistic heritage as a common national culture without picking out elements mirroring the ideology of the

feudal upper stratum means to accept the erroneous "single torrent" theory.[4]

The form of the national culture was expected to vary throughout the Soviet Union, depending upon the traditions of each nation. The content of the culture was to be the same throughout the Soviet Union, stressing values that were socialist, proletarian international and Soviet patriotic. The symbols of the national cultures could remain intact but they were to be reinterpreted in a way that the values linked to these symbols were to be linked to the values of socialism rather than "bourgeois nationalism" (i.e., the meanings of the past). The highly centralized and monolithic structure of decision making and policy execution made the goal of restructuring of all national cultures potentially realizable. The Soviet state controlled education, publication, and the media. The regime developed a multitarget policy of cultural reinterpretation which revamped linguistical, educational, historiographical, and literary theory. In Central Asia and Kazakhstan, these policies took the form of an attack on the prerevolutionary clanic and tribal leadership, the remnants of the Sultanates, the vestiges of the "feudal" authority structure and the Muslim religious hierarchy and those customary religious, economic and social practices which were considered to be feudal or exploitative of the lower classes. The Soviet authorities introduced an extensive educational network embracing all groups in the population, which combined efforts at socialization with the introduction of basic literacy. The linguistic policy introduced five new literary languages, Kazakh, Kirghiz, Tadzhik, Turkmen, and Uzbek,[5] one for each ethnic group in the area. This was designed to increase ethnic heterogeneity and to prevent the reemergence of pan-Turkism.[6] Five separate republics were established in the area.

The policies relating to history and literature were quite similar. The past was to be recalled in a selective and moralistic fashion which depicted history solely in class terms. The educational policy introduced a common curriculum throughout the USSR and was primarily directed toward producing a new national intelligentsia which was loyal to Soviet policies and ideals. It was dual language education in the native language and Russian, but the latter predominated at the higher levels. The literary past of the Central Asian peoples was recalled selectively with the socially redeemable qualities of a work determining its inclusion or exclusion.

In the 1920s Soviet cultural policy was directed toward the elimination of the survivals of bourgeois nationalism. By 1926, all Kazakhs who had been active in prerevolutionary national groups were removed from their positions of leadership in government, education, and the arts.[7] They were replaced by Kazakhs more closely identified with the Bolshevik or Communist party. There was an attempt to eliminate the praise or glorification of the past from literature and history. Beyond this there were few strictures applied to the emerging Kazakh intelligentsia, and the development of a Kazakh Soviet literature was encouraged.

The 1930s was a time of increasing attention to doctrinal purity. In 1934, at the First Writers Congress, the doctrine of "socialist realism" was introduced. Literature and the arts began to exist primarily to serve the needs of the state. In these years of economic dislocation resulting from collectivization and mass industrialization there was a real concern with establishing a loyal Soviet citizenry. Writers, artists, and historians were enlisted to aid the regime in this cause. The inevitable victory of socialism was heralded everywhere and inspirational stories of loyal and dedicated workers who gave their all for socialism to succeed dominated literature and the media. This policy superceded the nationality policy, i.e., the focus of the nationality policy was to be on producing a culture which was socialist (and uniform) in content. This remained the philosophy of the nationalities policy until the time of Stalin's death. There was a relative loosening up of restrictions for some of the nationalities at the time of World War II, but following the war there was a reassertion of vigilance, the Zhdanovshchina.[8] This policy affirmed superiority of ethnic Russians and the Russian culture which was to become a dominant element in all the national cultures.

Following Stalin's death, during the period of the Khrushchev thaw, there was a relaxation of control over all of society and as a part of this greater latitude was afforded to the cultural self-expression of the various nationalities, although these cultures had to remain socialist in form. In the late 1950s, Khrushchev displayed a seeming sensitivity to the needs of national minorities. He transferred some power to the federal republics. He also permitted the posthumous rehabilitation of some national communists who had been purged in the 1930s. Rather quickly, however, Khrushchev became alarmed by what he and other members of the central leadership considered a dangerous reemergence of "bourgeois nationalist" tendencies in the official histories and literary histories of various nationalities, including the Kazakhs, who were criticized for publishing poems by nineteenth century religiously inspired poets.[9] This led to a reconceptualization of the nationality theory, which was included in the party program adopted at the 22nd Party Congress in October 1961. It hailed the USSR as building communism and asserted that:

> The full scale communist construction signifies a new stage in the development of national relations in the USSR in which the nations will draw still closer together and their complete unity will be achieved.[10]

This new theory maintained that, as communism was being built and socialist culture came to predominate, the cultures of all the Soviet nationalities were coming closer together (sblizhenie) and this process would ultimately result in their merger (sliianie) when a single Soviet nation would emerge. This theory met with the disapproval of many national intellectuals who were increasingly concerned with tracing prerevolutionary history and restoring to prominence the "progressive" aspects of their cultural pasts. This effort has been made by a new generation of national leaders. These individuals, born and raised under socialism, are sincerely concerned with redefining their national cultures to make them national in form and socialist in content, and to define "socialist in content" in a way that reinforced many preexisting cultural values. In many national regions, including Kazakhstan, such activities had either the support or tacit approval of high level party and government officials, and were part of a growing tendency on the part of the leaders of various nationalities to assert greater cultural and even political control. Rather than provoke dissension on this issue, the central leadership chose to retreat from the advocacy of sblizhenie and sliianie, and admit that individual nationalities will continue to exist but that all cultures will have an increasingly more uniform and socialist content.[11] As Brezhnev himself stated:

> In speaking about the new historic community of people, we certainly do not mean that national differences are already disappearing in our country, or all the more, that a merging of nations and nationalities populating the Soviet Union retain

their features, national character traits, language and their best traditions.[12]

The development of Soviet cultural policy in Kazakhstan mirrors the general policy line. The execution of the policy of "nationalist in form" and "socialist in content" was achieved by the isolation of symbols from the prerevolutionary culture and seeking to replace the previous values or loyalties associated with them with new progressive values. The traditional Kazakh culture was firmly rooted in the nomadic past. The Kazakhs were composed of three hordes (tribal confederations) of pastoral nomads who occupied a semiarid Steppe located west of China, south of Siberia, and north of Turkestan. They were under constant threat from two more powerful forces, the Kalmyks in the east and the Kokand Khanate in the south. The Russians began to move south from Siberia into the Steppe in the nineteenth century. Their expansion was with the support of the local sultans as the Russian expansion provided the Kazakhs with protection from their traditional enemies. The Russians gradually acquired control over the Kazakh territory which in 1868 was incorporated as a province in the Russian Empire.[13] Throughout the nineteenth century, the pastoral nomadic economy declined at an ever-increasing rate and at the end of the century with the introduction of almost two million Russian and Ukrainian settlers, nearly seventy percent of the Kazakhs had abandoned year-round migration for a seminomadic lifestyle of livestock-breeding and limited agriculture. The changing economic situation, as well as the local administrative structure,[14] helped undermine the tribal and clanic authorities. Their position was further challenged by a newly emergent Kazakh intelligentsia.

The traditional Kazakh culture was directly linked to the practices of pastoral nomadism. Most rituals involved the slaughter of livestock or the celebration of a part of the annual migratory pattern. Kazakh religious practices were an important component of the culture. Although Islam had been introduced in the sultanic retinues as early as the seventeenth century, it didn't become widespread among the masses until the nineteenth century, and even then shamanism and ancestor worship continued to dominate the folk religion. Many tradiitonal practices acquired quasilegal status when they were incorporated into the *adat* (customary law).[15] These practices regulated marriage, inheritance, and the rituals surrounding the celebration of birth, death and matrimony. The provisions of the adat were directed toward maintaining the patterns of livestock ownership between generations. The Kazakhs were exogamous, with marriages being arranged by the families concerned and child marriage was common. All sons inherited equally. Each son received a share of his father's livestock as a wedding gift.[16] The adat also provided the standard of morality for the population. This part of the culture was directly linked to the preservation of the community, establishing a delicate balance between the rights of the individual and the needs of the community. The actions of the former could not threaten the status quo of the latter. The adat regulated relations between individuals and established the responsibilities of community members. It provided a structure for adjudicating disputes and levying penalties, which ranged from fines to the death sentence or ostracism. The Kazakhs had well-established patterns of authority. The role of the father in his household and the clan or tribal elder was an autocratic one, but authority had to be used wisely or else it was lost.[17]

The prerevolutionary oral epics provide the best documentation of the values and practices of traditional Kazakh culture. These tales record the myths that dominated the culture. Most of the epics are tributes to the bravery of Kazakh fighters who sought to protect the honor of their tribe or clan. Respect for one's elders and reverence toward the tribal past and customary practices were central to the construction of the tales. Many heroes were instilled with magical powers, and were likened to falcons or eagles, the symbols of bravery. Many of the tales dealt with tragic love affairs, and were about individuals unable to marry because of their unequal status. Despite the sad tone of these stories, the values of the community were always reaffirmed and the Kazakhs believed that everyone occupied a predetermined place in society, that economic and social distinctions existed but did not define an individual's worth. All members of a clan shared a common past and the common obligation to fight for the clan's preservation. This was the great equalizer. The desires or opinions of an individual were subject to contradiction by clan or aul (communal) authorities, who had to be obeyed, as an ostracized individual could not survive the harsh conditions of the Steppe.

In the last half of the nineteenth century, the Kazakhs began to develop a recorded literature, in fact two literatures; one influenced by Russian culture and the other by Islam. The former was the product of a small group of Russophiles, or Russian Democrats as they are now referred to in Soviet literary criticism.[18] These individuals were graduates of Russian secular schools and wrote in

Russian. They argued the virtues of Westernization, the transformation of Kazakh culture to make it compatible with the dominant economic and cultural values of the Russian empire. This was to be accomplished through secular education which, by the introduction of technical skills, would encourage sedentarization and would reduce the influence of the Muslim clergy. The writings of these individuals have received a great deal of attention during the Soviet period. The most prominent in this regard is Abai Kunanbaev (1845-1904), who advocated the social role of literature and used the oral poetic media to send his message to the masses.

At the same time, another group of intellectuals was emerging. These people wrote in Tatar or in a blend of Tatar and Kazakh and were graduates of Koran schools. They saw the Russian conquest and the conditions that consequently developed in the Steppe as threatening the moral fibre of Kazakh society. This position is best represented in the writings of the Zar Zaman (Time of Trouble) poets [19] who exorted the Kazakhs to seek solace in the teachings of Islam. Their writings are considered to be "reactionary" by the Soviet authorities and have been unavailable to the Kazakhs since the time of the revolution.

Finally, by the end of the century, a new generation of intellectuals emerged whose views in many ways were a combination of both positions. They advocated the modification of the Kazakh nomadic economy and the integration of the Kazakh people into the mainstream of the empire, but they were equally concerned with maintaining Kazakh cultural autonomy and argued for the refinement and preservation of a Kazakh culture through the development of Kazakh literary language and a recorded Kazakh history. They accepted the special relationship of Islam to Kazakh culture but argued for a reduction of its influence so that modern education could be introduced. These individuals, mostly young poets and writers, formed and staffed two Kazakh language newspapers, *Aikap* [20] and *Kazakh*.[21] After the Russian Revolution, the latter became the official organ of the *Alash Orda,* the Kazakh nationalist party and government which was in power during the civil war and was later absorbed by the Soviet government. Those Kazakh intellectuals who did not join the Communist party were fired by 1923 and their works were removed from circulation and literary history alike.[22] Those nationalists who joined the party and introduced "socialist" ideas into their works[23] remained in favor until the end of the twenties. From that time until Stalin's death, only those individuals who had not participated in prerevolutionary nationalist activities were considered true proletarians.

Many of the early Soviet goals were shared by the Kazakh reformers who believed that the traditional culture and many of its practices should be modified. They, too, were concerned by the diminishing standard of living of the Kazakh masses, which they attributed to the Russian land policy and not, as did the Soviets, to the exploitation by Kazakh *bais* and "feudal landowners." Like the Soviets, they believed that economic and social change could not occur without the establishment of a receptive cultural climate. As poets and writers, they defined their task as modifying the cultural values of the Kazkh masses. The plight of the Kazakh masses was a recurring theme in many prerevolutionary Kazakh works.

The Soviets thus were able to establish a link between the new Soviet literature, which was to be consciously political in content and at least one trend in contemporary Kazakh literature. The new Kazakh writers were called on to imitate the themes of earlier prerevolutionary works, such as those of Toraigirov, Donentaev, and Seifullin, but to see in the Soviet policies a solution to the oppression and depression that these authors depicted. The literature of the earlier centuries was reviewed critically and those oral epics which were free of religious references and glorified and heroic exploits of individuals rather than tribes were reprinted. In the late 1920s and early 1930s there was a particular attraction to those tales and odes which glorified resistance to tzarist oppression of the eighteenth-century writers.

The disastrous collectivization drive in 1929 revealed to the regime just how weak its support was among the Kazakh population. This led to a policy designed to systematically defeat the traditional leadership. This was to be accomplished through changing the settlement patterns to reduce clanic homogeneity, and by arresting recalcitrant leaders. The regime recognized that without some form of psychological change, without the transformation of the Kazakh culture, real loyalty to the new order would not be achieved. It was hoped that the dissemination of socialist realistic literature would help accomplish this. Artists and writers were transformed into technicians, as they were given specific themes to develop. They were also specifically charged with linking the new values to older cultural symbols, and to demonstrate that there was a basis for the new Soviet ethics in the old Kazakh culture.

Thus, an examination of the new Soviet literature is an excellent way to study the efforts of the regime to achieve cultural change. Literature was seen as an important educational tool. It was to be used in the schools and among the adult population as a way of spreading the new ideology, a more subtle form of propaganda than sloganeering. Because of the Kazakh literary tradition, poetry was the prime target of the regime. The oral epic tradition of the Kazakhs was well suited to Soviet purposes, as the epics had long served as a means to preserve myths and transmit morals. The new Soviet epics were also concerned with transmitting morals, but ones linked to the new Soviet morality. One way that this was accomplished was to use the oral epic form and give new endings to old tales. A good example of this is the epic *Sulushash* written in 1928 by Mukanov,[24] which is a retelling of the traditional love poem "Qozy Korposh and Baian Sulu." The theme of *Sulushash* is the unhappy love of a slave (Altai) for the daughter of a rich bai (Sulushash). In prerevolutionary epics, such tales ended with the two ill-fated lovers parting because of the need for the rich girl to marry a social equal, someone who would bring honor to her family. The tone would be sad but the fate of the two unquestionable, as marriage was regarded as a family obligation. In Mukanov's tale, Altai tries to capture Sulushash, wounding her in the struggle. She declares that their love can never be and kills herself. Rather than accept his fate philosophically, as did the hero in the prerevolutionary version, Altai blames his sad lot on the unjust and repressive social system in which he lives. He laments:

> To him who labors who has poured blood
> Over this entire earth not a crumb to him.
> The worker is a slave, let him die, he's a dog
> Let him sit his entire life in the smoke of manure fires
> Fate sent scratches and hunger
> Blows of the whip and a torn koshma
> While all the sheep, the entire Steppe and all the camels
> All the horses, everything belongs to the bai alone.[25]

The epic ends with Altai concluding that "private happiness can never be achieved under a social system which allows for economic exploitation," and criticizing himself for selfishly seeking personal happiness rather than seeking a new order, he stabs himself.[26] Altai was thus the personification of the values of the new order.

There were also new oral epics which retold Kazakh history. One celebrated one was *Kokshe Tau* by Saken Seifullin, a quasi-folk legend concerning the successful struggle of Khan Ablai (1714-1770) to expel the Kalmyks. Prior to the revolution, Khan Ablai was considered the greatest Kazakh leader of all and his feats were glorified in numerous epics and songs. In Seifullin's version, Ablai is depicted as a cruel expansionist whose plans are supported by equally heinous tribal leaders at the expense of the Kazakh masses. The hero in Seifullin's version is not Khan Ablai, but Adaq, a simple soldier who captures a beautiful Kalmyk girl from the abuse of the cruel Kazakh bais.[27] In the historiography of the Stalinist period, nobility could not be depicted in positive terms.

New oral epics were not the only type of literature to be experimented with in this period. Many Kazakh poets imitated the style of revolutionary Russian writers and introduced a variety of poetic forms into Kazakh literature. Many of these poems were also influenced by the political purposes of the regime. The impoverished position of the simple herdsman was a theme often stressed by Kazakh writers in the early years of Soviet rule. Their plight is blamed on the feudal structure of traditional society and the oppressive nature of the bais and Islamic clergy who sought to prosper at the expense of the Kazakh people. It was very important to stress and even overstate the downtrodden quality of life before the revolution. This theme emerges quite clearly in many of Saken Seifullin's works, including "My Poor Aul" (1926) when he speaks of how the mullahs and bais tried to corrupt the revolution by giving the government jobs to their children, but of course were ultimately foiled by loyal Communists. The conflicting messages of the Soviets and the clergy are compared in the poem "Journey to Stamboul" by Abdilda Tadzhibaev. The Soviets are seeking to improve the lot of the common man, whereas the mullah promises eternal salvation but nothing concrete to alleviate the Kazakhs' plight:

> The Mosque of Haja Sofia exists so take heed,
> Learn your prayer, read the Koran
> Pray to Allah, he is one, Allah
> Do not doubt the prophet you are a zorrax
> You are without bread? You are hungry. Good
> Do not look for food, Do not demand money
> Hope in this world, I do not hide,

Is not for you
Everything waits for you in Paradise.[28]

Although the new Soviet literature strips the Kazakhs of many of their past heroes, it substitutes new heroes in this void. Lenin and Stalin, as the authors of the new Soviet vision, are made to appear as having the same traits and virtues of many of the legendary Kazakh warriors. Lenin was the central hero of a new folk literature which contained numerous tales glorifying his life and death. Although described as a batyr (hero), the persona that was created for Lenin was a new one, that of a prophet rather than a warrior hero. He was depicted as a wise man with a great vision who would lead the Kazakhs to a bright new future. Much of the literature about Lenin employs the images of light and darkness, a common image in earlier Kazakh writings. Lenin brought light, the light of truth or understanding, and lighted up the dark existence of the Kazakhs.

In most poems and tales, Lenin is described as having those traits which characterized Kazakh legendary heroes. One vivid example of this is found in the poem "Song of a Simple Dzhigit" by Dzharakov. Lenin is described in terms that make him sound Turkish, sitting on the floor, drinking tea. He is depicted as sharing the concerns of most Kazakhs—herds, grain, and land. He is linked to the falcon, the symbol of heroism, and has a gun which never misses fire, as every hero has his weapon and Lenin's words are defended with might. What follows is the description of a meeting between Amengeldy Imanov [29] and Lenin:

> In the campfire heavy Steppe-wood is burning,
> The round-beaked falcon had dozed off on the saddle,
> And the hunters forgetting about their aul,
> Tell simple stories . . .
> The wind has died down, the howling has ceased.
> And in the court of Moscow beautiful
> Lenin meets the Steppe-hunters
> He strokes the falcon and presents to them
> His gun which never misses fire.
> He spreads out the rug on the floor,
> And fills the glasses with tea.

And till morning they talk in the Kremlin
Of herds, of grain, of land.[30]

During Stalin's lifetime, he too was depicted in heroic terms, as Lenin's handpicked successor and the person entrusted with Lenin's mission. In the poem "Two Eagles" (1935) by Mukanov, Stalin and Lenin are described as two eagles; and in the following song by the akyn [31] Bek, Stalin is described as a falcon and an eagle:

Bold beautiful and strong is the dzholbars,
The striped hero of the Steppe,
But many times stronger,
Many times braver than the dzholbars are you.

Sharp-sighted is the falcon, and the eagle of the Steppe.
Looking o'er the earth from soaring heights,
But it is you who have brought the people these heights,
More far-sighted than the falcon—are you! [32]

Although Lenin and Stalin were accorded a unique place in Kazakh folklore, those who fought on the Bolshevik side in the civil war were also awarded an honorific position. Mikhael Frunze, the Soviet general who led the army which was responsible for the unification of Kazakhstan and Turkestan with the center, became a new hero in the folk literature. Of particular importance is the place accorded to Amengeldy Imanov,[33] a leading Kazakh fighter in the Red army during the civil war. In the poem "Amengel'dy" by Nurkhan Akhmetbekov, he is described as a great batyr who, like the great batyrs of old, arose to lead the Kazakhs out from the time of troubles.[34] Amengeldy is described in traditional images as speaking in a powerful voice and having an eye like an eagle. His role in the civil war is depicted metaphorically as leading the Kazakhs from their past plight to a new future, by permitting them to be exposed to Lenin and his teachings:

There is a man who is bringing light to the people
There are no other people like him in the world.
Only he can give the people freedom
Only with him will come our dawn
For all the peoples that are oppressed

> For our wives who have not seen the spring
> The great batyr Lenin is fighting
> So that we will become ever equal.³⁵

In the years that followed collectivization, Kazakh literature was to focus increasingly on glorifying the new Soviet way of life, and sought to link these new economic pursuits with noncontroversial traditional practices and with traditional values. It was particularly important to try to achieve some support for the new collective farms. Collectivization in Kazakhstan had been achieved at a cost of nearly two million Kazakh lives and had led to the destruction of nearly the entire Kazakh herd. The Kazakhs had consented to join the collective farms only when all other economic options had been denied to them. Kazakh writers quickly took up the task of trying to show how life on the new collective farms was not dissimilar to that in the former nomadic aul. None worked harder on this theme than Dzhambul Dzhabaev (1846-1945), the people's akyn of the Kazakh SSR. In his poem "To the Dzhailu," written in 1935, he described the trek of the kolkhozniki (collective farmers) to the summer pasturage and attributed to this the symbolic importance of the long summer migration of the pastoral nomads.³⁶ In his "Song About Grain" (1939), he sought to glorify farming, as grain growing was the predominant pursuit of many Kazakhs on collective farms. Traditionally, agriculture was considered far inferior to livestock breeding, the latter being an inseparable part of the Kazakh conception of manhood. Kazakh writers also attempted to glorify industrialization and the new occupational roles that it introduced in the Steppe. The poem excerpted below makes a hero out of a former shepherd who now works on the Turksib (Turkestan-Siberian) railroad:

> Those who used to be slaves and serfs
> Have now been made heroes by the Turksib
> The simple shepherd, tempered by work,
> Has now become dispatcher of the train,
> And thus has gained batyr-like power.
> He used to shepherd the sheep, and beat them with a whip,
> But now with a steady hand
> He draws the diagram of railroad traffic.³⁷

In his poem "Ninety Years" Dzhambul reflects on the positive changes that occurred in the Kazakh Steppe during his lifetime, and how Soviet policy and the new economic system which was introduced has dramatically improved the quality of life. This is described through the use of traditional imagery, conjuring up a picture of the akyn, combra in hand, traversing the vast open Steppe. He writes:

> Since that time every Kazakh
> Has acquired a path for his movement
> His chest has inhaled into itself a soul
> This means that we have achieved wealth.
> We have become an honorable people
> And this with a dombra in my left hand
> My Kazakhstan as though it were my village
> In a smooth hyma like a river
> Sings Dzhambul who has grown young.[38]

In the prerevolutionary period, the loyalty of most Kazakhs was a very parochial one. Allegiance was to a clan or *aul* (the residential community). In praising the Soviets, Dzhambul expresses his patriotism in terms comprehensible to the ordinary Kazakh. He equates his love of Kazakhstan to the love of a village. One of the goals of Soviet policy was to expand these loyalties to include a concept of nationhood, which was politically and not ethnically based, and this loyalty is to be first a Soviet rather than Kazakh state. This is the theme in Seifullin's poem *Sovetstan*. Stan is the old Persian term for state, and is used in the names of four central Asian republics, Kazakh*stan*, Tadzkhiki*stan*, Turkmeni*stan*, and Uzbeki*stan*. In his poem Seifullin, through the use of metaphors, develops the theme that the Soviet Union is a "stan," a state which is rooted in the values and traditions of the Central Asian past.

The problem of instilling Soviet patriotism in the Kazakhs became particularly acute at the time of World War II when large numbers of Kazakhs were drafted into the Soviet army and were required to serve at the front.[39] Kazakh writers rapidly began to churn out works glorifying the heroism of the Kazakh fighters and appealing to the Kazakh soldiers to live up to the memory of the great batyrs. One particularly interesting work is the epic poem "The Twentyfive," a tribute to the Panfilov division which served on the Moscow front. The description of Tolengen, the hero, a steel worker, is like that of an ancient warrior:

> Powerful in his fighting flight,
> So Tolengen like a storm of the Steppes

Flew, circled, blinded.
And left on the field of battle
The thief now a spiritless corpse.
Like cane on the riverbank in the storm
The enemy trembles and bends to the ground.
Remember: as long as the battle lasts
The batyr will not tremble in the saddle!
Hundreds of Germans lie in the field. . . .
Tolengen the crag, Tolengen the giant
Is equal to hundreds of enemies;
"My anger will answer for me!" [40]

Stalin's regime seems to have been relatively successful in creating a form of Soviet patriotism among the Kazakhs. There is little or no evidence of disloyalty among the Kazakhs at the time of World War II. Furthermore, Stalin did emerge as a popular hero, and efforts to stamp out the Stalinist cult of personality have been less successful in the national regions than in Russia.[41] After World War II the leadership began to believe that the most basic of the new Soviet values, such as loyalty to the Soviet state, a belief in proletarian internationalism, and a commitment to a collectivist ideology, had been accepted by the postrevolutionary generation. It is difficult to know exactly what role the political content of literature played in this process. However, from this time on there began to be a de-emphasis on traditional forms in literature, although there remained a strong emphasis on the integration of traditional themes with socialist values.

There is little doubt that the Soviets managed to manipulate many of the symbols found in traditional Kazakh culture sufficiently to create a Soviet patriotism, i.e., political allegiance to the Soviet state. They appear to have been far less successful in creating a new Kazakh-Soviet culture, particularly in the rural areas. Cultural change has occurred but it has been more gradual than the regime anticipated. On the collective farms, many customary practices, particularly those involving livestock breeding, continue to be integrated into daily life. The three-generation family residing together is still common, even among party members and kolkhoz officials.[42] Sharp distinctions continue to exist between male and female social and economic tasks.[43] Many traditional marriage practices persist; exogamy is still prevalent, as is the payment of a symbolic kalym. Livestock still have great symbolic importance in the Kazakh community. Ritual slaughters highlight most holiday celebrations, and magic and charms are used to protect the herd.

From the point of view of the regime, it is very dangerous that religion continues to play an important role in the life of most Kazakhs. Kolkhoz chairmen commonly assume religious as well as political responsibilities. Local schools not only fail to teach scientific atheism, but often propagate religious ideas.[44]

In general, the Soviet cultural policies have been more successful in the cities. However, even in urban areas, as reported in a 1972 study, the overwhelming majority of Kazakhs identified themselves as Muslims.[45] Nonetheless, the urban dwelling Kazakh is largely indistinguishable from residents of other Asian cities in the Soviet Union. The traditional practices that remain are vestiges, a sign of respect for older relatives and a desire to honor the remote past.

The urban setting is ideal for the introduction of social change. The individual is isolated from the traditional economy and traditional culture, and consequently there is not the continual reinforcement of old myths and their supporting rituals that one finds in the countryside. But even though the customary practices have largely died out in the cities, the new Soviet myths and symbols have not been able to totally eclipse the traditional myths, in part because there are almost no new "Soviet" rituals to reinforce the symbols. Thus, although there are few direct links between the contemporary Kazakh city dweller and his nomadic predecessor, there is an increasing desire on the part of the Kazakhs, and particularly the Kazakh intellectuals, to reestablish and retain some connections with their prerevolutionary cultural heritage. This trend has the approval of many Kazakh communist leaders and is being led by official writers and historians who assert that there is a basic harmony between Kazakh cultural-Soviet political values. As stated by Olzhas Suleimenov, a celebrated contemporary Kazakh poet, at a speech delivered at the Sixth Conference of the Writers' Union of Kazakhstan in 1971:

> ... A people which has traversed a complex and tragic path going back thousands of years, which has maintained its spirit through the darkness of defeat and the bright flame of victory, which has protected its great land from Chinese, Muslim and Mongol emperors—this people deserves to know its past. And this past commands respect. If we look at the Russians we see a broad outlook on history. If you exclude

the princes Dmitry Donskoy and Alexander Nevsky, the czars Ivan the Terrible and Peter I, do you have serious history? We must know everything that happened, hiding nothing from the people. But we must know and appraise history from the Marxist class position.[46]

Most contemporary Kazakh writers and poets are thus faced with a complicated task in their capacity of official "mythmakers." The artist must (within the confines of his creative impulses) sort out three competing realities—the Soviet political present, the official past, and his individual romanticized vision of the past, and then emerge with a symbolic myth that satisfies the artist, the audience, and the censor.

The task of the artist has been simplified somewhat by compromises that have been made by the regime in the definition of the political present. As the poem "Native Land" by Abdilda Tadzhibaev excerpted below indicates, there has been a depoliticization of themes in the official Kazakh literature. Tadzhibaev is poet laureate of Kazakhstan, and the poem "Native Land" appeared in the 29 March 1979 issue of *Kazakhstanskaia Pravda,* the official organ of the Communist party of Kazakhstan. The theme of the poem is the poet's love of his motherland, expressed through his devotion to certain geographical places. He expresses his ties to this land in terms that recall the Kazakh practice of ancestor worship that was prevalent in the prerevolutionary period:

> Frosts gave me snows to the waist,
> And the dust devil in the Steppe twisted me around until I cried
> I turned in terror to the souls of my ancestors
> And for that reason doubtless did not freeze,
> Without a motherland, of which I have only one,
> I am not a galloping horse, but the skin of one.

The image of nationalism invoked in the poem is a relatively apolitical one, in that it is tied to a place and a people rather than to a set of values which are either ideologically (Soviet) or historically (prerevolutionary Kazakh) based. This emerges rather clearly in many poems written in the past fifteen years. The poets write about themes which have a strong historical referant, such as the Kazakh *dzhigit* (horseman), or the fate of a herdsman and his horse or camel. Traditional imagery is invoked, but the poems are vague, articulating a loyalty which is instinctive rather than learned, one which is tied to an undefined past rather than to a new revolutionary present or communist future. The link to the past is made through the memories and traditions of livestock breeding, as distinguished from nomadism, which one cannot glorify.

The central authorities seem to have effected a sort of compromise. The goal of the Soviet authorities was to politicize myths in a way that would change their content and lead to the creation of new myths. These new myths would alter the very nature of the Kazakh political belief system. The content of Kazakh myths, as expressed in contemporary poetry, is very different from pre-revolutionary poetry, but is its logical progression. The contemporary Kazakh Soviet culture is very definitely Kazakh and it is the *Kazakh* which determines and interprets the meaning of the *Soviet* for its audience. This is a new culture and as such has created its own new myths, but these are not really the same Soviet-based myths that the regime hoped would develop, or the myths found in many of the poems of the 1930s. An important "sliianie" has occurred, but it is between the cultural values of the Kazakh past and those of the Kazakh present rather than between Kazakh and Soviet (Russian) culture. The Kazakh present is the Kazakh understanding and reinterpretation of the Soviet culture in ways that make sense to Kazakh intellectuals. These intellectuals, the official poets of Kazakhstan, are loyal to the political order and most are even committed communists, but they are also tied to their Kazakh past and are determined to preserve those aspects of it which are potentially harmonious with socialist morality. What seems to result is the relatively apolitical writings of recent years, a political compromise or new cultural synthesis, depending upon the vantage point of the observer.

Thus, it appears that the Soviet cultural policy in Kazakhstan has enjoyed a rather mixed success. While it is the case that the Soviets have been able to create a new political identity, that of a Kazakh Soviet national, they have not succeeded in manufacturing a new cultural identity or a new culture. They have speeded up the process, and perhaps even the direction, of modification of traditional Kazakh culture but the Kazakh culture of today clearly represents the continuation of the cultural values of the Kazakh past.

Notes

1. Robert Conquest, *Soviet nationalities policies in practice* (New York, 1967), p. 63.

2. Thomas Winner, *The oral art and literature of the Kazakhs of Russian central Asia* (Durham, 1958), p. 174.
3. Teresa Rakowska-Harmstone, *Russia and nationalism in Central Asia: The case of Tadzkikistan* (Baltimore, 1970), p. 77.
4. *A leap through history* (Moscow, 1974), p. 137.
5. All but Tadzhik are Turkic languages.
6. The Basmachi revolt (1918-1924) and the activities of Enver Pasha had made the Bolsheviks fear pan-Turkism in Turkestan.
7. Including many who had been recruited personally by the Bolshevik leadership.
8. The policy of ideological purity associated with Andrei Zhdanov.
9. Including Shortembai Kanaev, Dulat Babataev, and Mashur-Zhusup Kopeev.
10. John Strong, *The Soviet Union under Brezhnev and Kosygin* (New York, 1971), p. 166.
11. *Current Digest of the Soviet Press*, 1972.
12. *Current Digest of the Soviet Press*, 1974.
13. This conquest was largely peaceful, with the notable exception of the 1846 revolt of Kenisary.
14. Which was defined by territory and not by clan.
15. Local customary law, *adat*, existed simultaneously with the Islamic *shariat* law.
16. Livestock was individually owned (although animals bore clan brands) but pasturage was under clan control.
17. Elders were elected by the heads of households and could be removed through majority vote.
18. The most prominent were Chokan Valikhanov, Ibragim Altynsaryn, and Abai Kunenbaev.
19. The most important of whom was Mullah Abdulgahir.
20. Edited by Seralin.
21. Edited by Ali Khan Bukeikhanov.
22. Today these men are considered to be more dangerous than even the nineteenth century reactionary poets.
23. These authors have been posthumously rehabilitated and some of their works are again being published.
24. *Antalogiia Kazakhskoi Poezii* (Alma Ata, 1958), p. 477.
25. *Ibid.*, p. 477.
26. Winner, p. 187.
27. Winner, p. 91.
28. *Antalogiia*, p. 581.
29. A Kazakh hero of the civil war.
30. Winner, p. 218.
31. An *akyn* was an itinerant poet who traveled from aul to aul, performing at feasts and ceremonies.
32. *Ibid.*, p. 161.
33. Whose support of the Bolsheviks was nonideological and part of an internecine struggle in the Steppe.
34. An illusion to eighteenth century history.
35. *Antalogiia*, p. 366.
36. *Ibid.*, p. 284.

37. Winner, p. 165.
38. *Antalogiia*, p. 286.
39. There was great fear of Kazakh unrest because of the 1916 draft riots.
40. *Ibid.*, p. 167.
41. During my travels through Central Asia in 1975 I saw Stalin's picture prominently displayed on several occasions, something that is not done in Russia.
42. *Kul'tura i byt Kazakhskogo kolkhoznogo aula* (Alma Ata: Nauka, 1967), p. 188.
43. *Ibid.*, p. 196.
44. P. Kshibekov, "O preodelenie perezhitkov Islama" *Izvestia AN Kaz SSR*, no. 4 (1957), p. 112.
45. T. Sarsenbaev, *Problemy internatsional'nogo vospitaniia lichnosti* (Alma Ata, 1973), p. 124.
46. George Simmonds, *Nationalism in the USSR and Eastern Europe* (Detroit, 1977), p. 297.

Index

Abdullah, Abu, 112
Abercrombie, Nicholas, 128
Abrahams, Roger, 41
Adams, Richard, 97, 108, 109, 112
Alavi, H., 155
Allen, David, 35
Althusser, Louis, 58, 121
Aronoff, Myron: 97, 142; on ideology and interest, 1-29; on the conceptualization of culture, 3-7; on the conceptualization of ideology, 7-13

Bailey, F.G., 59, 66, 72, 83
Beck, Brenda, 52
Barber, Bernard, 65
Barnett, Steve, 99
Barth, Frederik, 60, 127
Bauman, Z., 154
Beidelman, T.O., 128
Bell, Wendell, 47
Berger, Peter L., 4-8, 27, 121. See also Legitimation
Berreman, Gerald, 129, 130, 147

Bertocci, Peter, 13, 15; on the politics of community in Rural Bangladesh, 97-125; on a model of solidarity, 100-107; on a structure of power, 107-114; on models of solidarity and structures of power, 114-121
Beteille, Andre, 93
Block, Maurice, 92, 111
Blum, Jerome, 109
Blustain, Harvey, 2, 13-14; on caste, ideology, and power in North-Central Nepal, 127-150
Bocock, Robert, 20
Boyce, James, 112

Calkins, Philip B., 110
Caste, 101, 127-149
Cohen, Abner, 2, 31, 50, 157, 185
Coulanges, Fustel de, 3
Cross, Whitney, 45
Culture: and politics, 1, 98; Aronoff on, 3-7; culturalists on, 58; Geertz' definition of, 2; materi-

alists on, 58; on national culture, 193-211. *See also* Ideology, Interest, Myth, Ritual, Symbols
Cuthbertson, Gilbert M., 17

David, Kenneth, 147
Davis, Marvin, 2, 13, 16; on two-dimensional politics, 57-95; on fitting, 62; on systems of meaning and action, 58; on the politics of caste, 65; on the processual model, 72; on village and government politics, 59, 64-65; 101, 116
Dolci, Danilo, 111
Dolgin, Janet L., 97
Douglas, Mary, 52
Dow, James, 100, 122
Dumont, Louis, 93, 99, 128, 129, 146, 147
Durkheim, Emile, 20, 27, 102
Dutt, N.K., 93

Easton, David, 90
Ellickson, Jean, 106
Engles, Friedrich, 128
Epstein, T. Scarlett, 83

Faiz, Ahmed Faiz, 166
Fallers, L., 60
Fernandez, James, 52
Fortes, M., 156
Frake, C.O., 58
Frazier, E. Franklin, 43
Fuzzetti, Lina, 99

Garfinkle, Harold, 61, 62
Geertz, Clifford, 1, 2, 3, 6, 7, 9-10, 13, 14, 59, 62, 65, 92, 117
Glasse, Robert, 99, 102
Gluckman, Max, 60, 61, 156
Goffman, Erving, 21, 22
Goodenough, W.H., 58
Goody, Jack, 20
Gough, E.K., 72
Gulati, K.C., 186

Habermas, Jurgen, 184
Hara, T., 122
Harris, M., 58

Hartmann, Betsy, 112
Hossain, Mosharaff, 112

Ideology: and interest, 1-29; Aronoff on, 7-13; Geertz on, 9-10; 98; and power, 139-140; and alternate ideologies, 142-146; 165-167
Inden, Ronald B., 61, 92, 101, 110, 128
Interest, 13, 23, 59
Islam, A.K.M. Aminul, 101, 113

Jahangir, B.K., 120
Jannuzi, F. Tomasson, 111
Jenkins, Loren, 87

Keesing, R.M., 13, 92
Keil, Charles, 40, 48
Kemmitzer, David S., 97
Kochman, Thomas, 37
Kroeber, A., 98

Langer, Suzanne K., 10, 27
Lasswell, Harold, 59
Legitimation: definition of, 5; normative and cognitive dimensions of, 5; levels of, 5
Levi-Strauss, Claude, 52, 58
Locke, John, 179
Lukacs, G., 156
Luckmann, Thomas, 4-8, 121. *See also* Legitimation

Manning, Frank, 12-13, 23; on revivalist politics in Bermuda, 31-55. *See also* Symbols
Mannheim, Karl, 61, 62, 92, 184
Marcuse, H., 184
Marx, Karl, 128, 130
Marriott, McKim, 72, 128, 141, 142
McHugh, Peter, 92
McLane, John R., 110
Mead, George H., 92
Meillassoux, Claude, 129
Mencher, Joan, 129, 130, 147
Metaphor, 51-53
Metonymy, 51-53
Metzger, D., 58
Merleau Ponty, M., 180
Mills, G. Wright, 91, 115-116

Moon, P., 190
Moore, Sally F.: on secular ritual, 20, 21, 59, 60, 73, 82, 153
Myerhoff, Barbara: on secular ritual, 20, 21, 59, 60, 153
Myth, 16-19, 23-24, 193-211

Nations, Richard, 112
Nayar, B.R., 168
Nayar, K., 159
Nicholas, Ralph, 59, 60, 61, 92, 101, 109
Nieberg, H.L., 19

Olcott, Martha, 18-19, 130; on the fabrication of a social past, 193-213
Ortner, Sherry B.: on symbols, 10-12, 53, 59, 103
Ostor, Akos, 99

Parsons, Talcott, 98
Paterson, S., 156
Peach, James T., 111
Pettigrew, Joyce, 2, 9, 13, 14-15; on Sikh ideals and practice, 151-192

Ray, Ratna, 110
Retzlaff, Ralph, 83
Ricoeur, Paul, 61
Ritual, 19-23, 103, 107, 193
Robinson, Marqeurite, 47, 59

Sahlins, Marshall, 120
Schneider, David, 13, 61, 92, 97, 98, 99, 103
Schuon, Frithjof, 101, 106
Schutz, Alfred, 4
Scott, James, 119
Seliger, M., 15
Service, E., 58
Silverberg, James, 72

Singh, Gur Rattan Pal, 164
Smith, Anthony, 162
Sorel, G: on myth and ideology, 16-17
Spradley, James P., 58
Srinivas, M.N.: on Sanskritization and Brahmanization, 66, 140
Steward, J., 58, 108
Swartz, Marc, J., 90
Symbols: in relationship to ideology, 10-13, 22, 23-24, 31-55, 97-99, 103-105; manipulation of, 140-142, 208

Thorp, John P., 102, 106, 108, 110, 111, 112, 115, 119-120
Tuden, A., 90
Tudor, Henry, 16-17
Turner, Edith, 54
Turner, Victor W., 54, 59, 90, 104, 128

Vayda, A.P., 58
Veblen, Thorstein, 185
Velson, Van, 61

Wade, Frederick, 40
Wadley, Susan, 147
Watt, W. Montgomery, 103
Weber, Max, 3, 100, 115
Weingrod, A., 161
White, Leslie, 3, 6
Williams, G., 58
Wilson, Peter, 47, 48
Winckler E.A., 60
Wolf, Eric R., 108, 109
Wood, Geoffrey, 111
Wooding, Hugh, 35, 54

Zaidi, S.M. Hafeez, 106
Zaman, M.Q., 108, 112, 113
Ziring, L., 184